First World War
and Army of Occupation
War Diary
France, Belgium and Germany

61 DIVISION
182 Infantry Brigade
Royal Warwickshire Regiment
2/5th Battalion
1 September 1915 - 20 February 1918

WO95/3056/1

The Naval & Military Press Ltd
www.nmarchive.com
Published in association with The National Archives

Published by

The Naval & Military Press Ltd

Unit 10 Ridgewood Industrial Park,

Uckfield, East Sussex,

TN22 5QE England

Tel: +44 (0) 1825 749494

www.naval-military-press.com

www.nmarchive.com

This diary has been reprinted in facsimile from the original. Any imperfections are inevitably reproduced and the quality may fall short of modern type and cartographic standards.

© **Crown Copyright**
Images reproduced by permission of The National Archives, London, England, 2015.

Contents

Document type	Place/Title	Date From	Date To
Heading	WO95/3056/1		
Heading	61st Division 182nd Infy Bde 2-5th Bn R Warwicks 1915 Sep 1918 Feb (1916 Feb, Mar, Apr, Diaries Missing)		
War Diary	Danbury	01/09/1915	30/09/1915
Miscellaneous	Summary Of War Diary	03/09/1915	03/09/1915
Operation(al) Order(s)	Operation Order No.31 By Brigadier-General W.E.B. Smith C.M.G. Commanding 80th Infantry Brigade	10/04/1915	10/04/1915
War Diary	Danbury	01/10/1915	30/11/1915
Heading	War Diary of 2/5 Battalion Royal Warwickshire Regiment From 1st December 1915 To 31st December 1915 Volume 2		
War Diary	Danbury	01/12/1915	31/12/1915
Operation(al) Order(s)	182nd Inf. Bde Order No.30	29/12/1915	29/12/1915
Operation(al) Order(s)	2/5th R.War.R. Order No.30	30/12/1915	30/12/1915
Heading	War Diary of 2/5th Battalion Royal Warwickshire Regiment From 1st January 1916 To 31st January 1916 Volume 3		
War Diary	Danbury	01/01/1916	31/01/1916
Heading	War Diary 2/5 Royal Warwickshire Regt May 21st 1916 To May 31st 1916 Vol 1		
War Diary	Perham Down	21/05/1916	21/05/1916
War Diary	Havre	22/05/1916	23/05/1916
War Diary	Merville	24/05/1916	24/05/1916
War Diary	Bellerive	25/05/1916	30/05/1916
War Diary	Beuvry	31/05/1916	31/05/1916
Heading	War Diary 2/5 Warwick Regt June 1916		
Miscellaneous	Appendix		
War Diary	Beuvry	01/06/1916	09/06/1916
War Diary	Belle Rive	10/06/1916	12/06/1916
War Diary	Merville	13/06/1916	17/06/1916
War Diary	Fosse	18/06/1916	21/06/1916
War Diary	Moated Grange Sector	22/06/1916	30/06/1916
Operation(al) Order(s)	Red Square Operation Order No.1	05/06/1916	05/06/1916
Operation(al) Order(s)	Red Square Operation Order No.2	08/06/1916	08/06/1916
Operation(al) Order(s)	Red Square Operation Order No.3	21/06/1916	21/06/1916
Operation(al) Order(s)	Red Square Operation Order No.4	26/06/1916	26/06/1916
Operation(al) Order(s)	Red Square Operation Order No.5	29/06/1916	29/06/1916
Heading	2/5th Bn Royal Warwickshire Regmt War Diary Volume III From July 1st 1916 to July 31st 1916		
War Diary	Moated Grange Sector	01/07/1916	04/07/1916
War Diary	Croix Barbee	05/07/1916	09/07/1916
War Diary	Neuve Chapelle (Left)	10/07/1916	15/07/1916
War Diary	La Gorgue	16/07/1916	31/07/1916
Operation(al) Order(s)	Red Square Operation Order No.6	03/07/1916	03/07/1916
Operation(al) Order(s)	Red Square Operation Order No.7	09/07/1916	09/07/1916
Diagram etc	Diagram		
Miscellaneous			
Operation(al) Order(s)	Red Square Operation Order No.8	09/07/1916	09/07/1916
Operation(al) Order(s)	Red Square Operation Order No.9	15/07/1916	15/07/1916

Type	Description	Start	End
Operation(al) Order(s)	Operation Order No.30 By Brigadier-General W.E.B. Smith C.M.G. Commanding 80th Infantry Brigade	08/04/1915	08/04/1915
Heading	2/5th Bn Royal Warwickshire Regiment War Diary Volume IV From August 1st 1916 To August 31st 1916		
War Diary	La Gorgue	01/08/1916	01/08/1916
War Diary	Moated Grange	02/08/1916	09/08/1916
War Diary	Riez Bailleul	10/08/1916	18/08/1916
War Diary	Neuve Chapelle	19/08/1916	25/08/1916
War Diary	La Gorgue	26/08/1916	31/08/1916
Operation(al) Order(s)	Red Square Operation Order No.10	31/07/1916	31/07/1916
Operation(al) Order(s)	Red Square Operation Order No.11	08/08/1916	08/08/1916
Operation(al) Order(s)	Red Square Operation Order No.12	18/08/1916	18/08/1916
Miscellaneous	Red Square Operation Order	25/08/1916	25/08/1916
Miscellaneous	Brigade Routine Orders by Brigade W.B. Evans D.S.O. Commanding 182nd Infantry Brigade	13/01/1918	13/01/1918
Heading	War Diary of 2/5th Bn Royal Warwick Regt From Sept 1st To Sept 30th 1916		
War Diary	La Gorgue	01/09/1916	02/09/1916
War Diary	Laventie	03/09/1916	10/09/1916
War Diary	Fauquissart	11/09/1916	19/09/1916
War Diary	Laventie	19/09/1916	24/09/1916
War Diary	Fauquissart	25/09/1916	30/09/1916
Operation(al) Order(s)	Red Square Operation Order No.14	02/09/1916	02/09/1916
Operation(al) Order(s)	Red Square Operation Order No.15	10/09/1916	10/09/1916
Operation(al) Order(s)	Red Square Operation Order No.16	18/09/1916	18/09/1916
Operation(al) Order(s)	Red Square Operation Order No.17	24/09/1916	24/09/1916
Heading	War Diary of 2/5th Royal Warwickshire Regt From Oct 1st 1916 To Oct 31st 1916		
War Diary	Fauquissart	01/10/1916	01/10/1916
War Diary	Laventie	01/10/1916	07/10/1916
War Diary	Fauquissart	07/10/1916	13/10/1916
War Diary	Laventie	14/10/1916	19/10/1916
War Diary	Fauquissart	20/10/1916	23/10/1916
War Diary	Laventie	24/10/1916	27/10/1916
War Diary	Les Lauriers	28/10/1916	31/10/1916
Operation(al) Order(s)	Red Square Operation Order No.18	06/10/1916	06/10/1916
Operation(al) Order(s)	Red Square Operation Order No.19	12/10/1916	12/10/1916
Operation(al) Order(s)	Red Square Operation Order No.20	18/10/1916	18/10/1916
Operation(al) Order(s)	Red Square Operation Order No.21	22/10/1916	22/10/1916
Operation(al) Order(s)	Red Square Operation Order No.22	26/10/1916	26/10/1916
Operation(al) Order(s)	Red Square Operation Order No.18	30/09/1916	30/09/1916
Heading	War Diary of 2/5th Bn Royal Warwickshire Regt From Nov 1st 1916 To Nov 30th 1916		
War Diary	Les Lauriers	01/11/1916	02/11/1916
War Diary	Bellerive	03/11/1916	03/11/1916
War Diary	Cauchy-A-La-Tour	04/11/1916	04/11/1916
War Diary	Monchy Breton	05/11/1916	05/11/1916
War Diary	Houvin Houvigneul	06/11/1916	06/11/1916
War Diary	Villers-L'Hopital	07/11/1916	15/11/1916
War Diary	Berneuil	16/11/1916	16/11/1916
War Diary	Berteaucourt	17/11/1916	17/11/1916
War Diary	Rubempre	18/11/1916	18/11/1916
War Diary	Warloy-Baillon	19/11/1916	21/11/1916
War Diary	Albert	22/11/1916	22/11/1916
War Diary	Senlis	23/11/1916	30/11/1916
Operation(al) Order(s)	Red Square Operation Order No.23	01/11/1916	01/11/1916

Operation(al) Order(s)	Red Square Operation Order No.24	02/11/1916	02/11/1916
Operation(al) Order(s)	Red Square Operation Order No.25	03/11/1916	03/11/1916
Operation(al) Order(s)	Red Square Operation Order No.26	04/11/1916	04/11/1916
Operation(al) Order(s)	Red Square Operation Order No.27	05/11/1916	05/11/1916
Operation(al) Order(s)	Red Square Operation Order No.28	15/11/1916	15/11/1916
Operation(al) Order(s)	Red Square Operation Order No.29	16/11/1916	16/11/1916
Operation(al) Order(s)	Red Square Operation Order No.30	17/11/1916	17/11/1916
Operation(al) Order(s)	Red Square Operation Order No.31	17/11/1916	17/11/1916
Operation(al) Order(s)	Red Square Operation Order No.32	20/11/1916	20/11/1916
Operation(al) Order(s)	Red Square Operation Order No.33	21/11/1916	21/11/1916
Operation(al) Order(s)	Red Square Operation Order No.34	26/11/1916	26/11/1916
Heading	War Diary of 2/5th Bn Royal Warwickshire Regt From Dec 1st 1916 To Dec 31st 1916		
War Diary	Senlis	01/12/1916	02/12/1916
War Diary	Martinsart	03/12/1916	10/12/1916
War Diary	Mouquet Farm Sector	11/12/1916	15/12/1916
War Diary	Wellington Huts Nab Rd	16/12/1916	20/12/1916
War Diary	Martinsart	21/12/1916	22/12/1916
War Diary	Varennes	23/12/1916	31/12/1916
Operation(al) Order(s)	Red Square Operation Order No.35	30/11/1916	30/11/1916
Operation(al) Order(s)	Red Square Operation Order No.36	09/12/1916	09/12/1916
Operation(al) Order(s)	Red Square Operation Order No.37	11/12/1916	11/12/1916
Operation(al) Order(s)	Operation Order 38	14/12/1916	14/12/1916
Operation(al) Order(s)	Red Square Operation Order No.39	19/12/1916	19/12/1916
Operation(al) Order(s)	Red Square Operation Order No.40	21/12/1916	21/12/1916
Operation(al) Order(s)	Red Square Operation Order No.41	29/12/1916	29/12/1916
Heading	War Diary of 2/5th Bn Royal Warwickshire Regt From Jan 1st 1917 To Jan 31st 1917		
War Diary	Martinsart	01/01/1917	06/01/1917
War Diary	Mouquet Farm	07/01/1917	16/01/1917
War Diary	Val De Maison	17/01/1917	17/01/1917
War Diary	Fienvillers	18/01/1917	18/01/1917
War Diary	Coulonvillers	19/01/1917	19/01/1917
War Diary	Lamotte-Buleux	20/01/1917	31/01/1917
Operation(al) Order(s)	Red Square Operation Order No.42	05/01/1917	05/01/1917
Operation(al) Order(s)	Red Square Operation Order No.43	10/01/1917	10/01/1917
Operation(al) Order(s)	Red Square Operation Order No.44	15/01/1917	15/01/1917
Operation(al) Order(s)	Red Square Operation Order No.45	16/01/1917	16/01/1917
Operation(al) Order(s)	Red Square Operation Order No.46	17/01/1917	17/01/1917
Operation(al) Order(s)	Red Square Operation Order No.47	18/01/1917	18/01/1917
Miscellaneous	Issued with 30th Division Operation Order No 75	21/01/1917	21/01/1917
Heading	War Diary of 2/5th Bn Royal Warwickshire Regt From 1/2/17 To 28/2/17		
War Diary	Lamotte-Buleux	01/02/1917	05/02/1917
War Diary	Vauchelles-Les-Quesnoy	06/02/1917	15/02/1917
War Diary	Marcelcave	16/02/1917	19/02/1917
War Diary	Vauvillers	20/02/1917	25/02/1917
War Diary	Vermandovillers	26/02/1917	28/02/1917
Operation(al) Order(s)	Red Square Operation Order No.48	04/02/1917	04/02/1917
Operation(al) Order(s)	Red Square Operation Order No.49	12/02/1917	12/02/1917
Operation(al) Order(s)	Red Square Operation Order No.50	14/02/1917	14/02/1917
Operation(al) Order(s)	Red Square Operation Order No.51	18/02/1917	18/02/1917
Operation(al) Order(s)	Red Square Operation Order No.52	24/02/1917	24/02/1917
Heading	War Diary of 2/5th Bn Royal Warwickshire Regt From March 1st 1917 To March 31st 1917		
War Diary	Vermandovillers	01/03/1917	08/03/1917

War Diary	Harbonnieres	09/03/1917	15/03/1917
War Diary	Rainecourt	16/03/1917	17/03/1917
War Diary	Deniecourt	18/03/1917	18/03/1917
War Diary	Ablaincourt	19/03/1917	19/03/1917
War Diary	Marchelepot	20/03/1917	23/03/1917
War Diary	Epenancourt	24/03/1917	27/03/1917
War Diary	Montecourt	28/03/1917	28/03/1917
War Diary	Poeuilly	29/03/1917	31/03/1917
Operation(al) Order(s)	Red Square Operation Order No.59	02/03/1917	02/03/1917
Operation(al) Order(s)	Red Square Operation Order No.60	07/03/1917	07/03/1917
Operation(al) Order(s)	Red Square Operation Order No.61	14/03/1915	14/03/1915
Operation(al) Order(s)	Red Square Operation Order No.62	22/03/1917	22/03/1917
Operation(al) Order(s)	Red Square Operation Order No.63	27/03/1917	27/03/1917
Operation(al) Order(s)	Red Square Operation Order No.64	28/03/1917	28/03/1917
Heading	War Diary of 2/5th Bn Royal Warwickshire Regt From April 1st To April 30th 1917		
War Diary	Montecourt	01/04/1917	03/04/1917
War Diary	Monchy Lagache	04/04/1917	06/04/1917
War Diary	Marteville	07/04/1917	09/04/1917
War Diary	Fresnoy-Le-Petit	10/04/1917	11/04/1917
War Diary	Marteville	12/04/1917	12/04/1917
War Diary	Quivieres	13/04/1917	21/04/1917
War Diary	Savy	22/04/1917	24/04/1917
War Diary	Brown Line (St Quentin Sector)	25/04/1917	30/04/1917
Operation(al) Order(s)	Red Square Operation Order No.64	09/04/1917	09/04/1917
Operation(al) Order(s)	Red Square Operation Order No.65	11/04/1917	11/04/1917
Operation(al) Order(s)	Red Square Operation Order No.66	11/04/1917	11/04/1917
Operation(al) Order(s)	Red Square Operation Order No.67	20/04/1917	20/04/1917
Operation(al) Order(s)	Red Square Operation Order No.68	24/04/1917	24/04/1917
Operation(al) Order(s)	Red Square Operation Order No.69	29/04/1917	29/04/1917
Heading	War Diary of 2/5th Bn The Royal Warwickshire Regt From May 1st To May 31st 1917		
War Diary	St. Quentin Sector	01/05/1917	16/05/1917
War Diary	Billancourt	17/05/1917	17/05/1917
War Diary	Flesselles	18/05/1917	21/05/1917
War Diary	Gezaincourt	22/05/1917	23/05/1917
War Diary	Beaudricourt	24/05/1917	24/05/1917
War Diary	Berneville	25/05/1917	31/05/1917
Operation(al) Order(s)	Red Square Operation Order No.69	03/05/1917	03/05/1917
Operation(al) Order(s)	Red Square Operation Order No.70	06/05/1917	06/05/1917
Operation(al) Order(s)	Red Square Operation Order No.71	13/05/1917	13/05/1917
Operation(al) Order(s)	Red Square Operation Order No.72	15/05/1917	15/05/1917
Operation(al) Order(s)	Red Square Operation Order No.73	16/05/1917	16/05/1917
Operation(al) Order(s)	Red Square Operation Order No.74	20/05/1917	20/05/1917
Operation(al) Order(s)	Red Square Operation Order No.75	22/05/1917	22/05/1917
Operation(al) Order(s)	Red Square Operation Order No.76	23/05/1917	23/05/1917
Heading	War Diary of 2/5th Bn The Royal Warwickshire Regt From 1/6/17 To 30/6/17		
War Diary	Berneville	01/06/1917	01/06/1917
War Diary	Achicourt	02/06/1917	11/06/1917
War Diary	Dainville	12/06/1917	23/06/1917
War Diary	Vacqueriette & Erquieres	24/06/1917	30/06/1917
Operation(al) Order(s)	Red Square Operation Order No.76	31/05/1917	31/05/1917
Miscellaneous	To Reference Attached Operation Order	10/06/1917	10/06/1917
Operation(al) Order(s)	Red Square Operation Order No.77	10/06/1917	10/06/1917
Operation(al) Order(s)	Red Square Operation Order No.78	22/06/1917	22/06/1917

Heading	War Diary of 2/5th Bn The Royal Warwickshire Regt From 1/7/17 To 31/7/17		
War Diary	Vacqueriette And Erquieres	01/07/1917	24/07/1917
War Diary	Fortel	25/07/1917	26/07/1917
War Diary	Rubrouck	27/07/1917	31/07/1917
Operation(al) Order(s)	Red Square Operation Order No.79	23/07/1917	23/07/1917
Operation(al) Order(s)	Red Square Operation Order No.80	24/07/1917	24/07/1917
Heading	War Diary of the 2/5th Bn The Royal Warwickshire Regt From Aug 1st To Aug 31st 1917		
War Diary	Rubrouck	01/08/1917	16/08/1917
War Diary	Brandhoek	17/08/1917	25/08/1917
War Diary	Ypres. N.	26/08/1917	26/08/1917
War Diary	Wieltje	27/08/1917	28/08/1917
War Diary	Goldfish Chau. Ypres	29/08/1917	29/08/1917
War Diary	Goldfish Chateau Bank Farm	30/08/1917	31/08/1917
Operation(al) Order(s)	Red Square Operation Order No.80	15/08/1917	15/08/1917
Operation(al) Order(s)	Red Square Operation Order No.81	24/08/1917	24/08/1917
Operation(al) Order(s)	Red Square Operation Order No.82	26/08/1917	26/08/1917
Operation(al) Order(s)	Red Square Operation Order No.82	29/08/1917	29/08/1917
Heading	2/5 Bn Royal Warwickshire Regiment War Diary September 1917		
War Diary	Bank Farm	01/09/1917	02/09/1917
War Diary	Wieltje	03/09/1917	05/09/1917
War Diary	Bank Farm	06/09/1917	07/09/1917
War Diary	Brandhoek	08/09/1917	14/09/1917
War Diary	Tay Camp	15/09/1917	15/09/1917
War Diary	Watou	15/09/1917	17/09/1917
War Diary	St. Sylvestre Cappel	18/09/1917	18/09/1917
War Diary	Warlus	19/09/1917	22/09/1917
War Diary	Hull Camp St Nicholas	23/09/1917	23/09/1917
War Diary	Northumberland Lane	24/09/1917	28/09/1917
War Diary	Chemical Works	29/09/1917	30/09/1917
Operation(al) Order(s)	Red Square Operation Order No.83	02/09/1917	02/09/1917
Operation(al) Order(s)	Red Square Operation Order No.84	05/09/1917	05/09/1917
Operation(al) Order(s)	Red Square Operation Order No.85	07/09/1917	07/09/1917
Operation(al) Order(s)	Red Square Operation Order No.86	13/09/1917	13/09/1917
Operation(al) Order(s)	Red Square Operation Order No.87	16/09/1917	16/09/1917
Operation(al) Order(s)	Red Square Operation Order No.88	17/09/1917	17/09/1917
Operation(al) Order(s)	Red Square Operation Order No.89	21/09/1917	21/09/1917
Operation(al) Order(s)	Red Square Operation Order No.90	23/09/1917	23/09/1917
Operation(al) Order(s)	Red Square Operation Order No.91	29/09/1917	29/09/1917
Heading	War Diary of 2/5th Bn The Royal Warwickshire Regt From Oct 1st To Oct 31st 1917		
War Diary	Chemical Works	01/10/1917	05/10/1917
War Diary	Pudding Trench	06/10/1917	10/10/1917
War Diary	Chemical Works	11/10/1917	16/10/1917
War Diary	Lancaster Camp St. Nicholas	17/10/1917	20/10/1917
War Diary	Arras	21/10/1917	28/10/1917
War Diary	Greenland Hill Sector	29/10/1917	31/10/1917
Operation(al) Order(s)	Red Square Operation Order No.92	04/10/1917	04/10/1917
Miscellaneous	With Reference To Your Operation Order No.135	14/10/1917	14/10/1917
Operation(al) Order(s)	Red Square Operation Order No.93	10/10/1917	10/10/1917
Miscellaneous	Relief Table Issued With Red Square Operation Order No.93 October 10th 1917	10/10/1917	10/10/1917
Operation(al) Order(s)	Red Square Operation Order No.94	11/10/1917	11/10/1917
Diagram etc	Diagram		

Type	Description	Start	End
Miscellaneous	Map		
Map	Map		
Miscellaneous	Artillery Programme In Support of Raid By 2/5 Warwicks	15/10/1917	15/10/1917
Miscellaneous	Trench Mortar Programme In Support Of Raid By 2/5 Warwicks	15/10/1917	15/10/1917
Miscellaneous	Machine Gun Programme in Support of Raid By 2/5 Warwicks	15/10/1917	15/10/1917
Operation(al) Order(s)	Red Square Operation Order No.95	15/10/1917	15/10/1917
Miscellaneous	Relief Table Issued With Red Square Operation Order No.95 October 15th 1917	15/10/1917	15/10/1917
Operation(al) Order(s)	Red Square Operation Order No.96	27/10/1917	27/10/1917
Miscellaneous	Relief Table Issued With Red Square Operation Order No.96 October 27th 1917	27/10/1917	27/10/1917
Heading	War Diary of 2/5th Battn Royal Warwickshire Regt From Nov 1st To Nov 30th 1917		
War Diary	Green Land Hill Sector	01/11/1917	21/11/1917
War Diary	Arras	22/11/1917	28/11/1917
War Diary	Warlus	29/11/1917	30/11/1917
Operation(al) Order(s)	Red Square Operation Order No.97	02/11/1917	02/11/1917
Operation(al) Order(s)	Red Square Operation Order No.98	08/11/1917	08/11/1917
Operation(al) Order(s)	Red Square Operation Order No.99	14/11/1917	14/11/1917
Operation(al) Order(s)	Red Square Operation Order No.100	20/11/1917	20/11/1917
Operation(al) Order(s)	Red Square Operation Order No.101	28/11/1917	28/11/1917
Operation(al) Order(s)	Red Square Operation Order No.102	29/11/1917	29/11/1917
Heading	War Diary 2/5 Royal Warwickshire Regt December 1st To 31st 1917 Volume 20		
War Diary	Metz-En-Couture	01/12/1917	01/12/1917
War Diary	Heudecourt	02/12/1917	02/12/1917
War Diary	La Vacquerie	03/12/1917	04/12/1917
War Diary	Equancourt	05/12/1917	07/12/1917
War Diary	Havrincourt Wood	08/12/1917	10/12/1917
War Diary	La Vacquerie	11/12/1917	12/12/1917
War Diary	Beaucamp	13/12/1917	13/12/1917
War Diary	La Vacquerie	14/12/1917	15/12/1917
War Diary	Beaucamp	16/12/1917	19/12/1917
War Diary	Manancourt	20/12/1917	23/12/1917
War Diary	Vaux-Sur-Somme	24/12/1917	30/12/1917
War Diary	Cayeux-En-Santerre	31/12/1917	31/12/1917
Miscellaneous	Reference Gonnelieu Map Edn 3a.1/10000	02/12/1917	02/12/1917
Miscellaneous	Headquarters 182nd Infantry Brigade	30/12/1917	30/12/1917
Miscellaneous	Red Square Operation Order No	22/12/1917	22/12/1917
Operation(al) Order(s)	Red Square Operation Order No.104	29/12/1917	29/12/1917
Operation(al) Order(s)	Red Square Operation Order No 105	30/12/1917	30/12/1917
Heading	War Diary 2/5th Royal Warwickshire Regiment January 1918 Vol 20		
War Diary	Le Quesnel	01/01/1918	07/01/1918
War Diary	Nesle	08/01/1918	09/01/1918
War Diary	Vaux	10/01/1918	11/01/1918
War Diary	Holnon Wood	12/01/1918	14/01/1918
War Diary	Fayet	15/01/1918	17/01/1918
War Diary	Attilly	18/01/1918	25/01/1918
War Diary	Fresnoy Le Petit	26/01/1918	31/01/1918
Operation(al) Order(s)	Red Square Operation Order No.106	06/01/1918	06/01/1918
Operation(al) Order(s)	Red Square Operation Order No.106	08/01/1918	08/01/1918
Operation(al) Order(s)	Red Square Operation Order No.107	10/01/1918	10/01/1918

Operation(al) Order(s)	Red Square Operation Order No.107	14/01/1918	14/01/1918
Miscellaneous	2/5th Bn. Royal Warwickshire Regiment Report on Enemy Raid	18/01/1918	18/01/1918
Operation(al) Order(s)	Red Square Operation Order No.109	17/01/1918	17/01/1918
Operation(al) Order(s)	Red Square Operation Order No.110	25/01/1918	25/01/1918
Operation(al) Order(s)	Red Square Operation Order No.111	29/01/1918	29/01/1918
Heading	War Diary of 2/5th Battalion Royal Warwickshire Regiment February 1918		
War Diary	Fresnoy Le Petit	01/02/1918	10/02/1918
War Diary	Germaine	11/02/1918	16/02/1918
War Diary	Bray-St-Cristophe	17/02/1918	20/02/1918
Operation(al) Order(s)	Red Square Operation Order No.112	02/02/1918	02/02/1918
Operation(al) Order(s)	Red Square Operation Order No.113	06/02/1918	06/02/1918
Operation(al) Order(s)	Red Square Operation Order No.114	12/02/1918	12/02/1918
Operation(al) Order(s)	Red Square Operation Order No.114	15/02/1918	15/02/1918
Operation(al) Order(s)	Red Square Operation Order No.115	19/02/1918	19/02/1918

3095/3056/1

61ST DIVISION
182ND INFY BDE

2-5TH BN R. WARWICKS

~~MAY 1916 — FEB 1918.~~

1915 SEP — ~~1916 JAN~~
~~1916~~ 1918 FEB
(1916 FEB, MAR, APR, DIARIES MISSING)

DISBANDED

Army Form C. 2118.

WAR DIARY
or
INTELLIGENCE SUMMARY
(Erase heading not required.)

Instructions regarding War Diaries and Intelligence Summaries are contained in F. S. Regs., Part II. and the Staff Manual respectively. Title pages will be prepared in manuscript.

Hour, Date, Place		Summary of Events and Information	Remarks and references to Appendices
1915.			
September 1st. Danbury.	Company Training :	800 Field Dressings received from C.O.O.Weeden.	
2–3rd. "	Battalion "		
4th "	Company " :	1 water cart received from C.O.O.Colchester.	
6–7th "	Company Training		
8–9th "	Battalion "		
10th "	Brigade "		
11th "	Company "		
13–14th "	Battalion "		
15th "	Brigade "		
16th "	Brigade "		
17th "	Battalion " :	2 telephone sets received from C.O.O.Harwich and 4 horse shoe valises and 7 brake blocks from C.O.O.Colchester.	
20–21st "	Company "		
22nd "	Battalion "		
23rd "	Brigade "		
24th "	Battalion " :	One horse clipping Machine received from C.O.O. Colchester.	
25th "	Company "		
27th "	Company " :	Spare bicycle parts received from C.O.O.Colchester.	
28th "	Brigade "		
29–30th "	Battalion "		

Danbury,
3.10.15.

W. Coates, Lieut.Col.
Commanding 2/5 Royal Warwick Regiment.

SUMMARY OF WAR DIARY.

UNIT. 2/5th Battalion Royal Warwickshire Regiment.

BRIGADE. 182nd Infantry Brigade.

DIVISION. 61st (South Midland) Division.

MOBILIZATION CENTRE. Birmingham.

TEMPORARY WAR STATION. Danbury.

STATIONS SINCE OCCUPIED SUBSEQUENT TO CONCENTRATION.
Hoddesdon.
Coggeshall, Braintree, Colchester, Kelvedon, Chelmsford, Epping, Danbury.

(a). MOBILIZATION   Nil

(b). CONCENTRATION AT WAR STATIONS. Movements have been carried out by road as ordered.

(c). ORGANIZATION FOR DEFENCE   Satisfactory

(d). TRAINING.   Proceeding, but under great difficulties owing to the low strength of the Battalion.

(e). DISCIPLINE.   Much improved.

(f). ADMINISTRATION.

(1). Medical Services.   Nil.
(2). Veterinary Services   Nil.
(3). Supply services   Satisfactory.
(4). Transport   Improved.
(5). Ordnance Services   Nil.
(6). Billeting & Hutting   Nil.
(7). Channels of correspondence, routine matter. Nil
(8). Range Construction   Nil.
(9). Supply of remounts.   Nil.

(g). REORGANIZATION of T.F. INTO HOME & IMPERIAL SERVICE

Complete.

(h). PREPARATION OF UNITS FOR IMPERIAL SERVICE.

Nil.

Lieut.Col.
Commanding 2/5 Royal Warwick.Regt.

Danbury.
3.9.1915.

Copy No.

OPERATION ORDER No.31
by
Brigadier-General W.E.B.Smith C.V.O., Commanding 80th Infantry
Brigade.

Brigade Headquarters,
10th April, 1915.

1. The 3rd K.R.R.C., 4th K.R.R.C. and P.P.C.L.I. will be relieved to-morrow as follows -

	Trench.	Garrison.	To relieve.
2nd K.S.L.I. (H.Q.S.2)	74	40	4th K.R.R.C.
	75	40	"
	76	150	"
	77	80	"
	78	80	3rd K.R.R.C.
	79 (as far as commn. trench)	40	"
	S.1	1 Coy.	4th K.R.R.C.
	S.2	1 "	3rd K.R.R.C.
4th Rifle Bde (H.Q.S.3)	79 (From Commn. trench)	) 3 Coys.) (520 men)	
	A	)	3rd K.R.R.C.
	B	)	P.P.C.L.I.
	C	)	P.P.C.L.I.
	S.3	1 Coy.	"

O.C. 2nd K.S.L.I. will also arrange to put a secure garrison in the support trench immediately in rear of Trench 78 sufficient to keep the trench in order

2. On relief 2 Coys. 3rd K.R.R.C. will occupy the dug outs vacated by the K.S.L.I. West of ETANG DE BELLEWAARDE Square I 12 D. H.Q. and 2 remaining Coys. 3rd K.R.R.C. will return to billets in YPRES and will form Brigade Reserve.
    The 4th K.R.R.C. will return to billets in YPRES and the P.P.C.L.I. to VLAMERTINGHE and both Battalions will form part of the Composite Brigade in Divisional Reserve.

3. Relieving Battalions will pass the MENIN GATE as follows -
    4th Rifle Bde. at 7.30 p.m. and march via VERLORENHOEK.
    2nd K.S.L.I. at 8.30 p.m. and march via the railway.

4. The 2nd K.S.L.I. and 4th Rifle Bde. will remain in the trenches till the evening of the 14th April.

5. During the time Units remain in YPRES and VLAMERTINGHE each unit will detail 2 Officers and 12 men for instruction by the O.C. 17th Field Company R.E. in bomb throwing and the use of the trench mortar.

6. Trench reports by Officers in charge of trenches will be forwarded to the Brigade Office on the morning of the day on which units are to be relieved.

Major,

Brigade Major, 80th Infantry Brigade.

Army Form C. 2118.

WAR DIARY
or
INTELLIGENCE SUMMARY.

(Erase heading not required.)

Instructions regarding War Diaries and Intelligence Summaries are contained in F. S. Regs., Part II. and the Staff Manual respectively. Title pages will be prepared in manuscript.

Hour, Date, Place 1915.	Summary of Events and Information	Remarks and references to Appendices
October 1st. DANBURY.	Brigade Training.	
2nd. "	Battalion Training: 3 Rifles & 27 Bayonets & Scabbards received from C.O.O.Weedon.	
4th. "	Battalion Training.	
5th. "	Battalion Training: Brigade Tactical Exercise for Officers.	
6th. "	Battalion Training: 600 Bolster cases received from C.O.O.Colchester.	
7th. "	Brigade Training.	
8-9th. "	Battalion Training.	
11th. "	Battalion Training: 12 N.C.O's and men transferred to 81st Provisional Battalion.T.F.	
12-13th. "	Occupation of Trenches by 61st (South Midland) Division.	
14th. "	Battalion Training: Clothing to replace that condemned, received from C.O.O.Weedon: Material to make up shortages of Transport Equipment received from C.O.O.Colchester: 220 yards Telephone wire received from C.O.O.Colchester.	
15th. "	Battalion Training: Brigade Tactical Exercise for Officers.	
16th. "	Battalion Training: One man transferred to 81st Provisional Battalion.T.F.	
18th. "	Battalion Training.: Material to make up some of the shortages of Transport Equipment received from C.O.O.Colchester: Five Fencing Muskets received from C.O.O.Weedon: 480 S.A.Ball P.W.Cartridges received from O.O Colchr.	
19-21st. "	Divisional Exercise: Twwo men transferred to 81st Provisional Battalion T.F.	
22nd. "	Battalion Training.	
23rd. "	Battalion Training: 24 bicycles sent to C.O.O.Colchester.	
25-26th "	Battalion Training.	
28th. "	Battalion Training: 3 men transferred to 81st Provisional Battalion T.F.: 2 sets Harness received from C.O.O.Colchester: 36 Rifles, Bayonets and Scabbards and 10,800 rounds Jap. .256 Ball ammunition sent to 70th Provisional Batt.T.F. & 39 rifles, Bayonets & Scabbards & 11,700 rounds Jap. .256 Ball ammunition sent to 64th Provisional Batt.T.F.	
29-30th "	Battalion Training.	

Danbury.
2.11.15.

M Carlie Lieut.Col.
Commanding 2/5 Royal Warwick Regt.

Army Form C. 2118.

WAR DIARY

INTELLIGENCE SUMMARY.

(Erase heading not required.)

Instructions regarding War Diaries and Intelligence Summaries are contained in F.S. Regs., Part II. and the Staff Manual respectively. Title pages will be prepared in manuscript.

Hour, Date, Place		Summary of Events and Information	Remarks and references to Appendices
1915.			
Nov. 1 - 3.	Danbury.	Individual Training.	
4.	"	Brigade Training.	
5 - 6.	"	Individual Training.	
8.	"	Individual Training.	
9.	"	Individual Training. Inspection of Horses & Transport by Col. Long. W.O.	
10.	"	Individual Training. 65 Caps S.D. received from C.O.O. Weedon.	
11.	"	Individual Training.	
12 - 13.	"	Individual Training.	
15.	"	Individual Training. 525 M.L.M. Rifles Mk.1. received from O.O.Devonport.	
16.	"	Individual Training. 30 Headropes and Field Kitchen Accessories received from O.O.Colchester. 157920 rounds S.A.A.Ball .303 Mark VI received from C.O.O.Weedon.	
17 - 18.	"	Individual Training.	
19.	"	Individual Training. Branding Irons received from O.O.Colchester.	
20.	"	9 G.S.wagons received. (No vouchers).	
21.	"	Brigade Training.	
22.	"	Individual Training.	
23 - 24.	"	Individual Training. 43 Saddle Blankets received from O.O.Colchester. 525 Oil Bottles and Pullthroughs received from C.O.O.Weedon.	
25.	"	Individual Training. 108 Small sand-bags received from O.O.Colchester.	
26 - 27.	"	Individual Training.	
29.	"	Individual Training.	
30.	"	Individual Training.	

Danbury.
2.12.15.

[signature]
Lieut.Col.
Commanding 2/5 R. Warwick Regt.

C O N F I D E N T I A L.

War Diary of

2/5 Battalion, Royal Warwickshire Regiment.

from 1st December 1915, to 31st December 1915.

Volume 2.

Army Form C. 2118.

WAR DIARY
INTELLIGENCE SUMMARY.
(Erase heading not required.)

Instructions regarding War Diaries and Intelligence Summaries are contained in F.S. Regs., Part II. and the Staff Manual respectively. Title pages will be prepared in manuscript.

Hour, Date, Place		Summary of Events and Information	Remarks and references to Appendices
1.12.15.	Danbury	Individual Training.	R. S. M.
2.12.15.	"	Individual Training. Two rolls of Wire enamelled received from O.C. Colchester.	R. S. M.
3.12.15.	"	Individual Training. 9 Wagon Covers G.S. received from HdQRS Company 61st S.M.D. TRAIN	R. S. M.
4.12.15.	"	Individual Training. 325 Sword Bayonets } received from O.C. WEEDON. 525 Sight Protectors } Church Parade.	R S. M. R. S. M.
5.12.15 9-45 AM	"	Individual Training. 3 Men demobilised for Munition Work.	AUTHORITY W.O. LETTER 19/Gen.No/5414(A.G.1) RELEASES R. S. M.
6.12.15	"		
7.12.15	"	Individual Training. 200 Sword Bayonets } received from O.C. WEEDON. 525 Scabbards Sword Bayonet } Strength of the Battalion (N.C.O.s and MEN) 508.	R. S. M.

WAR DIARY
INTELLIGENCE SUMMARY.

(Erase heading not required.)

Army Form C. 2118.

Instructions regarding War Diaries and Intelligence Summaries are contained in F. S. Regs., Part II. and the Staff Manual respectively. Title pages will be prepared in manuscript.

Hour, Date, Place		Summary of Events and Information	Remarks and references to Appendices
8.12.15	Danbury	Individual Training. 1 Field Forge received from O. C. HARWICH	R. S. M.
9.12.15	"	Individual Training	R. S. M.
10.12.15	"	Individual Training. Inspection of Battalion Transport by Colonel CULLIS 6,st S.M.D A.S.C.	AUTHORITY 1 & 2nd INFBDE LETTER N0.4330/15 DATED 9.12.15. AUTHORITY COL H/C TF RECORDS. NO 8/17/50/ 3/12/15 R. S. M.
		1 Armourer & 61st Provisional Battalion	
11.12.15	"	Individual Training. 27 Blankets G.S. received from O. C. COLCHESTER	R. S. M.
12.12.15 9-45 AM	"	Church Parade	R. S. M.

Army Form C. 2118.

WAR DIARY
INTELLIGENCE SUMMARY.

Instructions regarding War Diaries and Intelligence Summaries are contained in F.S. Regs., Part II. and the Staff Manual respectively. Title pages will be prepared in manuscript.

(Erase heading not required.)

Hour, Date, Place	Summary of Events and Information	Remarks and references to Appendices
13.12.15 Danbury	Individual Training. 36 Tents Wagon Lanterns G.S. received from B.O. WARWICK. 2 Rim clenchfeges for howitzer Wheels	AUTHORITY. W.O. LETTER 19 (G.Em.no/SW137(A.F.1) RELEASES R.S.M.
14.12.15 "	Individual Training. Below received direct from Battalion. Strength of the Battalion (N.C.O.s and MEN) 505	AUTHORITY. LETTER Col I/c T.F. RECORDS NO 17655, DATED 14.12.15 R.S.M R.S.M
15.12.15 "	Individual Training	
16.12.15 "	Individual Training. 1 Case for Bedford G.S. Wagons received from T.H. 9 Daniels, STROUD {dispatched to (ORDNANCE DEPOT WEEDON 958 Bags Bayonet Infamous Pattern 49 Shovels G.S.	R.S.M.

WAR DIARY
INTELLIGENCE SUMMARY.

(Erase heading not required.)

Army Form C. 2118.

Hour, Date, Place	Summary of Events and Information	Remarks and references to Appendices
17.12.15 Danbury	Individual Training. 9 Standard G.S. Wagons received from T.H. & J. DANIELS. STROUD.	R.S.M.
18.12.15 "	Individual Training. Two Men demobilized for Munition Work	AUTHORITY. W.O. LETTER 19/Gen.No/5415(AG1) RELEASES. R.S.M. R.S.M
19.12.15. 9.45 A.M. "	Church Parade	R S M
20.12.15 "	Individual Training	R S M
21.12.15 "	Individual Training. 30 Sets Webbing Equipment complete received from O.C. COLCHESTER 1 Bag Ammunition. S.A. complete with Tools received from G.O.O WEEDON. Strength of the Battalion (N Co's and MEN) 503.	R.S.M

Army Form C. 2118.

WAR DIARY
INTELLIGENCE SUMMARY.

(Erase heading not required.)

Instructions regarding War Diaries and Intelligence Summaries are contained in F.S. Regs., Part II. and the Staff Manual respectively. Title pages will be prepared in manuscript.

Hour, Date, Place	Summary of Events and Information	Remarks and references to Appendices
22.12.15. Danbury	Individual Training. LIEUT-COL COATES proceeded to BIRMINGHAM on Recruiting duty. MAJOR E.A.M. BINDLOSS assumed Command of the Battalion. CAPT and ADJT R.C. SCOTT-MURRAY proceeded on leave of absence. CAPT. R.S. MACKENZIE Acting Adjutant.	R. S. M.
23.12.15. "	Individual Training. 3 Helmets (Anti Gas) received from O.O. CHELMSFORD.	R. S. M.
24.12.15 "	Individual Training. LIEUT-COL COATES returned from BIRMINGHAM and resumed Command of the Battalion. 96 chat Capes received from O.O. WEEDON.	
25.12.15. 10 AM "	Church Parade	R.S.M.
26.12.15 9.45 AM "	Church Parade.	R.S.M. R.S.M.
27.12.15. "	Individual Training.	R.S.M.
28.12.15. "	Individual Training	R.S.M.

Army Form C. 2118.

WAR DIARY
INTELLIGENCE SUMMARY.

(Erase heading not required.)

Instructions regarding War Diaries and Intelligence Summaries are contained in F. S. Regs., Part II and the Staff Manual respectively. Title pages will be prepared in manuscript.

Hour, Date, Place	Summary of Events and Information	Remarks and references to Appendices
29.12.15. Danbury	Individual Training. 16 Recruits arrived from BIRMINGHAM	R.S.M.
30.12.15 "	Orders for tactical exercise Received from 162 INF BDE. Company Training. CAPT and Adjt J.R.C. SCOTT-MURRAY returned from Gas of scheme.	APPENDIX A. R.S.M.
31.12.15 "	Battalion paraded at 6-30 A.M. for tactical exercise and returned to camp at 3.20 P.M.	APPENDIX B. R.S.M.

A.J. Coates
Lt. Col.,
Comd'g 2/5th. Bn. R. War. Reg.
4/1/16.

COPY.
SECRET.   B.M.W./144/15   Copy No.4.
29.12.15.

Appendix A

182nd Inf. Bde Order No.30.

Ref. ½" O.S.   29. 12. 15.
Sheet 30.

1. Information.
"B" Composite Brigade (less Artillery) will assemble at COLD NORTON at 11 a.m. Friday 31st December 1915.

2. Intention.
Troops will be prepared to occupy the position ALTHORNE Station-ALTHORNE BARNS-LAWLING HALL-MARSH HOUSE. Position will not be occupied, but while troops are resting and feeding mounted officers will carry out a reconnaissance of the position, the approaches thereto, and the artillery positions.

3. Detail.
Troops will assemble in fields immediately E of COLD NORTON Station as follows:-

Cyclist Co less 2 platoons by route as previously instructed.

2/2nd R.F.A.Bde (officers only) by route as previously instructed.

2/2nd Fld Co.R.E.RxExBy route as previously instructed joining DANBURY column at Rd junc N of 1st L in LITTLE GRANGE at 9.30 a.m.

182nd Inf Bde Bde Hdqrs, 2/5th & 2/7th Bn.R.War.R. will pass RUNSELL GREEN at 9.7 a.m. in order named. 2/6th and 2/8th Bns R.War.R. will join the Brigade at X Rds at HAZELEIGH CHURCH at 9.50 am in order named.

No.2 Fld Amb by route as previously instructed.

4. Protection.
O.C.Cyclist Co. will be responsible for the protection of the Brigade at point of assembly.

5. Reconnaissance
All mounted Officers will report to G.O.C. at the RED LION LATCHINGDON at 11.30 a.m.

6. Reports.
To head of 182nd Inf.Bde.

Time.............

Copies as per distribution list.
Sgd. O.P.L.Hoskyns.Capt.
B.M. 182nd Infantry Bde.

INSTRUCTIONS.

i. This is a practice march.
ii. Preserved meat and biscuit will be drawn for 31.12.15.
iii. Iron rations, Field Dressing and Operation Maps will NOT be issued but all arrangements will be made to do so.
iv. Units of 182nd Bde will report time taken to turn out to Bde Hdqrs by 6 p.m. 31.12.15.
v. Parade states will be handed to Staff Capt 182nd Inf.Bde at point of assembly.
vi. Units will report time of their departure direct to Divisional Headquarters.

SECRET *APPENDIX. B.*
2/5th R.War.R.Order No.30.
Ref.½" O.S.Sheet 30.
          Copy No...1...
          30. 12.1915.

1. **INTENTION.** The G.O.C. 182nd Infantry Brigade intends to assemble at COLD NORTON tomorrow and to occupy the position ALTHORNE STATION - ALTHORNE BARNS - LAWLING HALL - MARSH HOUSE.

2. **PARADE.** The Battalion will parade as for an "ALARM" at 8.30 a.m. tomorrow. Detailed parade states to be handed to the Adjutant at 8.15 a.m.

3. **AMMUNITION** .303 Ball ammunition in accordance with F.S.Manual will be carried and will be issued to Companies at the Quartermasters Stores at 8 a.m. tomorrow.

4. **IRON RATIONS FIELD DRESSINGS** Iron Rations and Field Dressings will be issued to Companies at the Quartermasters Stores at 7.30 a.m. tomorrow.

5. **MAPS.** ½" O.S. Maps sheet 30 will be issued by the Adjutant to Officers at the Orderly Room at 8 p.m. today.

6. **SICK RECRUITS** Lieut.M.W.O'Bryen will remain in Camp in charge of the Sick and the Recruits.

7. **RECONNAISSANCE** All mounted officers will report to the O.C. at the RED LION, LATCHINGDON at 11.30 a.m. tomorrow.

          (Signed) R.C.Scott-Murray.Capt & Adjt
          2/5th R.Warwick Regiment.

Copy No. 1 to War Diary.
  :   2-5 to O.C.Coys.
  :   6 to Transport Officer.
  :   7 to Signalling Officer.
  :   8 to Quartermaster.
  :   9 to Medical Officer.

per Private Evans at 6 p.m.

CONFIDENTIAL.

WAR DIARY OF

2/5th Battalion, Royal Warwickshire Regiment,

from 1st January 1916 to 31st January 1916.

Volume 3.

Army Form C. 2118

WAR DIARY or INTELLIGENCE SUMMARY
(Erase heading not required.)

Instructions regarding War Diaries and Intelligence Summaries are contained in F. S. Regs., Part II. and the Staff Manual respectively. Title Pages will be prepared in manuscript.

Place	Date	Hour	Summary of Events and Information	Remarks and references to Appendices
BANBURY	1.1.16		Individual Training. LIEUT-COL COATES proceeded on leave of absence. MAJOR E.A.M. B.IND bss assumed Command of the Battalion.	R.S.M.
"	2.1.16.	9.45am	Church Parade.	R.S.M.
"	3.1.16.		Individual Training. 1 N.C.O. and 1 M.N demobilised for Munition Work.	AUTHORITY W.O.LETTER 19/GEN.NO/5405(A.G.1) RELEASES. R.S.M.
"	4.1.16.		Individual Training. Orders for Tactical Exercise received from 162nd INF BDE	AUTHORITY BRIGADE TELEPHONE MESSAGE 98.M.A.15.3 4.1.16. R.S.M.

WAR DIARY
or
INTELLIGENCE SUMMARY

Army Form C. 2118

Place	Date	Hour	Summary of Events and Information	Remarks and references to Appendices
CAMBURY	3.1.16	9.30 AM	Battalion paraded for Tactical Exercise and returned to Camp at 12-30 PM	APPENDIX 1 R.S.M.
"	6.1.16		Individual Training. Class of Instruction for Junior N.C.O.'s commenced 1 hour electro-theoretical of Instruction Work.	AUTHORITY W.O. LETTER APP. EN No. 87/Gen.) RELEASES R.S.M.
"	7.1.16		Individual Training	R.S.M.
"	8.1.16	8.15 A.M.	Individual Training. Fire in the Officers Mess.	R.S.M.
"	9.1.16	9.45 A.M.	Church Parade. 1 N.C.O. went to 61st Provisional Battalion	AUTHORITY 24th T.F. RECORD 10/11/15
			LIEUT-COL COATES returned from leave of absence and resumed command of the Battalion.	R.S.M.

Army Form C. 2118

WAR DIARY
or
INTELLIGENCE SUMMARY
(Erase heading not required.)

Instructions regarding War Diaries and Intelligence Summaries are contained in F. S. Regs., Part II. and the Staff Manual respectively. Title Pages will be prepared in manuscript.

Place	Date	Hour	Summary of Events and Information	Remarks and references to Appendices
BANBURY	10.1.16		Individual Training. Strength of the Battalion 526 N.C.O.'s and Men	R.S.M.
"		3.0 p.m.	Court of Inquiry into the Fire in the Officers lines	
"	11.1.16		Individual Training. 9 men went to the 51st Provisional Battalion. Orders received for the Battalion to parade in NEEDHAM - WALTER Golf Links L⁴ O.S Map SHEET 30 at 11 a.m.	AUTHORITY COL. TIPPING PASSED ON BRIGADE ROUTINE ORDER. HEAD OFFICE. R.S.M.
"	12.1.16		Battalion paraded at 9 A.M. for Brigade Drill. Postponed on account of Wet Weather. Individual Training. 7 Recruits arrived from DEPOT. 1 Man returned from Demobilisation.	AUTHORITY BRIGADE TEL. MESSAGE W.M.193255B. R.S.M.
"	13.1.16		Parade for Brigade Drill at NEEDHAM - WALTER GOLF LINKS L⁴ O.S MAP SHEET 30. 2nd LIEUTS ROBERTSON and HOWARD transferred to 3/5 R. WAR. R. as from 12.1.16.	AUTHORITY BRIGADE TRAINING W.A.80 12.1.16 AUTHORITY C. Ford E.C. LETTER 1249 A/13. 135. R.S.M.

Army Form C. 2118

WAR DIARY
or
INTELLIGENCE SUMMARY
(Erase heading not required.)

Instructions regarding War Diaries and Intelligence Summaries are contained in F. S. Regs., Part II. and the Staff Manual respectively. Title Pages will be prepared in manuscript.

Place	Date	Hour	Summary of Events and Information	Remarks and references to Appendices
Purfleet	14.1.16.		Individual Training	
		M.AM.	190 Favorables received from T.F.A. WARWICK	R.S.M.
			15 Greencards & 5 received from D.D.O.S. WOOLWICH.	
			Medical Board at Medical Inspection Room Col BULL R.A.M.C. A.D.M.S. President	
"	15.1.16. 9 A.M.		Route March. Route GRACES WALK - GT BADDOW - SANDON - DANBURY COMMON 6 1/2 AS MAP SHEET. 30.	R.S.M.
"	16.1.16. 9.30 a.m.		Church Parade	R.S.M.
"	17.1.16.		Individual Training	
			2 men despatched for Transfer Work.	AUTHORITY W.O. LETTER 11/GEN/NO. 5145(A.H.) RELEASES.
			1 Man discharged [Para 392. K.R.]	In R.T.F. RECORDS D/SQUZI R.S.M.
"	18.1.16. 9 a.m.		Individual Training	
		M.A.M	Inspection of Battalion by MAJ-GEN DICKSON.	
		4 P.M.	Part of Signalling Office 3rd ARMY	
			240 Recruits arrived from 3/5 R. WAR. R.	
			4 Recruits arrived from D'pot	
			100 Blanket received from D.O. COLCHESTER.	R.S.M.

WAR DIARY or INTELLIGENCE SUMMARY

Army Form C. 2118

(Erase heading not required.)

Instructions regarding War Diaries and Intelligence Summaries are contained in F. S. Regs., Part II. and the Staff Manual respectively. Title Pages will be prepared in manuscript.

Place	Date	Hour	Summary of Events and Information	Remarks and references to Appendices
D.H.Q. DRY	19.1.16		Individual Training. 3 Recruits arrived from Depot.	R.S.M.
"	20.1.16		Inspection of Battalion at Physical Drill by Capt. SHARP, School of Gymnasia, ALDERSHOT. Individual Training. Strength 788 N.C.O.'s and M.E.N.	R.S.M.
"	21.1.16		Individual Training.	R.S.M.
"	22.1.16		Individual Training. 1 Man discharged.	AUTHORITY 10% WR RECORDS LETTER 6/F 6953/A.T.6. R.S.M.
"			Armourer Sergt attached from A.O.C. [A.O.C. Order 59. 19.1.16.]	R.S.M.
"	23.1.16	9-30 AM	Church Parade.	R.S.M.
"	24.1.16		Individual Training.	R.S.M.
"		2-30 PM	G.O.C. 182" INF. BDE. Inspected Books of the Battalion. 1 Recruit arrived from Depot.	R.S.M.
"	25.1.16		Individual Training. 6 Men to 51st Provisional Battalion.	AUTHORITY 10% WR RECORDS P2221/0.17/15 R.S.M.

Army Form C. 2118

WAR DIARY
or
INTELLIGENCE SUMMARY
(Erase heading not required.)

Instructions regarding War Diaries and Intelligence Summaries are contained in F. S. Regs., Part II. and the Staff Manual respectively. Title Pages will be prepared in manuscript.

Place	Date	Hour	Summary of Events and Information	Remarks and references to Appendices
BANBURY	26.1.16		Individual Training. No Short L.E Rifles from O.O. WEEDON. 2 Men returned from Demobilization	R.S.M.
"	27.1.16		Individual Training	
		2.30 pm	Inspection of Transport by O.C. A.S.C. 1 Man returned from Demobilization. 7 Sets Officers Saddlery from O.O. COLCHESTER.	R.S.M.
"	28.1.16		Individual Training. Farriers Tools and Wire Cutters from O.O. HARWICH	R.S.M.
"	29.1.16		Individual Training	R.S.M.
	30.1.16	9.45am	Church Parade. Strength 763. NCO's and MEN.	R.S.M.
"	31.1.16		Individual Training. 1 Man demobilised for munition work	AUTHORITY W.O. LETTER 19/52/N.R.O. 5415 (A.G.1) RELEASES R.S.M.

W. Coates, Lt. Col.,
Comd'g. 17th (S) Bn. R. War. Reg.
1/2/16.

Confidential.

War Diary
2/5 Royal Warwickshire Regt.

May 21st 1916 to May 31st 1916.

Vol. 1

Army Form C. 2118.

WAR DIARY
or
INTELLIGENCE SUMMARY.
(Erase heading not required.)

Instructions regarding War Diaries and Intelligence Summaries are contained in F. S. Regs., Part II. and the Staff Manual respectively. Title pages will be prepared in manuscript.

Place	Date	Hour	Summary of Events and Information	Remarks and references to Appendices
PERHAM DOWN	21/5/16	10 a.m.	Battn. Paraded to proceed overseas. Strength 30 Officers: 950 O.R.: 64 animals: 31 vehicles. Sailed from SOUTHAMPTON 5 p.m.	H.P.C.
HAVRE	22/5/16	2 a.m.	Arrived HAVRE. Disembarkation commenced at 7 a.m. Marched to Docks REST CAMP.	H.P.C.
"	23/5/16	6 a.m.	26 Officers: 698 O.R. and all transport commenced entrainment. 6 Officers: 250 O.R. entrained at 11 a.m. Orderly room Corpl. De Vane. 1 Man to Hospital.	H.P.C.
MERVILLE	24/5/16	—	1st party detrained at MERVILLE & marched to BELLERIVE arriving at 11 a.m. 2nd party arrived at BELLERIVE at 6 p.m.	H.P.C.
BELLERIVE	25/5/16	—	Company training. 2 officers attached.	H.P.C.
"	26/5/16	7.30 a.m.	Route march: BELLERIVE - CHOCQUES - GONNEHEM - Mt. BERNENCHON.	H.P.C.
"	27/5/16	—	Company training. Orders received for move to BETHUNE.	H.P.C.
"	28/5/16	11 a.m.	Church parade. Move to BETHUNE cancelled. 7 Officers visit trenches, AUCHY sector	H.P.C.
"	29/5/16	—	Company training. Orders received for attachment to 19th INF. BDE.	H.P.C.
"	30/5/16	2 p.m.	Marched to BEUVRY coming under orders of 19th INF. BDE. Two Companies remained in BEUVRY, one Company attached to 2nd R. Welch Fusiliers & one Company to 2nd R. Pioneers in AUCHY sector of trenches.	H.P.C.
BEUVRY	31/5/16	—	Company training.	H.P.C.

O. L. Coats
Maj.
Comdg. 1/5 Warwick Regt.
1/6/16.

WAR DIARY
2/5 WARWICK REGT
JUNE 1916

(b) The General Officers Commanding Brigades concerned will allot the garrisons necessary for the above sections which for the present are to be of minimum strength. (Companies calculated at 150 rifles).

Right Section and Left Section.

    Trenches   - - 6 Companies.
    Close support- - 4 Companies.
    Brigade Reserve- 4 Companies.

Centre Section.

    Trenches   - - 8 Companies.
    Close support- - 4 Companies.
    Brigade Reserve- 4 Companies.

(c) The remaining troops, which on above estimate would be about -

    80th. Infantry Brigade...1½ Battalions.
    82nd. Infantry Brigade...1½ Battalions.
    81st. Infantry Brigade...2 Battalions.

will be accommodated in billets -

One battalion of each Brigade at YPRES.

One half battalion of 80th. and 82nd. Brigades and one battalion of 81st. Brigade at VLAMERTINGHE.

These battalions will form a composite Brigade to act as Divisional Reserve under the command of the senior Battalion Commander.

An officer will be detailed to act as permanent Staff Officer, Headquarters, YPRES.

They will be at the disposal of their own Brigade Commanders to carry out reliefs. Further they will be available for work on the G.H.Q. or Second Line.

Army Form C. 2118.

2/5 WM/MKS Vol 2

WAR DIARY
or
INTELLIGENCE SUMMARY.
(Erase heading not required.)

Instructions regarding War Diaries and Intelligence Summaries are contained in F.S. Regs., Part II. and the Staff Manual respectively. Title pages will be prepared in manuscript.

Place	Date	Hour	Summary of Events and Information	Remarks and references to Appendices
BEUVRY	1/6/16	9 am	Company Training continued. A & C Coys in Trenches for instruction.	A.J.K.
"	2/6/16	9 am	Company Training continued. A & C Coys in Trenches. B & D Coys relieved A & C at 10 pm. Casualties 2 killed 2 wounded.	M/— M/— M/— M/—
"	3/6/16		Company Training	
"	4/6/16		CHURCH PARADE & Company Training. Also relieve at 11pm to A & C Coys.	
"	5/6/16		Battalion took over NIGHT RIGHT Sector, relief completed at 11 pm. Appendix 1	
"	6/6/16		Quiet on situation occupied.	M/—
"	7/6/16		Quiet. Visit of G.O.C. 33 Div. He went round Fire Trenches.	
"	8/6/16		at 2.30 am enemy sprung a small mine on battalion front close to our & out of trenches distance of our sap. A fair amount of Artillery activity during the afternoon in reply & our Trench Mortar & Rifle Grenade fire on the new mine crater. Relieved by 2 Yorks appendix in BARRACKS, BETHUNE,	M/— M/—
"	9/6/16		Battalion marched to Billets at BELLE RIVE.	
BELLE RIVE	10/6/16		Rest. Cleaning and Inspections.	R/—
"	11/6/16		Inspection at 10.30 am by Maj Gen Sir R.C.B. HAMING K.C.B. G.O.C. 11th Corps.	N/—
"	12/6/16		Battalion moved to MERVILLE. Maj CAPPER & 70 O.R. & TUNNELLING COY.	

Army Form C. 2118.

WAR DIARY or INTELLIGENCE SUMMARY.

(Erase heading not required.)

2/5 WARWICK Regt.

June 1916

Place	Date	Hour	Summary of Events and Information	Remarks and references to Appendices
MERVILLE	13/6/16		COMPANY TRAINING. Lt HOPKINS & 16 O.R. to 182 TRENCH MORTAR BATTERY	M.h
"	14/6/16		COMPANY TRAINING	M.h
"	15/6/16		COMPANY TRAINING	M.h
"	16/6/16		COMPANY TRAINING. 2 Lts CLASS & H.J. O'BRYEN & 18 O.R. to Machine gun Company	M.h
"	17/6/16		Battalion moved to FOSSE	
FOSSE	18/6/16		16 Officers 640 O.R. on hostile parts convoys for defender	R.h
"	19/4/16		10 officers 400 O R do Specialist Training	T.M
"	20/6/16		Company Training 2nd Lt CLASS & H.J. O'BRYEN & 16 O.R returned from H.Q. b.	R.h
"	21/6/16		Battalion took on MOATED GRANGE SECTION of trenches. Appendix III relief complete	11.30pm M.h
MOATED	22/6/16		minor operations	M.h
GRANGE	23/6/16		do	T.M
SECTOR	24/6/16		do	A.M
"	25/6/16		do	T.M
"	26/6/16		Artillery Bombardment of enemy with Trench Mortar & Rifle grenade cooperation. Bombing raid obtained much useful Appendix 4	M.h
"	27/6/16		information but owing to amount of wire un cut could not get through enemy trenches	M.h

Army Form C. 2118.

WAR DIARY
or
INTELLIGENCE SUMMARY.
(Erase heading not required.)

Instructions regarding War Diaries and Intelligence Summaries are contained in F. S. Regs., Part II. and the Staff Manual respectively. Title pages will be prepared in manuscript.

Place	Date	Hour	Summary of Events and Information	Remarks and references to Appendices
MORTED	28/4/16		Minor Operations	Othr
BRAYLE	28/4/16		do	TM2
SECTOR	29		do See Appendix 5. The wind was not favourable throughout the	TM2
			length of the line & the Regts. keeping discharged no smoke.	
	30		Minor Operations	Nil

O. Carth M.
Comdg. 1/5 Warwicks.

720

Appendix 1

SECRET.   Copy No. 15
RED SQUARE OPERATION ORDER No.1.   5.6.16.
Reference Map Combined No.36.

1. The Battalion will take over the AUCHY RIGHT sector tonight.

2. Dispositions :-   Right 'C' Coy. Centre 'D' Coy.
                     Left 'B' Coy.   Reserve 'A' Coy.

3. 'B' and 'D' Companies will move under orders of 1st Cameronians and 1/5 Scottish Rifles respectively. Guides for 'A' and 'C' Coys will be at CAMBRIN CHURCH at 8.30 p.m. numbered as follows :-
   Right front platoon   C — 1.
   Left   "   "   C — 2.
   Right support "   C — 3.
   Left   "   "   C — 4.
   RAILWAY RESERVE "   'A' — 7.
   RAILWAY KEEP   "   A — 8.
   FACTORY TRENCH platoons A — 5 and 6.
   These eight platoons will enter via LEWIS ALLEY.

4. 1 Officer and 4 N.C.O's of the 19th INF BDE will be attached to each Company. Those for 'B' and 'D' Companies will join them in the line. Those for 'A' Company will join it at CAMBRIN CHURCH at 8.30 p.m. Those for 'C' Company will join it at BEUVRY before leaving.

5. Company 2nds in Command, Company Sergeant Majors, Lewis Gunners and Bombers of 'A' and 'C' Companies and the Snipers and observers of all Companies together with the Regimental Sergeant Major Battalion Signallers and Cpl Bennett will be met at ANNEQUIN cross roads at 2 p.m. They will parade under Capt. Gibson at Battalion Headquarters at 1 p.m. Lewis Gunners and Bombers of 'B' and 'D' Companies will take over in accordance with orders to be issued by Lieuts Barnes and O'Bryen respectively.

6. All cooking will be done in FACTORY TRENCH, Dixies, rations and baggage will be dumped at BRAYS KEEP (A.25.d.1.1.) Cookers will return to BEUVRY. 'A' Company will detail 1 N.C.O. and 6 men to march with the Transport and unload, after which they will rejoin their platoons in the trenches.

7. Mess boxes and trench kits etc of 'A' and 'C' Companies will be ready for collection by 6 p.m. Stores or baggage not required in the trenches will be sent by Companies to the Quartermasters Stores by 6 p.m.

8. Lieut.W.G.C.Lane will hand over billets and obtain the usual certificates. He will afterwards remain in BEUVRY under the Quartermaster.

1.

2.

9. O.C. Companies will report relief complete by sending the one word "LONDON" on the buzzer. Instructions have been given to all signallers regarding the use of the telephones and these are not to be contravened by any officer.

                                          Capt & Adjt.
                                  Red Square Battalion.

Issued at 11 a.m.

Copy No. 1 to 1st Cameronians.
        2 to 1/5 Scottish Rifles.
        3 to 19th Inf Bde.
        4 to 182nd Inf Bde.
        5 to 'A' Coy
        6 to 'B' Coy.
        7 to 'C' Coy.
        8 to 'D' Coy.
        9 to L.Gun Officer.
       10 to Bombing Officer.
       11 to Sniping Officer.
       12 to Q.M.
       13 to T.O.
       14 to Signals.
       15 to War Diary.
       16 to File.

Appendix ii

SECRET.

RED SQUARE OPERATION ORDER No. 2. Copy No. 17.
Reference Map Combined No.36 (BETHUNE) 8.6.16.

1. The Battalion will be relieved tonight and will move into billets at BETHUNE.

2. Guides will meet incoming units at CAMBRIN CHURCH as follows :-
   Snipers, Bombers, Signallers, and Lewis Gunners at 3 p.m.
   H.Q. and 'A' Coys at 8.30 p.m.
   'C' Coy at 8.45 p.m.
   'D' Coy at 9 p.m.
   'B' Coy 9.15 p.m.

3. Trench Stores will be handed over to the relieving Battalion. Lists will be prepared beforehand in duplicate, one being sent to the Adjutant and the other being handed over.

4. Certificates that trenches are clean will be handed to the Adjutant immediately after relief.

5. O.C. Coys will report relief complete by code word.

D/Coates,
Lieut.Col.
Commdg Red Square Battalion

Issued at 12 noon.

Copy No. 1 to 182nd Inf Bde.
        2 to 'A' Coy.
        3 to 'B' Coy.
        4 to 'C' Coy.
        5 to 'D' Coy.
        6 to L.Gun Officer.
        7 to Bombing Officer.
        8 to Sniping Officer.
        9 to Q.M.
       10 to T.O.
       11 to Signals.
       12 to War Diary.
       13 to File.
       14 to 2nd Worcesters.

SECRET.   Appendix III

RED SQUARE OPERATION ORDER No. 3. Copy No. 12
Reference Map Combined No.36 (BETHUNE) 21.6.16.

1. The Battalion will take over the MOATED GRANGE sub-section tonight.

2. Dispositions :- Right 'C' Coy., Centre 'B' Coy.,
   Left 'A' Coy., Reserve 'D' Coy.

3. Guides will be provided at M.15.c.7.6. at the following hours:-
   'D' Coy .... 4 p.m.
   'A' Coy .... 9 p.m.
   'C' Coy .... 9.30 p.m.
   'B' Coy............ 10 p.m.
   The remainder of H.Q. Coy will move in rear of 'A' Coy.

4. Coy 2nds in Command, Regtl Sergt.Major, Coy Sgt Majors, Cpl Bennett, Lewis Gunners, Snipers, Signallers & Bombers will be met by guides at the Police Post in SOUTH TILLELOY STREET at 3 p.m.

5. All parties will move independently via BOUT DE VILLE and PONT DU HEM. Movements of troops along or east of the BELLE CROIX - LA BASSEE Road will be by platoons at 100 yards distance by day and 50 yards distance by night. Wagons and cars will move by threes at the same distances.

6. The Transport and Quartermasters Stores will move to R.23.b.9.2.
   The Battalion dump for rations and baggage will be at the junction of road and railway at M.21.d.7.2.
   The dump for R.E. materials is at the junction of road and railway about M.21.a.4.1. From these points all stores will be trolleyed by night only up to the Battalion dump about M.29.c.1.6.
   Ration and baggage parties for all companies will be provided by 'D' Coy.

7. Mess Boxes and Trench kits etc will be ready for collection at 6 p.m. Stores and baggage not required in the trenches, together with service dress caps (the latter to be packed without badges in the cases provided by the Quartermaster) will be sent by Companies to the Quartermasters Stores by 6 p.m. Cookers will be ready for collection at 7 p.m. These will proceed to the new Transport Field.

8. 2/Lieut.W.G.C.Lane will hand over billets and obtain the usual certificates. He will afterwards be attached for duty to the Quartermasters Stores.

9. O.C. Coys will report relief complete by the code word.

P. Coates, Lieut.Col.
Commdg Red Square Battalion.

Issued at 11 a.m.
Copy No. 1 to 182nd Inf Bde.
       2 to 'A' Coy.
       3 to 'B' Coy
       4 to 'C' Coy   Copy No.10 to T.O.
       5 to 'D' Coy   11 to Signals.
       6 to L.Gun Officer.   12 to War Diary.
       7 to Bombing Officer.   13 to File.
       8 to Sniping Officer.   14 to 2/4th Gloucesters.
       9 to Q.M.

SECRET.

RED SQUARE OPERATION ORDER No. 4.
Reference:- Trench Map J.

Copy No. 1
June 26th. 1916.

1. Minor operations will take place tonight.

2. Artillery fire on certain points of the enemys trenches and wire between 11.40 p.m. and 1.40 a.m. has been arranged by O.C. Right Group 61st. Divisional Artillery.

3. Three Light Trench Mortars firing at the rate of ten rounds per minute will fire five bursts of two minutes each at the following times :- Midnight, 12.5 a.m., 12.9 a.m., 12.17 a.m. and 12.28 a.m., on the enemys front line from M.30.c.5½.6½. to M.36.a.5.8.

4. Three regimental batteries of rifle grenades will fire at the same times at their fastest rate on the vicinity of M.30.c.5.8. and M.36.a.5.6.

5. The Lewis Guns will fire intermittently all night on the gaps in the enemys wire at points 53 and 45.

6. Between 11.45 p.m. and 12.5 a.m. a continuous smoke cloud will be kept up under arrangements to be made by Lieut. White on our parapet between M.36.a.0.4. and M.30.c.2½.3. Similar clouds will also be sent up by the Battalions on our right and left.

7. A bombing party from 'C' Coy will attack at midnight the ditch running from M.36.c.1½.9¾. to M.36.c.3.8½. and on to the enemys sap near M.36.c.3.8¾.

8. Detailed reports will be sent by all Companies in the front line to Battalion Headquarters at 6.30 a.m. tomorrow.

Coates,
Lieut. Col.
Commanding.

Issued at 8.45 p.m.

Copy No. 1 to War Diary.
2 to File.
3 to 'A' Coy.
4 to 'B' Coy.
5 to 'C' Coy.
6 to 'D' Coy.
7 to Bombing Officer.
8 to Lewis Gun Officer.

SECRET.

RED SQUARE OPERATION ORDER No.5. Copy No. 7
Reference:- New Trench Map. June 29th. 1916.

1. If the wind is favourable, smoke will be discharged tonight along the whole Brigade front from 2.50 a.m. to 3.25 a.m. (30th June)

2. One smoke bomb will be discharged at intervals of 25 yards along the whole Company front every minute for the 35 minutes, all arrangements being made by Company Commanders. It is important that the bombs should not be discharged too quickly as the smoke must not all be expended before the end of the time. The intervals given have been worked out by the Brigade but if it is found that the supply of bombs is insufficient ('A' Coy 36 boxes 'B' and 'C' Coys 35 boxes each) Company Commanders will make the best arrangements they can.

3. The smoke will only be discharged if the wind is between N.N.W. and W. and if the smoke is blown back over our trenches at any point the order to stop discharge at that particular point will be given by the nearest officer.

4. Short bursts of rapid fire at the enemys parapet are to be opened by rifles, Lewis Guns and Machine Guns along the whole Brigade front at 2.55 a.m., 3.5 a.m, 3.15 a.m., and 4.20 a.m.

5. The fire ordered in the previous para will be carried out in any event, but the following code will be used regarding the discharge of smoke :-
    F. Favourable.
    U. Unfavourable.
   e.g. 4 F means wind four miles per hour favourable, 4 U means wind four miles per hour unfavourable. Company Commanders will send a wind report by this code to H.Q. on the buzzer at about 2 a.m.
   The following code will be used from these H.Q. to cancel or carry on the discharge of smoke only :-
    C O Carry on.
    D W D Postponed for tonight.

6. O.C. Coys may send out any wiring parties or patrols they wish up to 2 a.m., arrangements being made with the Lewis Gun Officer to ensure the gaps in the enemys wire being kept open.
   'B' Coy will send out a patrol to examine the ground between the two ditches running S.E. from M35.b.9½.8. and M35.b.8½.6½. Information is required as to the state of the of the whole of the ditch running across these two from M36.a.1½.4. to M36.a.2½.5. and also about the gap in the enemys wire about M36.a.2½.4.

7. All R.E. working parties are cancelled tonight.

Issued at 8.45 p.m. Lieut.Col.
                     Commanding.

Copy No. 1 to 'A' Coy.   Copy No.5 to Lewis Gun O.
       2. to 'B' Coy.   6. to Bombing Officer.
       3. to 'C' Coy.   7 to War Diary.
       4. to 'D' Coy.   8. to File.

2/5th Bn Royal Warwickshire Regmt.

WAR DIARY.

VOLUME III.

From July 1st. 1916.

To July 31st. 1916.

WAR DIARY or INTELLIGENCE SUMMARY.

(Erase heading not required.)

Army Form C. 2118.

Place	Date	Hour	Summary of Events and Information	Remarks and references to Appendices
MOATED GRANGE SECTOR	1/7/16	9 p.m.	Germans opened intense bombardment of our front line & east end of main communication trench & placed a barrage on road in M.sq.d. They attempted raid but were driven off. Bombardment ceased 11.30 pm. Trenches for 50 yards were obliterated & serious damage along whole of line.	O/C
""	2/7/16	—	Quiet day generally.	O/C
""	3/7/16	—	" " "	O/C
""	4/7/16	11 a.m.	Relief by 1/6 Warwicks commenced. Battalion moved into support near CROIX BARBEE.	Appendix 11 O/C
CROIX BARBEE	5/7/16	—	Rest at CROIX BARBEE	O/C
""	6/7/16	—	Rest. Inspection by G.O.C. 61st Bn. 9 a.m.	O/C
""	7/7/16	—	Rest	O/C
""	8/7/16	—	Rest	O/C
""	9/7/16	—	Relief of enemy trenches at NEUVE CHAPELLE, 10 p.m. Party did not enter trenches owing to enemy's MG fire.	Appendix 2 O/C
NEUVE CHAPELLE (Left)	10/7/16	6.45 a.m.	Battn. took over left sub section of NEUVE CHAPELLE Sector.	Appendix 3 O/C
""	11/7/16	—	In trenches	O/C

WAR DIARY or INTELLIGENCE SUMMARY.

Army Form C. 2118.

Instructions regarding War Diaries and Intelligence Summaries are contained in F. S. Regs., Part II. and the Staff Manual respectively. Title pages will be prepared in manuscript.

(Erase heading not required.)

Place	Date	Hour	Summary of Events and Information	Remarks and references to Appendices
NEUVE CHAPELLE (L4,1)	12/7/16	—	In trenches	w/c
"	13/7/16	—	"	w/c
"	14/7/16	—	"	w/c
"	15/7/16	—	Relief by 13th EAST YORKS commenced at 3 pm. Battn proceeded to billets at LA GORGUE	w/c Appendix A
LA GORGUE	16/7/16	—	Rest	w/c
"	17/7/16	—	Rest. Battn route march	w/c
"	18/7/16	—	Rest. Company training	w/c
"	19/7/16	—	Battn in Divl Reserve for minor operations	w/c
"	20/7/16	—	Battn moved by buses to LAVENTIE (2 Coys at 3 am & HQrs & 2 coys at 6.20 am) marched back to LA GORGUE at 1 pm	w/c
"	21/7/16	—	Rest. Company training	w/c
"	22/7/16	—	Rest. Company training	w/c
"	23/7/16	11 am	Church parade	w/c
"	24/7/16	—	Company training	w/c
"	25/7/16	9.30 am	Route march : L17D – L10C – L3D – NEUF BERQUIN – L26C – LA GORGUE	w/c
"	26/7/16	—	Company training	w/c

736

Army Form C. 2118.

WAR DIARY
INTELLIGENCE SUMMARY.
(Erase heading not required.)

Instructions regarding War Diaries and Intelligence Summaries are contained in F. S. Regs., Part II. and the Staff Manual respectively. Title pages will be prepared in manuscript.

Place	Date	Hour	Summary of Events and Information	Remarks and references to Appendices
La Gorgue	27/7/16		Company Training	1916
"	28/7/16		"	1916
"	29/7/16		"	1916
"	30/7/16		Church Parade	1916
"	31/7/16		Route March La Gorgue – Estaires – L.17.d – L.11.c – L.4.a – L.3 – L.7.a – L.4.13 – La Gorgue	1916

3

W Coates M.
Comdg 1/5 Warwick Regt
2/8/16

777

Appendix 1

SECRET.
RED SQUARE OPERATION ORDER No.6.   Copy No. 12
    Reference:- New Trench Map.   July 3rd.1916.

1. The Battalion will be relieved tomorrow (July 4th) and will
   take over the billets in the RUE DU PUITS and defensive posts
   at present occupied by the 2/8th Warwicks.
   A Coy will be relieved by C Coy 2/8th Warwicks.
   D   do   D   do
   B   do   B   do
   C   do   A   do

2. Guides will meet the incoming unit in the RUE DU BACQUEROT
   at the entrance to SOUTH TILLELOY STREET in M.22.c. as follows:-
   One from Signallers and one from Lewis Gunners at 8 p.m.today.
   One per platoon from A Coy at 4 a.m. tomorrow.
           do   D Coy at 5 a.m. tomorrow.
           do   B Coy at 8 a.m. tomorrow.
           do   C Coy at 11 a.m. tomorrow.
   Under Company arrangements a chit will be given to each guide
   showing thereon the letter of the company being relieved, the
   letter of the Company relieving, and the position in line or
   support.
   Incoming traffic will be by SOUTH TILLELOY STREET only.
   All outgoing traffic will be via east half of SOUTH TILLELOY
   STREET - D COY RESERVE LINE - BALUCHI ROAD - M.27.d.8.3. -
   M.32.d.7.7.
   C.Q.M.Sergeants will meet their Companies on the LA BASSEE
   ROAD at the entrance to BALUCHI ROAD.
   H.Q. Coy will move out in rear of C Coy.

3. Intervals between sections of 50 yards will be maintained
   until arrival at B Coys new billets in M.33.a. Company
   Commanders will make arrangements to collect at that point all
   men temporarily attached to other Companies. A, C and D
   Coys will move on to their own billets with 50 yards interval
   between platoons.

4. The Machine Gun Sergeant and the Lewis Gun Team of C and D
   Coys will not be relieved until early tomorrow morning, those
   of A and B Coys proceeding immediately upon relief to take
   over the defensive posts of EUSTON and LORETTO respectively.
   A guide will be provided by the incoming unit.

5. All Company heavy baggage (including big dixies belonging to
   cookers) will be sent by Coys to the Battalion Rail-head by
   9 p.m. tonight. The Transport Officer will arrange for a
   limber to be at B Coys new billets at 6 a.m. to wait for and
   collect light baggage of H.Q.,A,C,and D Coys. As much as
   possible however will be sent out tonight.

6. A cold breakfast ration for all Companies will be sent up
   tonight and the only dixies to be retained are sufficient
   small ones for making tea in the morning. The Transport
   Officer will arrange to take the cookers of all Companies
   (complete with dixies) to new billets at daybreak. Two cooks
   per company will go out with the dixies tonight and will see
   that a hot meal is ready for all ranks on arrival in billets.

                        (SEE OVER)

7. Companies will report relief complete by the code word.

                                            W.L.Coates
                                                 Lieut.Col.
                                     Commdg 2/5th Warwicks.

Issued at 4 p.m.

Copy No. 1 to A Coy.
          2 to B Coy.
          3 to C Coy.
          4 to D Coy.
          5 to Quartermaster.
          6 to Transport Officer.
          7 to 182nd. Infantry Brigade.
          8 to ~~182nd Infantry Brigade~~. 2/8 Warwicks
          9 to Signals.
         10 to Machine Gun Sergeant.
         11 to War Diary.
         12 to File.

Appendix 2.

SECRET.

RED SQUARE OPERATION ORDER No.7.　　　　Copy No. 6
Reference :- New Trench Map.　　　　　　　July 9th. 1916.

1. C Composite Company will raid the portion of the
   enemy's line tonight at M.36.c.0.5. seizing the
   support trench and holding it for one hour in order to:-
   (a) Secure prisoners either wounded or unwounded.
   (b) Kill Germans.
   (c) Collect any papers, maps or marks of
       identification.
   (d) Capture if possible or to destroy any machine
       guns or trench mortars.
   (e) Secure specimens of German Very Light
       cartridges.

2. COMPOSITION OF PARTIES:-
   O.C. Raid.　Captain F.W. Foster.
   2 Signallers with telephone and duplicate wire of
     D5 cable.
   2 wire cutters to improve passage in wire for exit.
   8 parapet men.
   2 tape men.
   5 Lewis Gunners with gun.
   4 Stretcher Bearers with two stretchers.
   30 men to act as connecting files.

   Five Storming Parties as follows:-
   1 Officer or N.C.O.
   2 Bayonet men.
   2 Bombers.
   1 Carrier.
   1 R.E. with explosives for blocking.
   2 Intelligence men.

   Nos. 3 and 4 in addition 1 Bayonet man and 1 Bomber.

   No.5 in addition 1 Officer R.E.

   Torpedo party:-
   Lieut. VICKERAGE, 1 man R.E. and 8 men with 4 pipes
   25'X 1½" (the 8 men form part of the 30 connecting
   men afterwards and the 1 man R.E. joins No.5
   Storming party).

   Rear party (in our front line)
   C.O. Battn.　　　　　　　　　　　　　　　　)
   F.O.O. and Signaller with telephone) Near Bay 7.
   2 Signallers with telephone.　　　　　)
   2/Lieut. CHURCHOUSE and 30 other ranks for collection
     of stores, prisoners etc and for shooting 1½"
     Very Lights in direction of area occupied.
   2 Lewis Guns with teams on flanks in our front line.

3. DRESS:-
   Balaclava helmets and cardigan jackets: gas helmets:
   faces and hands blackened: no equipment, tunics or
   helmets.
   Officers:- Electric torches, revolvers, 15 bombs.
   Signallers:- 4 bombs, knobkerries.

1.

3. Continued.
   Parapet men.)
   Tape men.   ) Rifles and bayonets, 15 bombs.
   Bayonet men)
   Bombers.   )
   Carriers   ) 15 bombs, knobkerries.
   Torpedo men.)
   Machine Gunners. All but Nos.1 and 2 slung rifles
      and bayonets.
   S.Bearers. Stretchers: simulant.
   Intelligence men. Electric torches, revolvers or
      knobkerries, 15 bombs, slung haversacks.
   Wire cutters. Large clippers, 15 bombs.
   Connecting files. Rifle & bayonet & slung bandoliers.
   R.E. men. Knobkerries and 14 lbs guncotton.
      All rifles to be loaded with 1 round in chamber
   and ten in magazine.
   All bombs will be carefully cleaned and oiled.
   All ranks will wear white calico band xxxxxxxxxxx
   pinned firmly on both arms and covered lightly with
   a black cover. This cover will be removed on the
   order of O.C. Raid. No identity discs, pay books, papers
   badges or other marks will be taken or worn.

4. ARTILLERY PROGRAMME.
   Intense bombardment on other points from 11.5 to
   11.20 p.m. and from 11.25 to 11.30 p.m.
   A mine will be exploded just north of the BIRDCAGE
   at 11.23 p.m.
   Barrage on enemy support line in front from 11.30 p.m.
   to 12.35 a.m. and on enemy parapet in front from
   12.35 a.m. onwards.
   The medium trench mortars will fire 12 rounds on
   enemy wire in front from 11.9 to 11.15 p.m. during
   which time all ranks in front of our wire must lie flat.

5. At 9 p.m. the rear party will take over the front line
   between Bay 7 and the east end of BALUCHI ROAD both
   inclusive. The remaining parties will arrive in the
   front line at 10 p.m. Route via BALUCHI ROAD.

6. At 10.40 p.m. the O.C. Raid will lead through the
   sally port in Bay 2 in the following order:- Torpedo
   party, Nos.1,2,3 and 4 Storming Parties, Signallers,
   Parapet Party, No.5 Storming Party, Lewis Gunners,
   Stretcher Bearers, Tape men, wire cutters, connecting
   files and into assembly formation, just this side of
   the road. 2/Lieut.CHURCHOUSE will check the parties
   out.
   When all are in position and ready to move O.C.Raid
   will buzz "R" on the telephone.
   At 11.15 p.m. the parties will move up to the enemy
   wire at a steady walk in the same order as for exit
   through the sally port. If the O.C.Raid considers
   that any torpedos will be necessary the torpedo party
   will double ahead to lay and explode them.
   Upon arrival at the enemy wire the connecting files
   (including torpedo men) will be turned about by the
   N.C.O. i/c who will space them back in pairs along the
   tape at intervals of 16 yards. He will himself report
   to the C.O. in Bay 7 on arrival back.

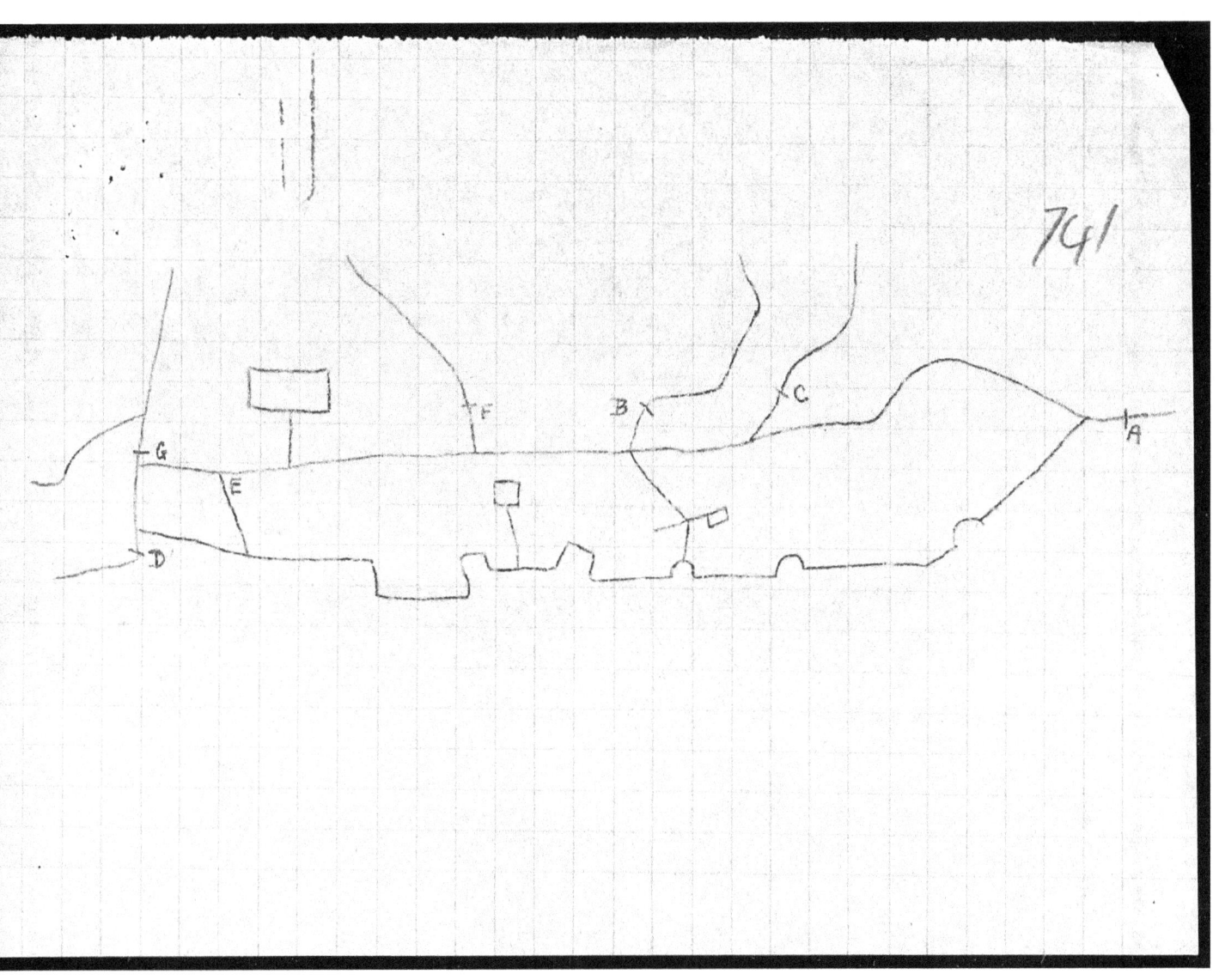
741

7. COMMUNICATION.
Two lines of D5 cable will be connected with a dugout in Bay 7 and carried out by the two signallers (one also having a telephone) who will be at least at 15 yards interval. They will both join up to O.C. Raid on the enemy parapet. If both wires are cut communication will be maintained by runner.
The two tape men will carry out a broad white tape through the gap in the wire to the enemy parapet, where they will divide and run outwards along the parapet as far as the Storming Parties have gone. After all parties are out 2/Lieut. CHURCHOUSE will run a white tape out through the sally port in Bay 4 to the other tape just our side of the road.
A password will be communicated to all ranks immediately beforehand.

8. DUTIES.
No.1 Storming Party to go to the right from point of entry and block at point A on sketch, bombing every dugout on the way.

No.2 Storming party to go to the left from point of entry and block at point D, detaching one bayonet man and bomber to clear communication trench to point E and to wait there until No. 4 Storming party has passed. All dugouts to be bombed on the way.

No. 3 Storming party to go to the right from point of entry and to go to the left down the first communication trench, where they will block at point B, then turn to the right and block at point C and carry on towards point A, bombing every dugout on the way.

No. 4 Storming Party to follow No.3 and turn to left just before point B, blocking point F and establishing a block at point G, bombing every dugout on the way.

No. 5 Storming Party will remain on the parapet under orders of O.C. Raid.

The Intelligence men will follow their own Storming parties and will systematically search all dug-outs and dead Germans collecting any papers, maps, identity discs etc.

R.E. men with Storming parties will carry explosives to destroy any trench mortars or machine guns if impossible to carry them away. They will also carry explosives for blocking purposes.
If the R.E. Officer is required for any special work they will send a message accordingly to the O.C. Raid.

Wire cutters will immediately improve the gap in the enemy wire as soon as all parties are through. They will devote their attention to the track made by the tape so, that exit is facilitated.

8. Continued.
Parapet men will line the enemy parapet and take any prisoners or salvage that may be handed up by the Storming Parties. They will (in conjunction with the Lewis Gunners) also see that the enemy do not come over the open ground in rear of their front line. Before retiring (and upon the order of O.C.Raid) they will drop tear bombs into the enemy trenches.

Stretcher bearers will remain with their stretchers near O.C. Raid.

Connecting men will be strung out in pairs at 16 yards distance across NO MANS LAND to our parapet to pass back any prisoners, heavy booty etc.

Tape men and signallers will act as per para 7. Both tape men will also act as parapet men when they have laid their tapes and will, in addition, cut the tape on their return just our side of the German wire.

9. RETURN.
When the O.C. Raid is satisfied that the area allotted has been thoroughly searched he will signal the withdrawal by blowing a whistle and ordering "C.I" both being repeated by the parapet men.
The Signaller with O.C.Raid signals "C.I" to our line when daylight rockets will be sent up from the flanks of our line.
Order of return as follows:-
Nos. 3 and 4 Storming Parties (and No.5 if previously sent in by O.C.Raid)
Nos. 1 and 2 Storming Parties.
  (each party dropping one tear bomb last thing before returning)
Parapet party (on order of O.C.Raid "Parapet Party C.I.").
   (O.C.Raid then signals that trench is vacated by buzzing "V")
Signallers.
Stretcher Bearers.
Lewis Gunners.
O.C.Raid.
Connecting men will be picked up by O.C. Raid as he returns.
Every effort will be made to bring in any casualties but this duty will not be performed by anybody except the stretcher bearers until after the signal to withdraw.

The word "Retire" will not be used and if heard will be considered as a German ruse. The order to return will be "C.I".

The O.C.Raid will exercise his discretion whether to come right in or to lie out until any artillery barrage has ceased.

744

9. CONTINUED.

Upon entering our line all leaders will check their men in and will report to 2/Lieut. CHURCHOUSE or to the C.O. at Bay 2 for directions.

10. Luminous watches will be carried by all leaders and will be synchronized by the C.O. at C Coys H.Q.'s at 8.15 p.m.

11. Men with coughs or colds will not be taken.

Coates
Lieut. Col.
Commdg Red Square Battalion.

Issued at 2.30 p.m.

Copy No. 1 to 61st Division (through 182nd Inf.Bde)
      2 to 182nd Inf.Bde.
      3)
      4) to C Coy.
      5 to War Diary.
      6 to file.
      7 to Lieut.Churchouse.
      8 to 2/8th R.Warwicks.
      9 to 2/7th R.Warwicks.
    10 to R.E.

SECRET.

RED SQUARE OPERATION ORDER NO.8. Copy No. 9
Reference:- New Trench Map. July 9th. 1916.

Appendix 3.

1. The Battalion will take over the left sub-section of the NEUVE CHAPELLE sector from the 2/6th Warwicks tomorrow,
    - A Coy 2/5th relieves D Coy 2/6th.
    - D Coy 2/5th " B Coy 2/6th.
    - B Coy 2/5th " C Coy 2/8th.
    - C Coy 2/5th " A Coy 2/6th.

    but with the new frontage pointed out to Company Commanders today.

2. Guides will be at the entrance to WINCHESTER TRENCH at the RUE DU BACQUEROT at the following times:-
    - Nos.1 to 4 for A Coy at 6.45.a.m.
    - 5 to 8 for D Coy at 9 a.m.
    - 9 to 12 for B Coy at 11.15 a.m.
    - 13 to 16 for C Coy at 11.30 a.m.

    Snipers will march with A Coy.
    Headquarters Company will move from billets at 8 a.m. 4 Lewis Guns and teams will march with D Coy unless sent in previously. One gun will remain in LORETTO and one in EUSTON POST, two men only staying with each. They will proceed to the trenches immediately on relief. The remainder of the days ration will be carried on the man.

3. The Garrisons of all posts will be reduced to 1 N.C.O. and 3 other ranks. These will be relieved by the 2/6th Warwicks later during the day and will then join the Battalion in the trenches at once.

4. All Companies will march by the following route:- CROIX BARBEE – Road junction M.19.d.6.7.– PONT DU HEM – LA FLINQUE – Road running south through M.16.d. to the entrance to WINCHESTER TRENCH. Usual distances will be kept.

5. 1 Officer and 1 N.C.O. per Company and the Bombing Officer will proceed to the trenches to take over at least 2 hours before the Companies are due to arrive

6. A limber will be sent to collect, before 8 o'clock tonight, anything that Companies may want to take into the trenches and which they can do without tonight. Empty round dixies for cooking in the trenches should be sent. Another limber will collect, at 7 a.m. tomorrow, the remainder of the baggage and mess boxes required in the trenches. These will all be taken to EPINETTE dump, one man per Company marching with each limber.

7. C.Q.M.S. will arrange to fetch all baggage for storage at the Q.M.Stores, making arrangements with the Transport Sergeant Major for the necessary vehicle. The Transport Sergeant Major will collect the field kitchens not later than 9 a.m. and take them to the Q.M.Stores.

8. Companies will report the relief completed by the new code word.

Coates
Lieut.Col.
Commdg Red Square Battalion.

Issued at 7 p.m.
Copy No.1 to A Coy.   Copy No.6 to M.G.Sergt.
    2 to B Coy.   7 to 2/8th Warwicks.
    3 to C Coy.   8 to War Diary.
    4 to D Coy.   9 to File.
    5 to H.Q.Coy.   10 to 2/6th Warwicks.

SECRET.

RED SQUARE OPERATION ORDER No. 9.
Reference:- BETHUNE Map.

Copy No. 10746
July 15th. 1916.

1. The sub-section will be taken over this afternoon by the 13th. E. York Regt, guides being provided as follows:-
   At the entrance to WINCHESTER TRENCH at 2 p.m. D Coy.
     do   SOUTH TILLELOY TRENCH at 3 p.m. B Coy.
     do   WINCHESTER TRENCH at 5 p.m. A Coy.
     do   WINCHESTER TRENCH at 6.30 p.m. C Coy.
   Guides will be given a chit marked Right platoon, centre platoon, left platoon and support platoon respectively.
   Incoming Lewis Gunners will be with their Companies.

2. Companies will move independently to billets at LA GORGUE.
   Route for all Companies except 'B' will be via LA FLINQUE - LE DRUMEZ.
   For 'B' Coy, via M.21.b.5.9. - PONT DU HEM - RIEZ BAILLEUL - R.5.a.9.2.
   Usual distances will be preserved, Companies reforming at a rendezvous to be arranged by Company Commanders.
   Headquarters Company will move in rear of 'C' Coy.

3. The Transport and Quartermasters Stores will remain as at present.

4. All Company baggage will be sent by Companies to railhead in the front line and will be left under a storeman. The Transport Officer will arrange to have this conveyed at dusk from the front line to the new billets.
   Cookers will be sent to new billets by 6 p.m. Two cooks per Company may be sent to the Quartermasters Stores immediately after dinner to march with them.

5. Companies will report relief complete by the code word.

              A. Coates
                Lieut.Col.
            Commdg Red Square Battalion.

Issued at 11 a.m.

Copy No. 1 to A Coy.
    2 to B Coy.
    3 to C Coy.
    4 to D Coy.
    5 to H.Q. Coy.
    6 to Transport Officer.
    7 to Quartermaster.
    8 to Lewis Gun Officer.
    9 to War Diary.
   10 to File.

Copy No.

OPERATION ORDER No.30
by
Brigadier-General W.E.B.Smith, C.M.G., Commanding 8th Infantry
Brigade.

Brigade Headquarters,
8th April, 1915.

1. The 2nd K.S.L.I. and 4th Rifle Brigade will be relieved to-morrow night as follows -

	Trench.	Garrison.	To relieve.
4th K.R.R.C.	74	45	K.S.L.I.
(H.Q. in S.1	75	35	"
Dug-outs.)	76	150 M.G.	"
	77	80 M.G.	"
	S.1	120 to 150.	"
	78	80 M.G.	"
3rd K.R.R.C.	79	40 M.G.	"
(H.Q. in S.2	A	160 2 M.G.	4th Rifle Bde.
Dug-outs).	S.2	100 to 200	K.S.L.I.
P.P.C.L.I.	B	160	4th Rifle Bde.
(H.Q. in S.3	C	160 2 M.G.	"
Dug-outs)	S.3	200	"

2. On relief 2 Companies K.S.L.I. will occupy the dug-outs vacated by the P.P.C.L.I. West of ETANG DE BELLEWAARDE Square @ I 12 D.
   Headquarters and 2 remaining companies K.S.L.I. and 4th Rifle Brigade will return to billets in YPRES.

3. Relieving Battalions will pass the MENIN GATE as follows -
   2 Coys. P.P.C.L.I.   at 7.30 p.m.
   3rd K.R.R.C.   at 8 p.m.
   4th K.R.R.C.   at 8.30 p.m.
   The O.C. 4th K.R.R.C. will arrange his march from VLAMERTINGHE so as to arrive at the MENIN GATE at 8.30 p.m.

Stewart
Major,
Brigade Major, 80th Infantry Brigade.

2/5th Bn Royal Warwickshire Regiment.

WAR DIARY.

Volume. IV.

From August 1st. 1916.
To   August 31st. 1916.

Army Form C. 2118.

WAR DIARY
or
INTELLIGENCE SUMMARY. O/5
(Erase heading not required.)

Instructions regarding War Diaries and Intelligence Summaries are contained in F. S. Regs., Part II. and the Staff Manual respectively. Title pages will be prepared in manuscript.

748

Place	Date	Hour	Summary of Events and Information	Remarks and references to Appendices
LA GORGUE	1/8/16	—	Battn. took over MOATED GRANGE Sub-section from 2/5 GLOUCESTERS. Relief complete 5"10pm	Appendix 1. O/S O/C
MOATED GRANGE	2/8/16	—	Quiet day in trenches.	O/C
—"—	3/8/16	—	G.O.C. 61 Div visits trenches about 10 a.m.	O/C
—"—	4/8/16	—	—"—	O/C
—"—	5/8/16	—	Some artillery active	O/C
—"—	6/8/16	—	—"—	O/C
—"—	7/8/16	—	—"—	O/C
—"—	8/8/16	3:30am	Enemy sprang a mine under our parapet at M.30.c.15.49, & attacked with a small party of infantry. This was repulsed & identification taken from German dead.	O/C
—"—	9/8/16	—	Battn. relieved by 2/8 WARWICKS and proceeded to billets in RIEZ BAILLEUL. Relief complete at 5 p.m.	Appendix 2. O/S
RIEZ BAILLEUL	10/8/16	—	Rest	O/C
—"—	11/8/16	—	Company training	O/C
—"—	12/8/16	—	—"—	O/C
—"—	13/8/16	—	Church parade 9 a.m.	O/C
—"—	14/8/16	—	Company training	O/C

Army Form C. 2118.

WAR DIARY or INTELLIGENCE SUMMARY. O/C

(Erase heading not required.)

Instructions regarding War Diaries and Intelligence Summaries are contained in F. S. Regs., Part II. and the Staff Manual respectively. Title pages will be prepared in manuscript.

749

Place	Date	Hour	Summary of Events and Information	Remarks and references to Appendices
RIEZ BAILLEUL	15/8/16	—	Company training	O/C
—"—	16/8/16	—	—"—	O/C
—"—	17/8/16	—	—"—	O/C
—"—	18/8/16	—	—"—	O/C
NEUVE CHAPELLE	19/8/16	—	Battn took over NEUVE CHAPELLE sub-section from 7/8 Warwicks. Relief complete 5 p.m.	Appendix 3. 9/C
—"—	20/8/16	—	Quiet day in trenches	O/C
—"—	21/8/16	—	—"—	O/C
—"—	22/8/16	—	—"—	O/C
—"—	23/8/16	—	In trenches; artillery active	O/C
—"—	24/8/16	—	Quiet day in trenches	O/C
—"—	25/8/16	—	—"—	O/C
LA GORGUE	26/8/16	—	Battn relieved by 2/7 Worcesters. Proceeded to billets at LA GORGUE.	Appendix 4 O/C
—"—	27/8/16	—	Rest	O/C
—"—	28/8/16	—	Company training	O/C
—"—	29/8/16	—	—"—	O/C
—"—	30/8/16	—	—"—	O/C
—"—	31/8/16	—	—"—	O/C

O/C Cmdg 1/5th Warwicks
Cmdg 1/5r Warwicks 1/9/16.

S E C R E T.

RED SQUARE OPERATION ORDER NO.10.   Copy No. 12
Reference Béthune Map 1/40000   July 31st.1916.

Appendix 1.

1. The Battalion will take over the MOATED GRANGE sub-section from the 2/5th Gloucesters tomorrow.
Right,'C' Company; centre 'D' Company; left 'A' Company; Reserve,-'B' Company, with 1 N.C.O. and 8 men in LAFONE POST and the same in SOUTH TILLELOY POST.

2. Guides will be provided by the 2/5th Gloucesters at the Police Post half way up SOUTH TILLELOY Trench at the following times:—
   A Company :- 1 p.m.
   D Company :- 3 p.m.
C Company will proceed without guides and will pass the Police Post at 4.30 p.m.
B Company, together with Signallers, Bombers, Lewis Gunners and Snipers will also proceed without guides, but via BALUCHI ROAD and BATTALION H.Q. and will reach the reserve line at 9.30 a.m.
The remainder of H.Q.Coy will move with C Company.

3. A, D and C Coys will march by the following route:-
R.5.a.— RIEZ BAILLEUL — M.14.c.6.6.— Emergency road from this point to M.20.b.6.9.— PONT DU HEM — M.21.b.— SOUTH TILLELOY Trench, leaving at 6.15 a.m., 6.30 a.m. and 6.45 a.m. respectively and halting under Company arrangements in the vicinity of PONT DU HEM for midday rest and dinners.
B Company will march via R.5.a.— BOUT DE VILLE — CROIX BARBEE and BALUCHI ROAD.
Usual distances will be kept.

4. 1 Officer and 1 N.C.O. per Company will proceed to the trenches to take over at least two hours before the Companies are due to arrive.

5. Company Quartermaster Sergeants will arrange to collect all baggage required in the trenches, the Transport Officer arranging for the necessary limbers. They will also arrange for other baggage (including service dress caps) to be stored in the Quartermasters Stores after the departure of the Companies.
The cookers of A, D and C Companies will proceed with their Companies to the vicinity of PONT DU HEM and will return after dinner. The large dixies from the cookers will x on no account be taken to the trenches. 1 limber will be placed at the disposal of H.Q.Mess at 10 a.m.

6. Companies will report relief complete by the new code word.

                                        N Coates   Lieut.Col.
                                        Commdg Red Square Battalion.

Issued at 10 p.m.
Copy No.1 to A Coy.   No.5 to H.Q.Coy.   No.9 to Signals.
     2 to B Coy.   6 to 2/5th Gloucesters. 10 to Bombing O.
     3 to C Coy.   7 Lewis G.Officer.   11 to War Diary
     4 to D Coy.   8 to Qmr & T.O.   12 to File.

S E C R E T.

RED SQUARE OPERATION ORDER NO.11. Copy No. 11
Reference:— Trench Map J and   August 8th.1916.
            BETHUNE Map 1
                      ─────
                      40000

1. The Battalion will be relieved tomorrow, the 2/6th
   Warwicks taking over the line from M.29.d.9½.to M.35.b.8½.6½.
   and the 2/8th Warwicks from M.35.b.8½.6½. to M.35.d.5½.6¼.

2. Guides for the Signallers, Snipers and three Lewis Gun Teams
   will meet the 2/8th Warwicks on the RUE DE BACQUEROT at the
   entrance to SOUTH TILLELOY STREET at 9.30 a.m.
   Guides for two Lewis Guns will meet the 2/6th Warwicks at
   the same time and place.
   Three guides from 'A' Company and one guide from 'D' Coy
   will meet 'D' Company of the 2/6th Warwicks at the above
   mentioned point at 11 a.m.
   Guides for the two right platoons of 'C' Company will meet
   two platoons of the 2/8th Warwicks at the above mentioned
   point at 1.30 p.m.
   'C' Company will provide one guide for the front line
   and 'D' Company will provide one guide for the support
   line to meet 'D' Company 2/8th Warwicks at above mentioned
   point at 3.30 p.m.
   Two platoons of the 2/8th Warwicks will relieve the Company
   in CARDIFF ROAD and in the two posts at about 3 p.m.
   Headquarters Coy. will march in rear of the reserve Company.

3. Routes:— Reserve Company relief in and out via BALUCHI
   ROAD, others via SOUTH TILLELOY.
   Companies will march independently to billets at RIEZ
   BAILLEUL via PONT DU HEM — the emergency road from M.20.b.4.8.
   to M.14.c.7.6., at which point they will be met by the
   billeting officer. Usual distances will be kept.

4. Arrangements have been made for the relieving Battalions
   to send an officer or N.C.O. to take over trench stores
   at 12 noon.

5. The Transport Officer will arrange to collect trench baggage.
   One limber will be placed at the disposal of Headquarter
   Mess and will be at the entrance to BALUCHI ROAD Trench
   at 2.30 p.m. The Transport Officer will arrange to take
   cookers to the new billets by 10 a.m.

6. Companies will report relief complete by the code word.

                                          Lieut.Col.
Issued at 6.30 p.m.   Commdg Red Square Battalion.
Copy No. 1 to A Coy.   Copy No.7 to 2/8th Warwicks.
         2 to B Coy.   8 to Lewis Gun Officer.
         3 to C Coy.   9 to Quartermaster & T.O.
         4 to D Coy.   10 to Signals.
         5 to H.Q.Coy.   11 to War Diary.
         6 to 2/6th Warwicks.   12 to File.

Appendix 3.

S E C R E T.

RED SQUARE OPERATION ORDER No.12.
Reference:- Trench Map J.

Copy No. 12
August 18th.1916.

1. The Battalion will take over the right sub-section (NEUVE CHAPELLE) from the 2/8th Warwicks tomorrow. Disposition:- Left 'C' Coy; Centre 'B' Coy; Right 'A' Coy; Reserve 'D' Coy, with 1 N.C.O. and 8 men in LAFONE, 1 N.C.O. and 8 men in CHURCH, 1 N.C.O. and 8 men in CHATEAU and 1 N.C.O. and 3 men in SOUTH TILLELOY Posts.

2. Guides will be on the LA BASSEE Road at the entrance to BALUCHI Trench as follows:-
   9.30 a.m. Signallers, Snipers, Lewis Gunners.
   1 p.m. 'A' Coy.
   3.30 p.m. 'B' Coy.
   Guides for D Coy will be at the DUE DU BACQUEROT at the entrance to SOUTH TILLELOY Trench at 3.30 p.m.
   No guides will be provided for 'C' Coy, but they will pass the entrance to SOUTH TILLELOY Trench at 1 p.m.
   The remainder of H.Q. Coy will move in with 'D' Coy.

3. Parties moving to and from RUE DU BACQUEROT will not exceed 10 at intervals of 100 yards.

4. 1 Officer and 1 N.C.O. per Company will proceed to the trenches to take over at least two hours before the Coys are due to arrive. Duplicate trench store lists (including Posts) to be sent to Battalion Headquarters as soon as possible.

5. Posts will be vacated with the exception of 1 man in each who will be left to hand over to the 2/8th Warwicks when they arrive.

6. Company Quartermaster Sergeants will arrange to collect all baggage required in the trenches, the Transport Officer arranging for the necessary limbers. They will also arrange for the other baggage to be stored in the Quartermasters Stores. One limber will be placed at the disposal of the Headquarter Mess at RIEZ BAILLEUL at 2 p.m. The Transport Officer will also arrange to collect the cookers after Companies have left.

7. Companies will report relief complete by the code word.

Issued at 4.30 p.m.

Lieut.Col.
Commdg Red Square Battalion.

Copy No.1 to A Coy.
2 to B Coy.
3 to C Coy.
4 to D Coy.
5 to H.Q. Coy.
6. to 2/8th Warwicks.
7 to 2/7th Warwicks.

Copy No.8 to 2/6th Gloucesters.
9 to Lewis Gun Officer.
10 to Signals.
11 to Transport O. & Quartermaster.
12 to War Diary.
13 to File.

S E C R E T.

RED SQUARE OPERATION ORDER.
Reference:— BETHUNE Map $\frac{1}{40000}$

Copy No. 12
August 25th. 1916.

Appendix 4

1. The Battalion will be relieved tomorrow by the corresponding Companies of the 2/7th WORCESTERS.

2. Guides for the Signallers, Snipers, Lewis Gunners and Bombers will be on the LA BASSEE Road at the entrance to BALUCHI Trench at 7 a.m. Our Lewis Gunners will move out with D Company and other Specialists with the nearest Companies. They will on no account move out as independent parties.
   One guide per platoon will be on the LA BASSEE Road at the entrance to BALUCHI Trench as follows:—
   D Company:— 8 a.m.
   B Company:— 10.30 a.m.
   One guide per platoon will be at the RUE DU BACQUEROT at the entrance to SOUTH TILLELOY Trench as follows:—
   C Company:— 8 a.m.
   A Company:— 10.30 a.m.
   One guide for Headquarter Company will be with A Company's guides. Headquarter Company will march out in rear of A Company.

3. Companies will move independently to previous billets in LA GORGUE, B and D Companies moving via BALUCHI Trench — CROIX BARBEE and BOUT DE VILLE.
   A and C Companies will move via SOUTH TILLELOY Trench — M.21.b.— M.20.b.— M.14.c. and RIEZ BAILLEUL.
   Usual distances will be kept.

4. Arrangements have been made for the relieving Battalion to send a N.C.O. to take over trench stores two hours before the time of relief. Statements of work in hand will be handed over to relieving Companies and copies of Trench Store list sent to Battalion Headquarters as soon as possible. The trench maps $\frac{1}{10000}$ will be handed in at Battalion Headquarters at LA GORGUE by noon on Sunday.

5. The Transport Officer will arrange to collect trench baggage, O.C. Companies informing Battalion Headquarters by 6 p.m. tonight their requirements.
   1 limber will be placed at the disposal of Headquarter Mess and will be opposite GREEN BARN Dressing Station at 9.30 a.m.; 1 limber at the same place at the disposal of the Machine Gun section at 10 a.m. and the Medical Cart at the same place at 11.30 a.m.
   The Transport Officer will arrange for cookers to be taken to LA GORGUE by 10 a.m. Company Commanders may send out two cooks per company ahead to prepare a hot meal upon arrival.

6. Companies will report relief complete by the code word.

Coates
Lieut.Col.
Commdg Red Square Battalion.

Issued at 5 p.m.
Copy No. 1 to A Company.
     2 to B Company.
     3 to C Company.
     4 to D Company.
     5 to H.Q.Coy.
     6 to 2/7th Worcesters.
     7 to 2/7th Warwicks.

Copy No. 8 to Lewis Gun Officer.
     9 to Quartermaster.
     10 to Transport Officer.
     11 to Signals.
     12 to War Diary.
     13 to File.

Appendix IV

BRIGADE ROUTINE ORDERS

BY

BRIG.-GEN. W. R. EVANS, D.S.O.

COMMANDING 182nd INFANTRY BRIGADE.

13.1.18.

64. HONOURS AND AWARDS.

IMMEDIATE AWARDS.

The following awards for gallantry and devotion to duty have been made.

THE MILITARY CROSS.

Lieut. (A/Capt) H.R.D. MAY.	2/5th R. War. R.
2/Lt. E.J. TRANTER.	-do-
Capt. A.P. THOMSON. R.A.M.C. att.	2/6th R. War. R.
Lieut. (A/Capt) R.A. JACKSON.	2/6th R. War. R.
T/2nd Lt. S.L. WARD.	do.
2nd Lt. D.L.A. PAINE.	2/7th R. War. R.
2nd Lt. T. CHAPMAN.	do.
T/2nd Lt. L. KIMBERLEY.	do.
T/2nd Lt. W.E. LOVEJOY.	do.
2nd Lt. T.C. DUCKWORTH.	2/8th R. War. R.

THE DISTINGUISHED CONDUCT MEDAL.

No. 200943 C.S.M. G. H. HOUGHTON.	2/5th R. War. R.
201542 Cpl. R. BARKER.	do.
242363 C.Q.M. R. H. BRYAN.	2/6th R. War. R.
240784 Sgt. A/C.S.M. W. BOURNE.	do.
242419 L/Sgt. H.C. MOODY.	do.
242044 Cpl. W. RAE.	do.
260311 Cpl. J. SOUTHERN.	do.
241419 L/Cpl. H. LANNEY.	do.
241477 Pte. (L/Cpl) D. SULLIVAN.	do.
241966 Pte. F. LACEY.	do.
13087 Pte. P.W. SHELDON	2/7th R. War. R.
307132 Pte. A. MORELAND.	2/8th R. War. R.

THE BAR TO MILITARY MEDAL.

No. 268472 Sgt. T.J. REYNOLDS.	2/7th R. War. R.
266417 L/Cpl. F.J. LOACH.	do.

THE MILITARY MEDAL.

No. 203286 Cpl. (L/Sgt) J.F. SOLLARS.	2/5th R. War. R.
200844 Cpl. (L/Sgt) H. HOBSON.	do.
203296 Cpl. A.J. GABB.	do.
201785 Pte. (L/Cpl) H.J.H. CLARKE.	do.
202443 Pte. E. PEACOCK.	do.
202507 Sgt. (A/C.S.M.) H. HADEN.	2/6th R. War. R.
241139 Pte. D. JONES.	do.
266065 Sgt. J.H. LARKS.	2/7th R. War. R.
266361 Sgt. G. CASHMORE.	do.
265855 Sgt. J. ROSS.	do.
29641 L/Cpl. W. HADLEY.	do.
300135 Pte. A. DUNNELL.	do.
307116 Sgt. R. ELLIOT.	2/8th R. War. R.
305103 Cpl. T. WORRALL.	do.
307462 Cpl. G. BUCKINGHAM.	do.
307160 L/Cpl. F. GATHERY.	do.
306320 Pte. H. PATCHETT.	do.
306995 Pte. T. SIMPSON.	do.
307060 Pte. U. EVANS.	do.
Pte. W.J. COUGHLIN	do.

THE MILITARY MEDAL (Continued).

No. 307277	Pte. R. HULME.	2/8th R. War. R.
306022	Pte. W. STEPHENS.	do.
307106	Pte. A. ANDERSON.	do.
307035	Pte. E. COOPER.	do.

NEW YEAR'S GAZETTE, 1918.

DISTINGUISHED SERVICE ORDER.
Lieut.-Col. W.E. ST. JOHN.   2/7th R. War. R.

The MILITARY CROSS.
Captain D.A.E. GRAHAM.	Bde. Major 182nd Inf. Brigade.
2nd Lieut. S. GRANT.	2/5th R. War. R.
Captain J.L. PADMORE.	2/6th R. War. R.
Lieut. D.J. LUTHIE.	do.
Captain C. LA TROBE.	2/7th R. War. R.
Hon. Capt. & Q.M. G.J. WILLIAMS.	do.
Major W.R.T. WHATMORE.	2/8th R. War. R.
2nd Lieut. A.C.F. WATSON.	do.

THE MERITORIOUS SERVICE MEDAL.
No. 305724 R.S.M. H.E.G. MEAD.   2/8th R. War. R.

AWARD OF DIVISIONAL COMMANDER'S PARCHMENT.

No. 200843	Sgt. A. EDWARDS.	2/5th R. War. R.
200356	Sgt. R. BLAYNEY.	do.
202369	Cpl. W. WESTWELL.	do.
200553	Pte. (L/Cpl) J. THOMSON.	do.
201448	Pte. (L/Cpl) C.W. SPILSBURY.	do.
203257	Pte. (L/Cpl) D. McDONALD.	do.
201478	Pte. H. MORSE.	do.
203250	Pte. E.J. LEONARD.	do.
15206	Pte. J.S. POULTON.	do.
30454	Pte. S. LISTER.	do.
203092	Pte. E.J. DUDLEY.	do.
241871	Sgt. P.R. SHORTER.	2/6th R. War. R.
242998	Pte. H. RYDER.	do.
242994	Pte. F. WARBUTON.	do.
242982	Pte. F. BYFORD.	do.
241892	Pte. W. BUIST.	do.
240906	Pte. A. WRIGHT.	do.
28906	Sgt. W.O. PATCH.	2/7th R. War. R.
266308	Pte. W. PRIESTLEY.	do.
23766	Pte. W. CLAY.	do.
300155	Pte. A. HEARN.	do.
305486	L/Cpl. W. DALE.	2/8th R. War. R.
307169	L/Cpl. J. ROBERTS.	do.
305610	Pte. A. LAWTON.	do.
306408	Pte. W. CHANDLER.	2/8th R. War. R. att. 182nd Inf. Bde.
243427	Pte. J.W. MOORE.	do.
500404	Spr. J.A. FRASER.	61st Div. Signal Coy. R.E. att. 182nd Inf. Bde.
500412	Pnr. W. LIDDICOAT.	do.

2/5 R War Regt
Vol 5

Confidential
War Diary
of
2/5 Bn Royal Warwick Regt.

from Sept 1st to Sept 30th 1916

WAR DIARY
or
INTELLIGENCE SUMMARY. O/C

(Erase heading not required.)

Army Form C. 2118.

Instructions regarding War Diaries and Intelligence Summaries are contained in F. S. Regs., Part II. and the Staff Manual respectively. Title pages will be prepared in manuscript.

Place	Date	Hour	Summary of Events and Information	Remarks and references to Appendices
LA GORGUE	1/4/16	—	Company training	O/C
	2/4/16	—	"	O/C
LAVENTIE	3/4/16	—	Bttn moved to LAVENTIE 9 a.m. taking over left sector of FAUQUISSART section	Appendix O/C
"	4/4/16	—	Company training	O/C
"	5/4/16	—	"	O/C
"	6/4/16	—	"	O/C
"	7/4/16	—	"	O/C
"	8/4/16	—	"	O/C
"	9/4/16	—	Church parade.	O/C
"	10/4/16 10 a.m.	—	Bttn took over left subsection of FAUQUISSART from 2/5 Warwicks. Relief complete 10.40 p.m.	O/C Appendix 2.
FAUQUISSART	11/4/16	—		O/C
"	12/4/16	—	Bttn holding left subsection of FAUQUISSART	O/C
"	13/4/16	—	"	O/C
"	14/4/16	—	"	O/C
"	15/4/16	—	"	O/C
"	16/4/16	—	"	O/C

WAR DIARY or INTELLIGENCE SUMMARY

Army Form C. 2118.

(Erase heading not required.)

Place	Date	Hour	Summary of Events and Information	Remarks and references to Appendices
FAUQUISSART	17/9/16	—	Batt. holding left subsection of FAUQUISSART.	S.P.C.
—	18/9/16	"	"	O.in.C.
—	19/9/16	—	Batt. relieved by 2/8th R. Warwick R. in left subsection FAUQUISSART. Relief complete 4 p.m.	S.P.C. Appendix 3
LAVENTIE	—	—	Batt. moved into Divisional Reserve at LAVENTIE.	S.P.C.
—	20/9/16	—	Working parties and Company training	M.C.
—	21/9/16	—	"	O.in.C.
—	22/9/16	—	"	O.in.C.
—	23/9/16	—	"	O.in.C.
—	24/9/16 10 a.m.	Church Parade and working parties	O.in.C.
FAUQUISSART	25/9/16	—	Batt. took over left subsection of FAUQUISSART from 2/5 Warwicks. Relief complete 6.30 p.m.	O.in.C. Appendix 4
—	26/9/16	—	Batt. holding left subsection of FAUQUISSART	O.in.C.
—	27/9/16	—	"	O.in.C.
—	28/9/16	—	"	O.in.C.
—	29/9/16	—	"	O.in.C.
—	30/9/16	—	"	O.in.C.

Appendix 1

SECRET.

RED SQUARE OPERATION ORDER No.14.   Copy No. 10
Reference:- $\frac{1}{40000}$ Sheet No.36.   September 2nd.1916.

757

1. The Battalion will move to LAVENTIE tomorrow as left reserve Battalion of the FAUQUISSART section, relieving the 2/4th OXFORDS.

2. Companies will march independently via BELLE CROIX and G.32.b.1.4. arriving at LAVENTIE at the following times:-
   A Company 9.15 a.m.
   B Company 9.25 a.m.
   C Company 9.35 a.m.
   D Company 9.45 a.m.
   H.Q.Coy. 9.55 a.m.
   Battalion Headquarters will be at M.4.b.1.8.
   The billeting officer and billeting parties will proceed to LAVENTIE to take over billets tonight.

3. D Company will furnish a permanent working party of 50 other ranks under 2/Lieut.R.K.SPURRELL for duty under the O.C. 1/3rd Field Company R.E. with billets at M.4.b.4.10. They will arrive in new billets not later than 10 a.m.
   C Company will take over the following posts:-
   HOUGOUMONT.   1 platoon.
   DEAD END.   1 platoon.
   PICANTIN.   1 platoon.
   LAVENTIE.   4 men.
   Personnel of the first three posts will be available for working parties.

4. Cookers will march with Companies, Company Commanders arranging with the Transport Officer for conveyance of other stores.

5. Billets will be left in a scrupulously clean condition and a certificate to this effect rendered to the Adjutant before marching off.

R/Coates,
Lieut.Col.
Commdg RED SQUARE BATTALION.

Issued at 11.45 a.m.
Copy No.1 to A Coy.
       2 to B Coy.
       3 to C Coy.
       4 to D Coy.
       5 to H.Q.Coy.
       6 to Signals.
       7 to Lewis Gunners.
       8 to Quartermaster.
       9 to Transport Officer.
      10 to War Diary.
      11 to File.

appendix 2.

SECRET.

RED SQUARE OPERATION ORDER No.15.   Copy No. 11
Reference:—   1/40000   Sheet No.36.   September 10th.1916.

1. The Battalion will relieve the 2/8th WARWICKS in the FAUQUISSART Left Sub Section tomorrow. Dispositions:- Left, D Company; Centre, B Company; Right, A Company, and Reserve C Company.

2. Guides for specialists will be at the RED HOUSE at 11.30 a.m. One guide per platoon will meet D Company on the RUE DU BACQUEROT at the entrance to PICCADILLY at 2.30 p.m. One guide per platoon will meet B Company on the RUE DU BACQUEROT at the entrance to GREAT NORTH ROAD at 2.30 p.m. One guide per platoon will meet A Company on the RUE DU BACQUEROT at the entrance to EDGEWARE ROAD at 2.30 p.m. C Company will take over HOUGOMONT, DEAD END, PICANTIN, and LAVENTIE Posts by 3.30 p.m., no guides being provided. H.Q. Company will arrive at the RED HOUSE at 3 p.m.

3. Companies will move independently via the most convenient emergency or other road, the usual distances being kept.

4. One Officer and one N.C.O. will proceed to the trenches to take over trench stores two hours before the Companies are due to arrive. The duplicate trench store lists are to be sent to the Orderly Room by 4 p.m. tomorrow.

5. Company Commanders will arrange direct with the Transport Officer for the conveyance of baggage. One limber will be placed at the disposal of the Headquarter Mess at 2 p.m.

6. Certificates to the effect that billets have been properly cleaned will be rendered to the Adjutant before marching off.

7. Companies will report relief complete by the code word.

P.J. Coates,
Lieut. Col.
Comdg RED SQUARE BATTALION.

Issued at 5 p.m.
Copy No.1 to A Coy.
    2 to B Coy
    3 to C Coy
    4 to D Coy
    5 to H.Q. Coy
    6 to Signals
    7 to Lewis Gunners
    8 to Quartermaster
    9 to Transport Officer
    10 to 2/8 Warwicks
    11 to War Diary
    12 to File.

Appendix 3

SECRET.   Copy No. 11
RED SQUARE OPERATION ORDER. No.16.   September 18th. 1916.
Reference 1/40000   Sheet No.36.

1. The Battalion will be relieved by the 2/8th. WARWICKS tomorrow and will be the Battalion in the Brigade in Divisional Reserve.

2. Guides from Signallers, Lewis Gunners, Snipers, and Bombers will be at RED HOUSE at 11 a.m. C Company will send a guide to meet D Company of the 2/8th. at the junction of the GREAT NORTH ROAD and RUE TILLELOY at 2.30 p.m. B and D Companies will each send a guide to meet C and D Companies respectively of the 2/8th at the junction of the PICANTIN ROAD and RUE TILLELOY at 2.30 p.m. and 3.30 p.m. respectively. A and H.Q. Companies will be relieved at 3.30 p.m.

3. Companies will move independently by the most convenient way and keeping the usual distances to their old billets. The Billeting Officer will arrive at LAVENTIE at 9 a.m. to take over the billets of the 2/8th.

4. Companies will send all their heavy stores to Rail Base by 9 p.m. today. The Transport Officer will arrange for the necessary limbers at that time and also will send one limber to be at the disposal of C and B Companies at the GREAT NORTHERN Rail Base at 3.30 p.m. tomorrow and one limber for A Company to be at DEAD END at 3.30 p.m., afterwards going to the GREAT NORTHERN Rail Base for the remainder of D Company's stores. The Transport Officer will also send a limber for the Lewis Guns to be at RED HOUSE at 11.15 a.m. and one limber to be at the disposal of Headquarter Officers' Mess at 2.30 p.m. The Officers' Mess Cart will be at the GREAT NORTHERN Rail Base at 2.30 p.m.

5. Rifle grenade stands with details of registration will be handed over.

6. The 1/10000 trench maps will not be handed over.

7. Companies will report relief complete by the code word.

8. D Company will, as soon as relieved, send one N.C.O. and 6 men to relieve LAVENTIE Post.

                                                                Capt.,
                                                        Commdg. 2/8th Warwicks.

Issued at 4 p.m.
Copy No. 1 to A Coy.
         2   B Coy.
         3   C Coy.
         4   D Coy.
         5   H.Q.Coy.
         6   Signals.
         7   Lewis Gunners.
         8   Q.M.
         9   T.O.
        10   2/8th.R.War.R.
        11   War Diary.
        12   File.

SECRET.

RED SQUARE OPERATION ORDER. No. 17.   Copy No...13....
Reference 1/40000 Sheet 36.   September 24th. 1916.

1. The Battalion will relieve the 2/8th. WARWICKS in the FAUQUISSART Left Sub Section tomorrow. Dispositions:- Right, C Company; Centre, D Company; Left, A Company; and Reserve, B Company.

2. The permanent R.E. Working Party (1 Officer and 50 O.R.) will return to the Battalion at 5 a.m. tomorrow.

3. All blankets will be returned to the Quartermaster's Store by 9.30 a.m. tomorrow.

4. Guides for specialists will be at the RED HOUSE at 11 a.m. Guides for other Companies will be as follows:-

From 2/8th.	For 2/8th.	Place.	Time.
B Coy.	C Coy.	Junction of GREAT NORTH ROAD and RUE TILLELOY.	2.30 p.m.
C Coy.	D Coy.	Junction of PICANTIN ROAD and RUE TILLELOY.	2.30 p.m.
D Coy.	A Coy.	Junction of PICANTIN ROAD and RUE TILLELOY.	3.30 p.m.

No guides will be provided by A Company of the 2/8th. for B Company and H.Q. Company, who will complete the relief by 3.30 p.m.

5. LAVENTIE Post will be relieved by the 2/8th WARWICKS by 4 p.m., no guides being provided. The Garrison will, on relief, at once join their Company.

6. Companies will move independently, the usual distances being kept.

7. One Officer and one N.C.O. will proceed to the trenches to take over trench stores 2 hours before the Companies are due to arrive. The duplicate trench store lists are to be sent to the Orderly Room by 4.30 p.m. tomorrow.

8. Company Commanders will arrange direct with the Transport Officer for the conveyance of baggage. One limber will be placed at the disposal of the Headquarter Mess at 2 p.m.

9. Certificates to the effect that billets have been thoroughly cleaned will be rendered to the Adjutant before moving off.

10. Companies will report relief complete by the code word.

                                                      Major.
                                      Comndg. Red Square Battalion.

Issued at 2 p.m.
Copy No. 1. to A Coy.   No. 8 to Bombers.
        2   B Coy.   9   Snipers.
        3   C Coy.   10   Q.M.
        4   D Coy.   11   T.O.
        5   H.Q. Coy.   12   2/8th Warwicks.
        6   Signals.   13   War Diary.
        7   Lewis Gunners.   14   File.

Confidential

War Diary
of
2/5th Royal Warwickshire Regt

from Oct 1st 1916 to Oct 31st 1916

WAR DIARY or INTELLIGENCE SUMMARY.

Army Form C. 2118.

Instructions regarding War Diaries and Intelligence Summaries are contained in F. S. Regs., Part II. and the Staff Manual respectively. Title pages will be prepared in manuscript.

(Erase heading not required.)

Place	Date	Hour	Summary of Events and Information	Remarks and references to Appendices
FAUQUISSART	1/10/16	—	Battn relieved by 2/6 R Warwick R in left subsection FAUQUISSART. Relief complete 2.45 PM	See Appendix 1
LAVENTIE	2/10/16	—	Battn moved into Divisional reserve at LAVENTIE	″
″	3/10/16		Working parties and company training	S.S.C.
″	4/10/16		″ ″ ″	S.S.C.
″	5/10/16		″ ″ ″	S.S.C.
″	6/10/16		″ ″ ″	S.S.C.
″	7/10/16		Battn relieved 2/6 Warwicks in left subsection FAUQUISSART. Relief complete at 2.55 pm.	See Appendix 2
FAUQUISSART	7/10/16		Battn holding left subsection FAUQUISSART.	S.S.C.
″	8/10/16			S.S.C.
″	9/10/16			S.S.C.
″	10/10/16			S.S.C.
″	11/10/16			S.S.C.
″	12/10/16			S.S.C.
″	13/10/16		Battn relieved by 1/8 Lon R in left subsection FAUQUISSART and moved in reserve billets at LAVENTIE. Relief 2	See Appendix 3
LAVENTIE	14/10/16		Working parties and Company training	S.S.C.

7/6/2

Army Form C. 2118.

WAR DIARY or INTELLIGENCE SUMMARY. App C

(Erase heading not required.)

Place	Date	Hour	Summary of Events and Information	Remarks and references to Appendices
LAVENTIE	15/9/16	—	Company Training and working parties	App C
—	16/9/16	—	—	App C
—	17/9/16	—	—	App C
—	18/9/16	—	—	App C
—	19/9/16	—	Batt relieved 2/ist R War R in PREQUISSART left subsection Relief completed at 2.55 pm Appendix H	App C
—	19/9/16	—	Coates assumed command of the Battn upon being relieved at 182 Infantry Brigade	2 1/2 pm Ph
FREQUISSART	20/9/16	—	Battn holding left subsection FREQUISSART.	App C
—	21/9/16	—	—	App C
—	22/9/16	—	—	App C
—	23/9/16	—	Batt relieved by 4/st Yorkshires in left subsection FREQUISSART & moved to billets at LAVENTIE. Relief complete	App 9/16 2.25 pm App C
LAVENTIE	24/9/16 8am	—	Company Battalion parade followed by Company Training	App 9/16 App C
—	25/9/16 9am	—	Batt. paraded for inspection by G.O.C. 182 Inf Bde. Company Training	App C
—	26/9/16	—	Company Training	App C
—	27/9/16	—	Batt relieved in LAVENTIE by 1st LONDON SCOTTISH and moved into Corps Reserve at LES LAURIERS arriving on	App C App C
LES LAURIERS	28/9/16	—	billets at 1.30 pm Company Training	App C

T.131. W. W708-776. 500000. 4/15. Sh.J.C.&9.

WAR DIARY or INTELLIGENCE SUMMARY.

Army Form C. 2118.

(Erase heading not required.)

Place	Date	Hour	Summary of Events and Information	Remarks and references to Appendices
F.S. KRRIERS	2/4/16	9.30am	Company Training	
	3/4/16	9.30am	Battn parade followed by Company Training	

764

Appendix 2
766
Copy No. 15

SECRET.
RED SQUARE OPERATION ORDER. No. 18.
Reference 1 Sheet 36.
        40000
October 6th. 1916.

1. The Battalion will relieve the 2/8th WARWICKS in the FAUQUISSART Left Sub Section tomorrow. Dispositions:- Right, C Company; Centre, B Company; Left, A Company; and Reserve, D Company.

2. The permanent R.E. Working Party (1 Officer and 50 O.R.) will return to the Battalion at 3 a.m. tomorrow.

3. All blankets will be returned to the Quartermaster's Store by 9.30 a.m. tomorrow.

4. Guides for specialists will be at the RED HOUSE at 11 a.m. There will be no guides for Companies, but they will pass the points mentioned below at the times stated:-

C Company.	Junction of GREAT NORTH ROAD and RUE TILLELOY.	1.30 p.m.
B Company.	Junction of PICANTIN ROAD and RUE TILLELOY.	1.30 p.m.
A Company.	Junction of PICANTIN ROAD and RUE TILLELOY.	2.15 p.m.

D Company will complete relief by 3 p.m.

5. LAVERIE Post will be relieved by the 2/8th WARWICKS by 4 p.m., no guides being provided. The Garrison will, on relief, at once join the Company.

6. Companies will move independently, the usual distances being kept.

7. One Officer and one N.C.O. will proceed to the trenches to take over trench stores 2 hours before the Companies are due to arrive. A duplicate copy of trench store lists to be sent to the Orderly Room by 4.30 p.m. tomorrow.

8. Company Commanders will arrange direct with the Transport Officer for the conveyance of baggage. One limber will be placed at the disposal of the Headquarter Mess at 2 p.m.

9. Certificates to the effect that billets have been thoroughly cleaned will be rendered to the Adjutant before moving off.

10. Companies will report relief complete by the code word.

Capt.
Commdg. RED SQUARE Battn.

Issued at 4 p.m.
Copy No. 1 to A Coy.
    2   B Coy.
    3   C Coy.
    4   D Coy.
    5   H.Q. Coy.
    6   Signals.
    7   Lewis Gunners.
    No.8 to Bombers.
        9   Snipers.
       10   Q.M.
       11   T.O.
       12   M.O.
       13   2/8th. Warwicks.
       14   War Diary.
       15   File.

SECRET.
RED SQUARE OPERATION ORDER No.12.   Appendix 3.
Reference 1/40000 Sheet 36.   Copy No. 14.
                                                           October 12th. 1916.

1. The Battalion will be relieved by the 2/8th. WARWICKS tomorrow and
    will be the Battalion in the Brigade in Divisional Reserve.

2. Guides for Lewis Gunners, Snipers, and Bombers will be at RED HOUSE
    at 11 a.m.
    Companies will not provide guides.
    C Coy. will be relieved by D Coy. 2/8th.
    B Coy.   do.   do.   A Coy. 2/8th.
    A Coy.   do.   do.   B Coy. 2/8th.
    D Coy.   do.   do.   C Coy. 2/8th.
    The reliefs will arrive at the entrances of the Communication
    Trenches by 1.30 p.m., relief being completed by 3 p.m.
    B and H.Q. Coy. will be relieved by 2.30 p.m.

3. Companies will move independently by the most convenient way,
    keeping the usual distances, to their old billets.
    O.C. D Coy. will detail 2/Lieut. SENIOR to act as Billeting Officer
    and arrive at LAVENTIE at 9 a.m. to take over the billets of the 2/8th.
    Instructions for the relief of LAVENTIE POST will be issued later.

4. Companies will send all their heavy stores to rail head by 8.30 p.m.
    today. The Transport Officer will arrange for the necessary limbers
    at that time and will also send one limber to be at the disposal of
    each Company at times and places to be arranged by Companies.
    The Transport Officer will also send a limber to be at RED HOUSE at
    1.30 p.m. for H.Q. Officers' Mess. The Officers' Mess Cart will be
    at the Great Northern Railway Dump at 1.30 p.m.
    Rifle grenade stands, with details of registration, and Snipers' maps
    1/10000 will be handed over. Other 1/10000 trench maps will not be
    handed over.
    Receipts for trench stores, maps (except 1/10000 trench maps), defence
    schemes, and air photographs will reach Brigade H.Q. 24 hours after
    handing over.
    A copy of the trench stores to be handed over will reach Battalion
    H.Q. by 10 a.m., the signed copy to be delivered at Battalion H.Q.
    by the time stated for relief.

5. C Company will find a permanent R.E. Working Party of one Officer
    and 50 O.R., daily, while out of the trenches. The Officer in
    charge of the R.E. Working Party for the 14th. inst., will report to
    the O.C. 1/3rd. Field Coy. at 6 p.m. on the day of relief.

6. Companies will report relief complete by the code word.

                                              M. Bosley
                                                           Capt.,
Issued at 5.30 p.m.   Commdg. Red Square Battalion.
Copy No.1 to A Coy.   Copy No.8 to Snipers.
        2   B Coy   9   Q.M.
        3   C Coy   10   M.O.
        4   D Coy   11   2/8th. Warwicks.
        5   H.Q. Coy.   12   Sgt. Carless
        6   Signals   13   War Diary
        7   Lewis Gunners.   14   File.
                                            15   M.O.

SECRET.
RED SQUARE OPERATION ORDER. No.20.   Copy No....15
Reference 1   Sheet 36.   October 18th. 1916.
          40000

1.   The Battalion will relieve the 2/8th WARWICKS in the PASQUISSART
        Left Sub Section tomorrow. Dispositions:- Right, D Company;
        Centre, B Company; Left, A Company; and Reserve, C Company.

2.   The permanent R.E. Working Party (1 Officer and 50 O.R.) will
        return to the Battalion at 8 a.m. tomorrow.

3.   All blankets will be returned to the Quartermaster's Store by
        9.30 a.m. tomorrow.

4.   Guides for specialists will be at the RED HOUSE at 11 a.m.
        There will be no guides for Companies, but they will pass the
        points mentioned below at the times stated:-

            D Company.   Junction of ROTTEN ROW and
                          RUE TILLELOY.   1.30 p.m.
            B Company.   Junction of PICANTIN ROAD
                          and RUE TILLELOY.   1.30 p.m.
            A Company.   Junction of BOND STREET
                          and RUE TILLELOY.   1.30 p.m.

        C Company will complete relief by 2.30 p.m.

5.   LAVERRIE Post will be relieved by the 2/8th WARWICKS by 6 p.m.,
        no guides being provided. The Garrison will, on relief, at
        once join the Company.

6.   Companies will move independently, the usual distances being
        kept.

7.   One Officer and one N.C.O. will proceed to the trenches to take
        over trench stores 2 hours before the Companies are due to
        arrive. A duplicate copy of trench store lists is to be sent
        to the Orderly Room by 4.30 p.m. tomorrow.

8.   Company Commanders will arrange direct with the Transport
        Officer for the conveyance of baggage. One limber will be
        placed at the disposal of the Headquarter Mess at 2 p.m.

9.   Certificates to the effect that billets have been thoroughly
        cleaned will be rendered to the Adjutant before moving off.

10.   Companies will report relief complete by the code word.

                                                    J.H. Churchouse Lieut
                                                    for Lieut. Col.
Issued at 12 noon.   Comdg. Red Square Battalion.
Copy no.1 to A Coy.   Copy No.8 to Bombers.
        2   B Coy.   9   Snipers.
        3   C Coy.   10   Q.M.
        4   D Coy.   11   T.O.
        5   H.Q. Coy.   12   M.O.
        6   Signals.   13   2/8th. Warwicks.
        7   Lewis Gunners.   14   War Diary.
                                                   15   File.

Appendix 5
769

SECRET.
RED SQUARE OPERATION ORDER. No.21.   Copy No........
Reference 1   Sheet 36.   October 22nd. 1916.

          40000

1.   The Battalion will be relieved by the 2/8th WARWICKS tomorrow
        and will move to billets in LAVENTIE, the usual distances being
        kept.

2.   Guides for specialists will be at RED HOUSE at 11 a.m.
        No guides will be provided for Companies, the dispositions of
        the 2/8th being;- A Company, Left; B Company, Centre; and
        C Company, Right. These will arrive at the entrances of the
        communication trenches at 1.30 p.m.
        D Company (Reserve) and H.Q. Company will complete relief by
        2.30 p.m.

3.   2/Lieut. R.C. BARLOW will proceed to LAVENTIE to take over
        billets, arriving there at 9 a.m. tomorrow.

4.   All heavy stores will be sent to the Rail Base by Companies
        by 8.30 p.m. today, the Transport Officer arranging for the
        necessary limbers at the same time. Limbers will be placed at
        the disposal of Companies on direct request to the Transport
        Officer. One limber will be placed at the disposal of the
        Headquarter Mess at RED HOUSE at 1.30 p.m. The Officers' Mess
        Cart will be at the Great Northern Rail Base at the same time.

5.   Stores and maps will be handed over as last. Trench store
        lists will reach Battalion Headquarters by 10 a.m.

6.   A Company will find a permanent R.E. working party of 1 Officer
        and 50 O.R. daily. The Officer in charge of this party for the
        24th. inst. will report to the O.C. 1/3rd. Field Company at
        6 p.m. on the 23rd. inst.
        A Company will also relieve LAVENTIE EAST POST by 6 p.m.
        tomorrow with the usual Garrison.

7.   The M.O. will arrange to spray all dug-outs, which will first be
        thoroughly cleaned and sandbags removed.

8.   Companies will report relief complete by the code word.

                                                        Lieut. Col.
                                                Commdg. Red Square Battalion.

Issued at 4 p.m.
Copy No.1 to A Coy.
     2   B Coy.
     3   C Coy.
     4   D Coy.
     5   H.Q. Coy.
     6   Signals.   Copy No.11 to 2/8th Warwicks.
     7   Lewis Gunners.   12   Sgt. Carless.
     8   Snipers.   13   M.O.
     9   T.O.   14   War Diary.
    10   Q.M.   15   File.

SECRET.
RED SQUARE OPERATION ORDER No.22.   Copy No....9...
Reference 1/40000   Sheets 36 & 36a.   October 26th. 1916.

1. The Battalion will be withdrawn into Corps Reserve at LES
    LAURIERS tomorrow, being relieved in LAVENTIE and N LAVENTIE
    EAST Post by the LONDON SCOTTISH.
    Route :- BELLE CROIX - L.36.a. - L.35.a. - Canal bank by
    Divisional Theatre - MERVILLE.
    Route for Transport :- BELLE CROIX - BEAUPRE.

2. Starting Point :- LAVENTIE Station Railway Crossing - 9 a.m.
    Order of March :- H.Q., A, B, C, D, Companies. As far as
    BELLE CROIX Companies will move independently at 200 yards
    distance. After passing that point the Battalion will move as
    a whole.

3. On any hostile aeroplane coming in sight all troops will halt and
    clear the road as far as possible.

4. O.C. D Company will detail 6 men, under Sgt. BLAYNEY, as a Rear
    Party.

5. Billetting Parties will meet Companies at MERVILLE road
    junction (K.20.b.0.5.)

6. Blankets will be rolled tightly into bundles of 10 and sent to
    the Quartermaster's Store at 8 a.m. Officers' kits will be
    sent to the Quartermaster's Store by 7.30 a.m. and the Mess Cart
    will call for Officers' mess boxes at Company Headquarters at
    8 a.m. All box periscopes and other stores not being carried
    on the man tomorrow will be sent to the Quartermaster's Store
    tonight.

7. Billets will be ready for inspection by 8.30 a.m. tomorrow and
    certificates that they are thoroughly clean will be handed to
    the Adjutant at the starting point.

8. Falling Out Returns, in accordance with Divisional Standing
    Orders Section 2 (7) and Company sketches in accordance with
    Section 5 (§ 4.e.) will reach Battalion Headquarters by 5 p.m.
    tomorrow.

                                              for Lieut. Col.
                                         Commdg. Red Square Battalion.

Issued at 7 p.m.
Copy No.1 to A Coy.
     2   B Coy.
     3   C Coy.
     4   D Coy.
     5   H.Q. Coy.
     6   Billetting Officer.
     7   Q.M.
     8   T.O.
     9   War Diary.
    10   File.

S E C R E T.

RED SQUARE OPERATION ORDER No.18.   Copy No.
Ref. $\frac{1}{40000}$ Sheet No.36.   September 30th. 1916.

1. The Battalion will be relieved by the 2/8th Warwicks tomorrow and will be the Battalion in the Brigade in Divisional reserve.

2. Guides for the Lewis Gunners, Snipers and Bombers will be at RED HOUSE at 11 a.m.
   Companies will not provide guides.
   C Coy will be relieved by A Coy 2/8th at 2.30 p.m.
   D Coy   do   do   D Coy 2/8th at 2.45 p.m.
   A Coy   do   do   C Coy 2/8th at 3 p.m.
   B and H.Q. Coys will be relieved at 3.15 p.m.

3. Companies will move independently by the most convenient way, keeping the usual distances, to their old billets.
   The Billeting Officer will arrive at LAVENTIE at 9 a.m. to take over the billets from the 2/8th.
   C Coy will as soon as relieved send 1 N.C.O. and six men to relieve LAVENTIE POST.

4. Companies will send all their heavy stores to mil base by 8.30 p.m. today. The Transport Officer will arrange for the necessary limbers at that time and will also send one limber to be at the disposal of each Company at times and places to be arranged by Companies. The Transport Officer will also send a limber to be at RED HOUSE at 2.30 p.m. for H.Q.Officers Mess. The Officers Mess Cart will be at the Great Northern Railway base at 2.30 p.m.
   Rifle grenade stands, with details of registration, and Snipers maps $\frac{1}{10000}$ will be handed over. Other $\frac{1}{10000}$ trench maps will not be handed over.
   Receipts for trench stores, maps (except $\frac{1}{10000}$ trench maps) defence schemes and air photographs will reach Brigade Headquarters 24 hours after handing over. A copy of the trench stores to be handed over will reach Battalion H.Q. by the time stated for relief.

5. Companies will report relief complete by the code word.

                                                Major.
Issued at 4 p.m.   Commdg Red Square Battalion.
Copy No.1 to A Coy.   Copy No.8 to Snipers.
       2 to B Coy   9 to Quartermaster.
       3 to C Coy   10 to Transport Officer.
       4 to D Coy   11 to 2/8th Warwicks.
       5 to H.Q.Coy   12 to Bombers.
       6 to Signals.   13 to War Diary.
       7 to Lewis Gun Officer.   14 to File.

Vol 7

Confidential

War Diary

of

2/5th Bn Royal Warwickshire Regt.

from Nov 1st 1916   to   Nov 30th 1916

Lieut Col.
Comdg 2/5th R. War R.

WAR DIARY
or
INTELLIGENCE SUMMARY. 106

(Erase heading not required.)

Army Form C. 2118.

Instructions regarding War Diaries and Intelligence Summaries are contained in F. S. Regs., Part II. and the Staff Manual respectively. Title pages will be prepared in manuscript.

Place	Date	Hour	Summary of Events and Information	Remarks and references to Appendices
LES LAURIERS	1/11/16	9.0 am	Battn paraded. Artillery formations. Company Training.	A.P.C.
"	2/11/16	—	182 Brigade marched to billets in BUSNES – BONNEHEM area; the Battn proceeded via CALONNE and ROBECQ to billets in ISBERGUE arriving 1.5 p.m.	A.P.C. appen. 1
RAINBERT	3/11/16	—	182 Brigade marched to billets in AUCHEL area; the Battn proceeded via LA VALLEE – BAS RIEUX – BURBURE and RAIMBERT to billets at CAUCHY-A-LA-TOUR arriving 1.25 p.m.	A.P.C. appendix 2
CAUCHY-A-LA-TOUR.	4/11/16	—	182 INF. BDE. marched to billets in LA THIEULOYE area; the Battn proceeded via FLORINGHEM – PERNES – VALHUON – LA THIEULOYE to MONCHY-BRETON arriving in billets at 2.50 p.m.	A.P.C. appendix 3.
MONCHY-BRETON	5/11/16	—	182 INF BDE. marched to billets in HOUVIN – HOUVIGNEUL area; the Battn proceeded via BAILLEUL – LE QUESNEL – AVERDOINGT – MAZIERES – MAGNICOURT to billets at HOUVIN-HOUVIGNEUL arriving 12.45 p.m.	A.P.C. appendix 4
HOUVIN – HOUVIGNEUL	6/11/16	—	182 INF BDE. marched to billets in BONNIÈRES area; the Battn proceeded via FREVENT – BONNIÈRES to billets at VILLERS L'HÔPITAL arriving 12.45 p.m.	A.P.C. appendix 5
VILLERS – L'HÔPITAL	7/11/16	—	Company Training	A.P.C.
"	8/11/16	—	"	A.P.C.
"	9/11/16	—	"	A.P.C.
"	10/11/16	10 am	Battn paraded on VILLERS – L'HÔPITAL – FROHEN road & practised artillery formations. Company Training.	A.P.C.
"	11/11/16	—	Company Training	A.P.C.

Army Form C. 2118.

WAR DIARY
or
INTELLIGENCE-SUMMARY.

(Erase heading not required.)

Instructions regarding War Diaries and Intelligence Summaries are contained in F. S. Regs., Part II. and the Staff Manual respectively. Title pages will be prepared in manuscript.

Place	Date	Hour	Summary of Events and Information	Remarks and references to Appendices
VILLERS —	11/11/16	10 a.m.	Battn. Church Parade on open ground S. of VILLERS.	Appx 6
L'HÔPITAL —	13/11/16	9.30 a.m.	Battn. paraded on open ground S. of VILLERS and practised the Attack. Company Training	Appx 6
"	14/11/16	10 a.m.	Battn. " " " " and practised same for demonstration of advancing under cover of an artillery barrage. The demonstration was carried out at 2.30 p.m.	Appx 6
"	15/11/16	—	182 INF BDE march to billets in FIENVILLERS area; battn proceeded via FROHEN-LE-GRAND — FROHEN-LE-PETIT — LE MEILLARD — BERNAVILLE to billets in BERNEUIL arriving at 12.55 p.m.	Appx 6 Appendix 6
BERNEUIL —	16/11/16	—	182 INF BDE marched to billets in BERTEAUCOURT; battn proceeded via DOMART-en-PONTHIEU — ST LEGER — to BERTEAUCOURT arriving 12.55 p.m.	Appx 6 Appendix 7
BERTEAUCOURT —	17/11/16	10.25 a.m.	182 INF BDE gp marched to RUBEMPRÉ — HERISSART area; battn proceeded via HALLOY — HAVERNAS — NAOURS — TALMAS to billets in RUBEMPRÉ arriving 3.15 p.m.	Appx 6 appendix 8
RUBEMPRÉ	18/11/16	9 a.m.	182 INF BDE. marched to WARLOY area; battn. proceeded via HERISSART — CONTAY to billets in WARLOY arriving 12.30 p.m.	Appx 6 appendix 9
WARLOY-BAILLON	19/11/16	10 a.m.	Working parties and Company Training	Appx 6
"	20/11/16		Company Training	Appx 6
"	21/11/16	12.25 p.m.	182 INF BDE marched to ALBERT area; the battn proceeded via HENENCOURT — MILLENCOURT to billets in ALBERT arriving 3.10 p.m.	Appx 6 appendix 10
ALBERT.	22/11/16	10 a.m.	Part of 182 INF BDE marched to SENLIS area, the battn proceeded via BOUZINCOURT to billets in SENLIS arriving 12.50 p.m.	Appx 6 appendix 11
SENLIS	23/11/16		Company Training	Appx 6

Army Form C. 2118.

WAR DIARY
or
INTELLIGENCE SUMMARY. JM6
(Erase heading not required.)

Instructions regarding War Diaries and Intelligence Summaries are contained in F.S. Regs., Part II. and the Staff Manual respectively. Title pages will be prepared in manuscript.

Place	Date	Hour	Summary of Events and Information	Remarks and references to Appendices
SENLIS	24/9/16	—	Working parties & Company Training.	JM6.
—"—	25/9/16	—	Company Training	JM6.
—"—	26/9/16	11:30 am	Church parade at THEATRE, SENLIS	JM6.
—"—	27/9/16	11 am	Batn. moved from billets, under canvas at SENLIS. Move completed at 12 noon	JM6 appendix 12
—"—	28/9/16	—	Company Training.	JM6.
—"—	29/9/16	—	" "	JM6.
—"—	30/9/16	—	" "	JM6.

H Crawley Lt Col
Commdg 1/6 R Warwick R
2/10/16

SECRET

Appendix 1

RED SQUARE OPERATION ORDER, No. 23
Reference, Bethune Map, sheet 36a.

Copy No. 10
Nov. 1/1916

---

1. The Brigade will march to billets in BUSNES-GONNHEIM area tomorrow and the Battalion will proceed to its old billets at BELLE RIVE via CALONNE and ROBECQ.

2. Companies will march in the following order:-
    - A. Coy.
    - B. "
    - C. "
    - D. "
    - H.Q. "
    - Transport

    the head of the Column passing the Starting Point, road junction at K.29.a.6.7. at 9.19 a.m. Baggage wagons will march with the Battalion. After leaving Brigade Column at ROBECQ the O.C. Headquarters Coy. will detail six men under an Officer as rear party.

3. The Billeting party will report to the Staff Captain at the cross roads 300 yards north of ROBECQ Church at 8 a.m. tomorrow. One extra guide for the supply wagons will proceed with it and will be at the road junction ½ mile north of BUSNES Church at 10 a.m. after ascertaining the position of the new Quartermaster's Stores.

4. The Transport Officer will arrange to collect Officers' kits, Officers' Mess boxes and blankets (tightly rolled in bundles of ten). Blankets will be ready for collection at 6.30 a.m. and other goods by 7 a.m.

5. Watches will be synchronised by a special D.R. sent from Battalion Headquarters about 7.30 a.m.

6. Billets will be ready for inspection at 8.30 a.m. tomorrow and certificates that they are thoroughly clean will be handed to the Adjutant at the Starting Point.

7. The usual Falling Out states and other particulars to be forwarded to Battalion Headquarters immediately upon arrival.

D.L. Coates,
Lieut.Col.
Comdg. 2/5th R. Warwick. Regt.

Issued at 6 p.m.

Copy No. 1 to H.Q. Coy
    2 " " Mess
    3 " A. Coy.
    4 " B. "
    5 " C. "
    6 " D. "
    7 " Quartermaster
    8 " Transport Officer
    9 " Billeting "
   10 " War Diary
   11 " File

SECRET

RED SQUARE OPERATION ORDER, NO.24   Copy No. 10
Map reference - Hazebrouck Map 1/100000   Nov. 2/1916.

Appendix 2

1. The Brigade marches to billets in the AUCHEL area tomorrow. The Battalion will be billeted for the night in CAUCHY-A-LA-TOUR. Route:- LA VALLEE - VAS RIEUX - BURBURE and RAIMBERT.

2. Companies will march in the following order:- B, D, A, Headquarter, C and Transport, the head of the Column passing the starting point (road junction 200 yards N.E. of the "M" in GONNEHEIM) at 9.16 a.m. C. Coy. will detail off a rear guard under an Officer in accordance with Divisional Standing Orders, section 2, para.8, to march in rear of the Brigade Column.

3. The Billeting party will report to the Staff Captain at the road junction immediately north of RAIMBERT at 8 a.m. Guides will be taken to meet the baggage and supply wagons at RAIMBERT after they have found the Battalion billets.

4. The Transport Officer will collect Officers' kits, Officers mess boxes and blankets from Company headquarters. Goods will be ready for collection by 7.39 a.m.

5. Billets will be ready for inspection by 8.45 a.m. The usual certificates that they are thoroughly clean will be handed to the Adjutant at the Starting Point.

6. Watches will be synchronised by Despatch Rider sent to Companies about 7.30 a.m.

7. The usual Falling Out states and other particulars will be forwarded to Battalion Headquarters immediately upon arrival.

D.L. Coates
Lieut.Col.
Comdg. 2/5th. R. Warwick. Regt.

Issued at 6 p.m.
Copy No. 1 to Headqrs. Coy.
      2 to Headqrs. Mess
      3 to A. Coy.
      4 to B. Coy.
      5 to C. Coy.
      6 to D. Coy.
      7 to Quartermaster
      8 to Transport Officer
      9 to Billeting Officer
    10 to War Diary
    11   File

appendix 3

SECRET

RED SQUARE OPERATION ORDER, NO. 25   Copy No. 10
Reference - HAZEBROUCK & LENS Maps 1/100000   Nov. 3/1916

1. The Brigade marches to billets in the LA MONCHY-BRETON area tomorrow. The Battalion will be billeted for the night in MONCHY BRETON. Route:- FLORINGHEM - PERNES - VALHUON - LA THIEULOYE.

2. Companies will march in the following order:- C, D, H.Q, B and A Companies, Transport. The head of the Column will pass the Starting Point (cross roads 600 yards W. of CAUCHY Church) at 9.23 a.m. Haversack ration will be carried. Lewis Gun hand-carts will follow the 1st. line transport. Baggage wagons will assemble under O.C. No. 2 Coy. Train at cross roads 400 yards N. of Y in CAUCHY at 10 a.m.

3. The Billeting party will report to the Staff Captain at BRYAS Church at 8.0 a.m. One cyclist guide will meet the baggage and supply wagons at VALHUON after they have found their billets.

4. The Transport Officer will collect Officers' kits, Officers' mess boxes and blankets from Company Headquarters. Mess boxes will be ready at 8.30 a.m. remainder at 8.0 a.m.

5. Billets will be ready for inspection at 9.0 a.m. The usual certificates that they are thoroughly clean will be handed to the Adjutant at the Starting Point.

6. Watches will be synchronised by Despatch Rider sent to Companies about 7.30 a.m.

7. The usual Falling Out states and other particulars will be forwarded to the Battalion Headquarters immediately upon arrival.

                M. Coates
                Lieut.Col.
                Comdg. 2/5th. R. Warwick. Regt.

Issued at 6.0 p.m.
Copy No. 1 to H.Q. Coy.
       2 to H.Q. Mess
       3 to A. Coy.
       4 to B. Coy.
       5 to C. Coy.
       6 to D. Coy.
       7 to Quartermaster
       8 to Transport Officer
       9 to Billeting Officer
     10   War Diary
     11   File

SECRET

Appendix 4

RED SQUARE OPERATION ORDER, NO. 26 Copy No. 10
Reference — LENS Map 1/100000 Nov. 4/18.

1. The Brigade marches to th HOUVIN–HOUVIGNEUL area tomorrow in two Columns. The Battalion will billet for the night in HOUVIN. Route:— BAILLEUL — LE QUESNEL — AVERDOINGT — MAIZERES — MAGNICOURT.

2. Companies will march in the following order:— D, B, H.Q, A and C Companies, Transport. The head of the Column will pass the Starting Point (cross roads ½ mile S. of the E in MONCHY–BRETON) at 8.30 a.m. Baggage wagons will march with the Battalion.

3. The Billeting party will meet the Staff Captain at MONCHEAUX at 8.0 a.m. A guide will be taken to meet the supply wagons at BUNEVILLE.

4. The Transport Officer will collect Officers' kits, Officers' mess boxes and blankets. Mess boxes will be ready for collection at 7.15 a.m. other goods by 6.45 a.m. All motor vehicles will proceed via cross roads ½ mile S. of E in MONCHY–BRETON — ST.POL — ARRAS road — TERNAS — HILAIRE — HOUVIN. They will assemble on the ST.POL — ARRAS road between road junction ¼ mile N. of the U in LE HAUE BARLET FM. and road junction ½ mile N.E. of 4th E in LA BELLE EPINE but will not move S. of ST.POL–ARRAS road before 9.30 a.m.

5. Billets will be ready for inspection by 7.30 a.m. The usual certificates that they are thoroughly clean will be handed to the Adjutant at the Starting Point.

6. Watches will be synchronised by Despatch Rider sent to Companies about 7.30 a.m.

7. The usual Falling Out states and other particulars will be forwarded to the Battalion Headquarters immediately upon arrival.

                                    Lieut.Col.
                                Comdg. 2/5th. R. Warwick. Regt.

Issued at 11 p.m.
Copy No. 1 to H.Q. Coy.
       2 to H.Q. Mess
       3 to A. Coy.
       4 to B. Coy.
       5 to C. Coy.
       6 to D. Coy.
       7 to Quartermaster
       8 to Transport Officer
       9 to Billeting Officer
    10   War Diary
    11   File

SECRET.

RED SQUARE OPERATION ORDER, NO.27   Copy No. 10
Reference - LENS Map 1/100000   November 5/1916

Appendix 5

1. The Brigade marches to the BONNIERES area tomorrow. The Battalion will be billeted in REMAISNIL. Route:- FREVENT and BONNIERES. VILLERS L'HÔPITAL

2. Companies will march in the following order:- H.Q. C, B, A and D Companies, Transport. The head of the Column will pass the Starting Point (cross roads 650 yards S. of the O. in HOUVIGNEUL) at 9.1 a.m. Baggage wagons will march with the Battalion. Motor lorries will move via CANETTEMONT - REBREUVIETTE - BOUQUEMAISON - BARLY - MEZEROLLES.

3. The Billeting party will meet the Staff Captain at BONNIERES at 8.30 a.m. A guide will meet the supply wagons at BONNIERES.

4. The refilling point will be on the ST.POL-FREVENT road just north of NUNCQ. REfilling commences approximately at 8.30 a.m.

5. The Transport Officer will arrange to collect Officers' mess boxes, Officers' kits and blankets. Mess boxes will be ready for collection at 8.0 a.m. remainder at 7.30 a.m.

6. Billets will be ready for inspection at 8.30 a.m. The usual certificates that they are thoroughly clean will be handed to the Adjutant at the Starting Point.

7. Watches will be synchronised by Despatch Rider sent to Companies about 7.30 a.m.

8. The usual Falling Out states and other particulars will be forwarded to Battalion Headquarters immediately upon arrival.

           Coates,
           Lieut.Col.
           Condg. 2/5th. R. Warwick. Regt.

Issued at 7.30 p.m.
Copy No. 1 to H.Q. Coy.
        2 to H.Q. Mess
        3 to A. Coy.
        4 to B. Coy.
        5 to C. Coy.
        6 to D. Coy.
        7 to Quartermaster
        8 to Transport Officer
        9 to Billeting Officer
       10   War Diary
       11   File

appendix 6

2nd/6th WARWICK OPERATION ORDER NO. 25   Copy No. 10
Reference :- LENS Map 1/100000   November 15th 1916.

1. The Brigade marches to the PIERVILLERS area today in
   two columns. The Battalion will be billeted in
   BERNAVILLE. Route:- FROHEN-LE-GRAND - FROHEN-LE-PETIT
   LE MEILLARD - BERNAVILLE.

2. Companies will march in the following order:- B, C, D,
   A and H.Qrs. Companies, Transport. The head of the
   column will pass the Starting Point (road junction
   400 yards N. E. of VILLERS Church) at 8.21 a.m.
   Baggage wagons will march with the Unit. Supply wagons
   will march independently to billets from the refilling
   point via MEZEROLLES and LE MEILLARD. Motor lorries
   will move via WAVANS - MEZEROLLES - LE MEILLARD -
   BERNAVILLE.

3. The Billeting Party and guide for the supply wagons
   will report to the Staff Captain at PIERVILLERS Church
   at 10 a.m.

4. The Transport Officer will arrange to collect Officers'
   mess boxes, Officers' kits and blankets. Mess boxes
   will be ready for collection at 8.15 a.m. remainder at
   7.45 a.m.

5. Billets will be ready for inspection at 9.0 a.m. The
   usual certificates that they are thoroughly clean will
   be handed to the Adjutant at the Starting Point.

6. Watches will be synchronised by Despatch Rider sent
   to companies about 7.30 a.m.

7. The usual Falling Out states and other particulars will
   be forwarded to the Battalion Headquarters immediately
   upon arrival.

                                    R. Coates,
                                        Lieut. Col.
                                   Comdg. 2/6th R. Warwick. Regt.

Issued at 4.0 a.m.
Copy No. 1 to H.Q. Coy.
         2 to H.Q. Mess
         3 to A. Coy.
         4 to B. Coy.
         5 to C. Coy.
         6 to D. Coy.
         7 to Quartermaster
         8 to Transport Officer
         9 to Billeting Officer
        10   War Diary
        11   File

SECRET

Appendix 7

RED SQUARE OPERATION ORDER, NO.29
Reference   LENS Map 1/100000

Copy No. 10

Nov. 16th 1918

1. The Brigade marches to the BERTEAUCOURT area today in two columns. The Battalion will be billeted in BERTEAUCOURT. Route :— DOMART-EN-PONTHIEU — ST. LEGER —

2. Companies will march in the following order :— C, D, A, H.Qrs. and B Companies, Transport. The head of the column will pass the Starting Point (road junction 1/8 mile E.N.E. of the E in ST. HILAIRE) at 9.0 a.m. Baggage wagons will march with the Unit. Supply wagons will march independently to billets from the refilling point.

3. The Billeting party and guide for the supply wagons will report to the Staff Captain at BERTEAUCOURT Church at 9 a.m.

4. The Transport Officer will arrange to collect Officers' Mess boxes, Officers' Kits and blankets. Mess boxes will be ready for collection at 8.0 a.m. remainder at 7.30 a.m.

5. Billets will be ready for inspection at 8.0 a.m. The usual certificates that they are thoroughly clear will be handed to the Adjutant at the Starting Point.

6. Watches will be synchronised by Despatch Rider sent to Companies about 7.30 a.m.

7. The usual Falling out states and other particulars will be forwarded to Battalion Headquarters immediately upon arrival.

R.L.Coates.
Lieut. Col.
Comdg. 2/5th. R. Warwick. Regt.

Issued at 1.0 a.m.
Copy No. 1 to H.Q. Coy.
       2 to H.Q. mess
       3 to A. Coy.
       4 to B. Coy.
       5 to C. Coy.
       6 to D. Coy.
       7 to Quartermaster
       8 to Transport Officer
       9 to Billeting Officer
      10   War Diary
      11   File

appendix 8

SECRET

RED SQUARE OPERATION ORDER No.30.   Copy No. 10
Reference – LENS Map 1/100000   Nov. 17/1916.

1. The Brigade marches today to the RUBEMPRE – HERISSART area.   The Battalion will be billeted in RUBEMPRE. Route:- HALLOY – HAVERNAS – NAOURS – TALMAS.

2. Companies will march in the following order:- D, A, H.Qr. B, C Companies and Transport.   The head of the column will pass the Starting Point (cross roads 1/8 mile S.S.W. of BERTEAUCOURT Church) at 10.25 a.m. Baggage wagons will march with the unit.   Supply wagons after refilling will proceed to RUBEMPRE Church where they will be met by guides.

3. The Billeting party and guide for the supply wagons will report to the Staff Captain at RUBEMPRE CHURCH at 11.0 a.m.

4. All Officers' kits will be taken to the Quartermaster's Stores by 9.0 a.m.   The Transport Officer will arrange to collect Officers' mess boxes and blankets.   The latter will be ready for collection at 9.0 a.m. the former at 9.30 a.m.

5. Billets will be ready for inspection at 9.0 a.m.   The usual certificates that they are thoroughly clean will be handed to the Adjutant at the Starting Point.

6. Watches will be synchronised by Despatch rider sent to Companies about 7.30 a.m.

7. The usual Falling Out states and other particulars will be forwarded to Battalion Headquarters immediately upon arrival.

R/ Coates,
Lieut. Col.
Comdg. 2/5th R. Warwick. Regt.

Issued at 8.0 a.m.
Copy No. 1 to H.Q. Coy.
        2 to H.Q. Mess
        3 to A. Coy.
        4 to B. Coy.
        5 to C. Coy.
        6 to D. Coy.
        7 to Quartermaster
        8 to Transport Officer
        9 to Billeting Officer
        10   War Diary
        11   File

Appendix 9

SECRET

RED SQUARE OPERATION ORDER, NO. 31.　　　　Copy No. 10
Reference – LENS Map 1/100000　　　　　　　Nov. 17/1916

---

1. The Brigade marches to the WARLOY area tomorrow. The Battalion will be billeted in WARLOY. Route:– HERISSART – CONTAY.

2. Companies will march in the following order:– H.Qr. A, B, C, and D Companies, Transport. Distances of 200 yards between Companies and between the last company and Transport will be maintained on the march. Cookers and Lewis Guns will march with their own companies. The head of the column will pass the Starting Point (road junction 200 yards E.N.E. of RUBEMPRE Church) at 9.4 a.m. Baggage wagons will march with the unit. Supply wagons after refilling will proceed independently to WARLOY.

3. The Billeting party will report to the Staff Captain at WARLOY Church at 9.30 a.m. A guide will be taken for the supply wagons.

4. Officers' kits will be taken to the Quartermaster's Stores by 7.30 a.m. Blankets will be ready for collection by the motor lorry at company headquarters at 7.30 a.m. Officers' mess boxes will be ready at 8.30 a.m.

5. Billets will be ready for inspection at 8.30 a.m. The usual certificates that they are thoroughly clean will be handed to the Adjutant at the Starting Point.

6. Watches will be synchronised by Despatch Rider sent to companies about 7.30 a.m.

7. The usual Falling Out states and other particulars will be forwarded to Battalion Headquarters immediately upon arrival.

　　　　　　　　　　　　　　P.L. Coates,
　　　　　　　　　　　　　　Lieut. Col.
　　　　　　　　　　Comdg. 2/5th. R. Warwick. Regt.

Issued at 10.30 p.m.
Copy No. 1 to H.Q. Coy.
　　　　2 to H.Q. Mess
　　　　3 to A. Coy.
　　　　4 to B. Coy.
　　　　5 to C. Coy.
　　　　6 to D. Coy.
　　　　7 to Quartermaster
　　　　8 to Transport Officer
　　　　9 to Billeting Officer
　　　10　 War Diary
　　　11　 File

SECRET.   Appendix 10

RED SQUARE OPERATION ORDER, NO.32   Copy No. 10
Reference – LENS & AMIENS Maps 1/100000   November 20/1916.

1. The Brigade marches to ALBERT tomorrow. The Battalion will be billeted in ALBERT. Route HENENCOURT – MILLENCOURT

2. Companies will march in the following order:- A, B, C, D & H.Qr. Coy/S, Transport. Distances of 200 yards between Companies and between the last Company and Transport and 500 yards between Battalions will be maintained on the march. Scouts and Lewis Gunners will march with their own companies. The head of the column will pass WARLOY Church at 12.25 p.m. All main roads in WARLOY will be kept clear until companies are actually on the march to the Starting Point. Baggage wagons will march with the unit. Supply wagons will be met by a guide at the Railway Bridge at the western entrance to ALBERT. Motor lorries will proceed independently in advance of the column, which starts at 11.0 a.m.

3. Haversack rations will be carried and dinner will be served on arrival at ALBERT.

4. The Billeting party will meet the Staff Captain at ALBERT Church at 11.0 a.m. Each company (except H.Qr. company) will detail three other ranks to accompany the Billeting party.

5. Officers' kits will be taken to the Quartermaster's Stores by 11.0 a.m. Blankets will be ready for collection by the motor lorry at company headquarters at 9.0 a.m. Officers' mess boxes will be collected at 11.30 a.m.

6. Billets will be ready for inspection at 11.45 a.m. The usual certificates that they are thoroughly clean will be handed to the Adjutant at the Starting Point.

7. Watches will be synchronised by despatch rider sent to companies about 7.30 a.m.

8. The usual Filling Out states and other particulars will be forwarded to Battalion Headquarters immediately upon arrival.

                                                    W.Churchouse
                                                    Lieut. & Adjt.

Issued at 10.0 p.m.
Copy No. 1 to H.Q. C.
         2 to H.Q. Mess
         3 to A. Coy.
         4 to B. Coy.
         5 to C. Coy.
         6 to D. Coy.
         7 to Quartermaster
         8 to Transport Officer
         9 to Billeting Officer
        10   War Diary
        11   File

Appendix 11

SECRET
RED SQUARE OPERATION ORDER, NO.35   Copy No. 10
Reference - LENS Map 1/100000   November 21/1916.

1. Part of Brigade group marches to SENLIS tomorrow. The Battalion will proceed via BOUZINCOURT to billets in SENLIS.

2. Companies will march in the following order:- B, C, D, H.Qrs. and A. Companies. The leading company will pass the Starting Point (road junction on the ALBERT - BOUZINCOURT road 5/8 mile S.S.W. of the S in SEA) at 10.40 a.m. Cookers and Lewis Gunners will march with their companies. There will be no halt between 10.50 a.m. and 11.0 a.m. It is essential that streets in ALBERT be kept clear. Companies will march to the Starting Point in file without falling in on a main road, and will time their march so that a halt at the Starting Point will not be necessary. 200 yards distance will be maintained between companies.

3. The Transport will follow the column in order of units, which is, Brigade Headquarters, 5th Warwicks, 7th Warwicks, 182nd. Machine Gun Coy. & 182nd. Trench Mortar Battery. 500 yards interval will be kept between transport units. Baggage wagons will march with the unit. Supply wagons after refilling will march direct to billets. Motor lorries will move independently in advance of the column.

4. The Billeting party will meet the Staff Captain at SENLIS Church at 10.0 a.m.

5. Blankets and Officers' kits will be taken to the Quartermaster's stores by 9.30 a.m. Mess boxes will be ready for collection at 9.50 a.m.

6. Billets will be ready for inspection at 10.0 a.m. The usual certificates that they have been thoroughly cleaned will be handed to the Adjutant at the starting point.

7. Watches will be synchronised by Despatch rider sent to companies about 7.50 a.m.

8. The usual Falling Out states and other particulars will be forwarded to Battalion Headquarters immediately upon arrival.

                                        [signature]
                                        Lieut. & Adjt.

Issued at 10.15 p.m.
Copy No. 1 to H.Q. Coy.
         2 to R.Q. Mess
         3 to A. Coy.
         4 to B. Coy.
         5 to C. Coy.
         6 to D. Coy.
         7 to Quartermaster
         8 to Transport Officer
         9 to Billeting Officer
        10   War Diary
        11   File.

SECRET

RED SQUARE OPERATION ORDER, NO. 34   Copy No. 10
Reference — Sheet 57d. 1/40000   November 26/1916.

Appendix 12

1. The Battalion will move under canvas at SENLIS (V.10.d.2.1.) tomorrow.

2. Company Commanders will meet the Adjutant at the Camp at 10.0 a.m. when tents will be allotted to Companies. Companies will move as follows:—
   - H.Qrs. Coy.   11.0 a.m.
   - A. Company   11.15 a.m.
   - B.   "   11.30 a.m.
   - C.   "   11.45 a.m.
   - D.   "   12 noon

   The Transport and Quartermaster's Stores will remain in their present billets.

3. Blankets will be carried by the men. The Transport Officer will collect Officers' kits and mess boxes at 10.30 a.m.

4. Sec.Lieut. Clegg will hand over billets to the incoming Battalion.

5. Billets will be ready for inspection at 10.45 a.m. The usual certificates that they have been thoroughly cleaned will be rendered to the Orderly Room.

6. Watches will be synchronised by Despatch rider sent to Companies about 8.0 a.m.

                                   Lieut. & Adjt.
                                   2/5th R. Warwick. Regt.

Issued at 7.30 p.m.

Copy No. 1 to H.Q.Coy.
        2 to H.Q. Mess
        3 to A. Coy.
        4 to B. Coy.
        5 to C. Coy.
        6 to D. Coy.
        7 to Quartermaster
        8 to Transport Officer
        9 to Billeting Officer
     10   War Diary
     11   File.

Vol I

Confidential

War Diary

of

1st Bn. Royal Warwickshire Regt.

from Dec 1st 1916   to Dec 31st 1916

WAR DIARY or INTELLIGENCE SUMMARY.

(Erase heading not required.)

Army Form C. 2118.

Place	Date	Hour	Summary of Events and Information	Remarks and references to Appendices
SENLIS	1/1/16	10 a.m.	182 INF. BDE. Practised Attack from trenches at HEDAUVILLE. Company Training	1/1/16
"	2/1/16	9 a.m.	182 INF. BDE. Relieved 182 INF BDE in support, Batn. marched via BOUZINCOURT to huts at MARTINSART arriving 11.15 a.m. Working Parties.	2/1/16 appendix 1
MARTINSART	3/1/16	11.30 a.m.	Church Parade at CHURCH ARMY HUT.	3/1/16
"	4/1/16	—	Working Parties. 25 Reinforcements arrived from Base.	4/1/16
"	5/1/16	—	" "	5/1/16
"	6/1/16	—	" "	6/1/16
"	7/1/16	—	Company Training & Bathing	7/1/16
"	8/1/16	—	Working Parties	8/1/16
"	9/1/16	—	" "	9/1/16
"	10/1/16	—	Battalion relieved 9th GLOUCESTERS in MOUQUET FARM AREA, Centre subsection. Relief complete at 11.30 p.m.	10/1/16 appendix 2
MOUQUET FARM SECTOR	11/1/16	—	Battn. extended front to the left relieving 2/6th WARWICKS. Relief complete 6 a.m. 12/1/16	11/1/16 appendix 3
"	12/1/16	—	Batn. holding left subsection MOUQUET FARM SECTOR	12/1/16
"	13/1/16	—	" "	13/1/16
"	14/1/16	—	" "	14/1/16
"	15/1/16	—	Batn. was relieved by 2/6th Warwicks & moved into left support. Relief complete 3.15 a.m. 16/1/16	15/1/16 appendix 4

WAR DIARY
or
INTELLIGENCE SUMMARY. JP6

Army Form C. 2118.

Place	Date	Hour	Summary of Events and Information	Remarks and references to Appendices
WELLINGTON HUTS MARTD	16/9/16	—	Battn in left support	JP6
"	17/9/16	—	"	JP6
"	18/9/16	—	"	JP6
"	19/9/16	—	"	JP6
"	20/9/16	—	Battn was relieved by 2/4th OXFORD & BUCKS REGT & moved into support at MARTINSART. Relief complete 5.30pm	JP6. appendix 5
MARTINSART	21/9/16	—	Working parties.	
"	22/9/16	—	Battn was relieved by 2/4th GLOUCESTER. R. & marched into Reserve at VARENNES arriving 1.10 pm.	JP6 appendix 6
VARENNES.	23/9/16	—	Company Training	JP6
"	24/9/16	10 am	Church Parade in Church Army tent.	JP6
"	25/9/16	10 am	Church Parade " " "	JP6
"	26/9/16	—	Company Training	JP6
"	27/9/16	—	" "	JP6
"	28/9/16	—	" "	JP6
"	29/9/16	—	" "	JP6
"	30/9/16	10 noon	Battn relieved 2/4th OXFORD & BUCKS.R in reserve & marched to huts in MARTINSART WOOD arriving 1 pm.	JP6 appendix 7
"	31/9/16	—	Working parties	JP6

MPole
Maj: Cmdg 2/5 R.War.R.

SECRET

RED SQUARE OPERATION ORDER, NO.35　　　　　Copy No. 10
Reference - Map 57D. S.E. 1/20000　　　　　　Nov. 30/1916.

appendix 1

1. The Brigade will relieve the 184th Infantry Brigade in support on December 2nd 1916. The Battalion will march via BOUZINCOURT to huts at W.2.d.8.9.

2. Companies will march in the following order:- H.Qrs. A, B, C and D Companies, Transport, the head of the column passing the Starting Point (SENLIS CHURCH) at 9.0 a.m. The usual distances will be maintained between companies, Cookers and Lewis Gunners proceeding with them.

3. Blankets and Officers' kits will be taken to the Quartermaster's stores by 8.0 a.m. Mess boxes will be ready for collection at 8.30 a.m.

4. The Billeting Officer will reconnoitre the new area sometime tomorrow.

5. Camp and billets will be ready for inspection at 8.45 a.m. The usual certificates that they have been thoroughly cleaned will be handed to the Adjutant at the Starting Point.

6. Watches will be synchronised by Despatch rider sent to Companies about 7.30 a.m.

7. The usual Falling Out states and other particulars will be forwarded to the Orderly Room immediately upon arrival.

　　　　　　　　　　　　　　　Lieut. Col.
　　　　　　　　　　　　Comdg. 2/5th R. Warwick. Regt.

Issued at 6.30 p.m.
Copy No. 1 to H.Q.Coy.
　　　　　2 to H.Q.Mess
　　　　　3 to A. Coy.
　　　　　4 to B. Coy.
　　　　　5 to C. Coy.
　　　　　6 to D. Coy.
　　　　　7 to Quartermaster
　　　　　8 to Transport Officer
　　　　　9 to Billeting Officer
　　　　　10　 War Diary
　　　　　11　 File.

SECRET

RED SQUARE OPERATION ORDER, No.36   Copy No. 10
Reference — Map 57D. S.E.   December 9th 1916.

appendix

INFORMATION. The 182nd Infantry Brigade will relieve the 183rd Infantry Brigade in the line on 10th & 11th December 1916.

1. The 2/5th R. Warwickshire Regt. will relieve the 2/6th Gloucester Regt. in accordance with the following relief table:—

   "D" Coy. plus 4 Lewis Guns   4 Guides at Gravel
   will relieve "D" Coy. Gloucester Regt.   Pit at 5.0 p.m.

   "B" Coy. plus 2 Lewis Guns   5 Guides at Gravel
   will relieve "B" Coy. Gloucester Regt.   Pit at 5.30 p.m.

   "A" Coy. plus 2 Lewis Guns   4 Guides at Gravel
   will relieve "A" Coy. Gloucester Regt.   Pit at 6.0 p.m.

   "C" Coy. plus 2 Lewis Guns   4 Guides at Gravel
   will relieve "C" Coy. Gloucester Regt.   Pit at 6.30 p.m.

   Parties will be organised ready for leading into the trenches before leaving MARTINSART. From MARTINSART to rest position, companies may be moved closed up, from thence onwards with 150 yards between platoons.

2. Dinner will be served in time to allow troops to move off at 1.0 p.m. Companies will move in the following order:—

   1 platoon of "A" Coy. & 1 platoon of "C" Coy. who are to act as ration and carrying party to report to Lieut. Farmer at Gravel Pits.

   "D" Coy, "B" Coy, 3 platoons of "A" Coy and 3 platoons of "C" Coy. Lewis Guns are to march in front of their companies.

   Cookers then to proceed to a point on NAB ROAD by a Bomb Dump (about X.2.a.) there to halt, and men to be fed with a hot meal before going into the trenches. Remainder of days rations will be carried into the trenches by the men.

3. The following Officers will proceed to the trenches today to take over:—
       Lewis Gun Officer
       1 Officer per Company
       1 N.C.O. per platoon
   The Sniping Officer will arrange for 6 snipers also to proceed today under himself or Sergt. of snipers. All signallers and H.Qrs. Coy. will proceed to Gravel Pits on the day of relief arriving there at 12 noon.

4. The Quartermaster will arrange for rations to be delivered by the Transport personnel at the Gravel Pits daily at 4.0 p.m. They must be there on the day of relief in time for the ration carrying parties to follow their platoons into the trenches during relief.

5. **DRESS:-** Marching order, less packs, which are to be labelled, packed in sacks and labelled by platoons and collected by the Transport at 9.0 a.m. at MARTINSART Camp and stored by the Quartermaster.

6. All blankets to be tightly rolled in 10's, tied in two places and will be collected by Transport not later than 9.0 a.m. on the morning of the 10th.

7. The Transport Officer will collect Officers' kits and mess boxes at 1.0 p.m.

8. Sec.Lieut. Donaldson will be attached to "A" Coy. while in the trenches, but his primary duties will be Battalion Bombing Officer.

9. Sergt. Blayney and 6 men of the police will report to the Staff Captain or representative at CRUCIFIX CORNER to issue Gum-boots to companies as they pass, reporting not later than 1.0 p.m.

10. Sec.Lieut. Farmer will supervise receipt and issue of rations and work generally by the H.Qrs. Coy. and 2 platoons attached for carrying duties at the Gravel Pits.

11. Companies will report relief complete by code word. Relief to be completed by 6.0 a.m.

12. The Confidential Box and Stationery boxes will be removed by the Orderly Room staff, less Sergt. Simpson who will proceed to the trenches, to space allotted by the 2/8th R. Warwickshire Regt. in Wellington Huts. Transport Officer to provide limber space for the above material to be moved up with the rations for the 11th.

Capt.
Comdg. 2/5th R. Warwick. Regt.

Issued at 12 noon.
Copy No. 1 to H.Q. Coy.
2 to H.Q. Mess
3 to A. Coy.
4 to B. Coy.
5 to C. Coy.
6 to D. Coy.
7 to Quartermaster
8 to Transport Officer
9 War Diary
10 File

SECRET.

RED SQUARE OPERATION ORDER. No. 57. Copy No. 7
Reference – Trench Map 11 M.25.   December 11th, 1916.

Appendix 3.

1. After 12 midnight 11/12th. Dec. the disposition of the Battalion will be as follows. From 16 street exclusive to Lucky Way at R20 b5.8 and a line drawn S. of this point.

2. The following relief will take place on night of 11/12th. Dec. Reliefs to be completed by midnight and to be reported by Codes.

3. Arrangements for reliefs will be made by O.C., Coys with the Coys. concerned on each flank.

4. "B" Coy will relieve two platoons of 2/6th. Warwicks in Stuff Trench.
"C" Coy will relieve two platoons of 2/6th. Warwicks in Bainbridge Trench.
"D" Coy will relieve one platoon of "B" Coy in DESIRE Trench and may withdraw troops from GLASGOW Trench.
One platoon of "A" Coy. E. of SIXTEEN St. will be relieved by 2/7th. Warwicks.
"A" Coy will relieve one platoon of "C" Coy W. of FIELD Trench.

5. Guides for "C" Coy. relieving platoon will be at junction of STUMP Rd. and BAINBRIDGE Tr. at 8 p.m. Guides for remainder must be arranged for by Coys. concerned, all movement being from the right.

6. Meeting of Coy. Comdrs. in HESSIAN is cancelled for tonight. From evening of 12th. inclusive, Coy. Comdrs. will report at 4 p.m. at Batt. H.Q.

7. As soon as Coys. have settled down, rations guides will be sent to GRAVEL PITS.

8. Sketch of new position required from Coy. Comdrs. by Noon 12th. inst.

Captain,
Comdg. 2/5th.R.Warwick.Regt.

Copy No. 1 to A. Coy.
         2 to B. Coy.
         3 to C. Coy.
         4 to D. Coy.
         5 to 2/6th. R.War.Reg.
         6 to 2/7th. R.War.Reg.
         7   File
         8   War Diary.
         9   Lieut. Farmer.

Operation Order 38.   Appendix 4
Issued at 7.00 p.m   Ref y No. 8
Map Ref. Sheet 57D.SE.   14.12.16.

(1) The battalion will be relieved in the left sector by the 2/6 R.War.R. on the night of 15/16 Dec.16; relief to be completed by 6 a.m.
Coys will proceed to quarters as follows:-
A Coy. 1 platoon & Coy HQ in Zollern Trench. 3 platoons at the front.
B Coy Wellington Huts
C Coy Mouquet Farm
D Coy Wellington Huts
HQ Coy Wellington Huts

(2) C.Coy 2/6 R.War.R. & 6 Lewis Guns relieves D Coy 2/5 R.War.R. in
                                        Right Front Trench.
4 Guides at Duckboards 100 yds S of junction of FIELD & HESSIAN TR. at 5 p.m.

B Coy 2/6 R.War.R. & 4 Lewis Guns relieves B Coy 2/5 R.War.R. in
                                        Left Front Trench
4 Guides at Gravel Pits at 5 p.m.

D Coy 2/6 R.War.R. & 4 Lewis Guns relieves A Coy 2/5 R.War.R. in
                                        Right Support
4 Guides at Gravel Pit at 6 p.m.

A Coy 2/6 R.War.R. & 4 Lewis Guns relieves C Coy 2/5 R.War. in
                                        Left Support
4 Guides at Gravel Pit at 6.30 p.m.

Gravel Pit & Bn HQ Staff will be

relieved by opposite numbers at ~~12 noon~~ 2pm, buy books with Diaries & utensils proceeding to their new billets, No 3 & 10 platoons being available for carrying parties.

Special care is to be taken that departing troops do not enter Gravel Pit or loiter in the vicinity.

(3) 1 Officer & 2 NCOs from A Coy will leave the trenches early and take over Zollern & Thiepval Dugouts from B Coy 2/6 R.War.R.

1 Officer & 1 NCO from C. Coy will also leave early and take over the billets at Mouquet Farm

The Q.M Sgts of each Coy will assist & obtain instructions direct from their Coys as to ration supplies. Where cookers can be put into use they should be used. Hot food to be ready for troops on arrival at billets. Orderly Room Staff at present with 2/8 R.War.R. will move into new HQ early on day of relief. L.Cpl Hackett being responsible for custody of Confidential Box.

(4) The following men detailed for leave will be attached to HQ Coy on leaving the trenches

    3442 Sgt. G.S. Miller   A Coy
    3976 Pte. J. Bramwell   B "
    3676 " E. Bishop   C "
    122 L.Cpl W. Fake   D "

Coys in support line will not move out

until troops relieving Front line have passed
to the front.
Outgoing troops will make way on the
duckboards and paths to incoming troops
Battle Orders will be carried in front of the
platoon to which they are attached.
Platoons must be kept closed up and 20 yds
distance between platoons observed until S
of the Thiepval-Pozières Road.
Each word of completed relief to be sent to
Batt. HQ by runner or telephone
1 Officer per Coy and 1 NCO per platoon of ½ R.War.R
will visit the trenches to take over the night
before relief.
Coys will hand in Trench Store Lists to Bn HQ
by 12 noon on day of relief.
The T.C. will arrange for the Maltese Cart to
be at junction of duckboards & Nab Road
at 12 noon. All Officers kits & Mess boxes &
Blankets for E, B & HQ Coys will be delivered
at Wellington Huts by 10 pm on day of relief.
Stores ex from Gravel Pit to be collected later
from junction of duckboards & Nab Road later.
Coy bombers will arrange direct with T.O. for
delivering of mins packs if required.
Gum Boots will not be handed over except
at the special request of N. incoming Coys
when a receipt will be obtained.
Transport Farmer will apportion the Huts & Tents
at Wellington Huts to the Coys quartered there

(5) Tactical Progress Reports up to the time of relief will be rendered to Bn HQ by 10 am. on the following morning.

M Giles Capt.
O.C. 2/5 R War R.

Copies to

1 to A Coy
2 to B "
3 to C "
4 to D "
5 to TO + Qmr.
6 to MO + 2nd/Capt Farmer
7 to 2/6 R War R.
8 to File
9 to War Diary.

SECRET.
RED SQUARE OPERATION ORDER. No. 59. December, 19th. 1916.
Reference - Sheet 57D. S.E. Copy No. 11

Appendix 5

1. The Battalion will be relieved tomorrow by the 4th. Bn. Oxfordshire Regiment, and will march to old billets in MARTINSART WOOD.

2. <u>Guides</u>. Four guides from "C" Coy. to be at junction of duckboards and NAB ROAD at 2 p.m. Four guides from "A" Coy. to be at junction of duckboards and NAB ROAD at 2 p.m. No guides required for remainder.

3. A party under 2nd. Lieut. Farmer of 12 O.R. to proceed to MARTINSART WOOD and take over billets there, arriving not later than 10 a.m.

4. "A" and "C" Coys. are to be careful to explain rationing and water arrangements, and to obtain signatures for all watercans handed over to relieving troops.

5. <u>Gum Boots</u>. Gum Boots in possession of the Companies, and any others which can be found, are to be gathered together and handed in tomorrow as follows. Transport will be provided by Transport Officer for B. D. & H.Qrs. Coys. at 9 a.m. at WELLINGTON HUTS; for A and C Coys. at 11 a.m. at NAB ROAD Duckboard Junction. Counting of all Gum Boots will be under 2nd. Lieut. Blanchard, who will obtain signatures from CRUCIFIX CORNER Dump for all Gum Boots handed over and report to Adjutant.

6. Transport for Officers' Mess Boxes and Kits and Orderly Room Boxes and Blankets at WELLINGTON HUTS at 10 a.m.

7. Horses for Watercarts at WELLINGTON HUTS at 10.45 a.m.

8. Transport for "C" and "A" Coys. dixies and Company baggage and Machine Guns, at NAB ROAD Duckboard junction at 3 p.m.

9. Medical Cart at WELLINGTON HUTS at 10 a.m.

10. Companies are to commence moving away from WELLINGTON HUTS at 10.45 a.m., and to be clear at 11.30 a.m.

11. Officer Commanding "A" Coy. will be responsible for the relief of "A" and "C" Coys. and will send a message with the Code word for the relief complete - "Christmas", to Brigade Headquarters at MOUQUET FARM. This will cover the relief of the Battalion.

Issued at 7 p.m.
Copy No. 1 to H.Q. Coy.
       2 to H.Q. Mess.
       3 to A. Coy.
       4 to B. Coy.
       5 to C. Coy.
       6 to D. Coy.
       7 to Quartermaster.
       8 to Transport Officer.
       9 to Billeting Officer.
     10   War Diary.
     11   File.

R. Coates,
Lieut.-Col.
Comdg. 2/5th. R. Warwick. Regt.

Appendix 6

SECRET.

RED SQUARE OPERATION ORDER No. 40. Copy No. 10
Reference. Sheet 57 D. S.E. 1/20000. December 21st.1916.

---

1. The Battalion will be relieved tomorrow by the 2/6th. Glosters, and will march to Huts in VARENNES. Route:- BOUZINCOURT - HEDAUVILLE.

2. Companies will march in the following order H.Qrs. A, B, C, and D Companies and Transport; the head of the column passing the Starting Point (W.2.b.6.0) at 10.20 a.m. The usual distances will be maintained between Companies and transport; Cookers and Lewis gunners proceeding with their Companies.

3. Blankets and Officers' Kits will be ready for collection by 9 a.m., and Mess boxes by 9.30 a.m. Blankets will be dumped at a spot to be selected by Sgt. Blayney, who will refuse any not properly tied. Ammunition, bombs and tools (less picks) will be exchanged with the 2/6th. Glosters.

4. Lieut. T.W. Blanchard with the billeting party, will report to the Staff Captain at the Town Major's Office HEDAUVILLE, at 9 a.m. tomorrow.

5. The Camp will be ready for inspection by 9.45 a.m. The usual certificates that all Huts and surroundings have been thoroughly cleaned, will be handed to the Adjutant at the Starting Point.

6. Watches will be synchronised by Despatch Rider sent to Companies about 8 a.m.

7. The usual falling-out states and other particulars will be forwarded to the Orderly Room immediately upon arrival.

   Lieut.-Col.
   Comdg.2/5th.Bn.R.Warwick.Regt.

Issued at 7 p.m.
Copy No. 1. to H.Q. Coy.
        2. to H.Q. Mess.
        3. to A. Coy.
        4. to B. Coy.
        5. to C. Coy.
        6. to D. Coy.
        7. to Quartermaster.
        8. to Transport Officer.
        9. to Billeting Officer.
       10.   War Diary.
       11.   File.

SECRET.

RED SQUARE OPERATION ORDER No. 41.   Copy No. 10
Reference, Sheet 57 D. S.E. 1/20000.   December, 29th, 1916.

---

1. The Battalion will relieve tomorrow the 2/4th. Oxford & Bucks. Regt., and will march to huts previously occupied at MARTINSART WOOD. Transport lines and Quartermaster's Stores will be taken over from the 2/4th. Oxford and Bucks. Regt.

   Route:— HEDAUVILLE—BOUZINCOURT—MARTINSART.

2. Companies will march in the following order, "A", "B", "H.Qrs." and Transport; the head of the Column passing the starting point, cross roads P.26.c.½.4. at 10.40 a.m.
   The usual distances will be maintained between companies, and Transport.
   Field Kitchens and Lewis Gunners will proceed with their companies.

3. Blankets and Officers' Kits will be ready for collection by 9 a.m. Mess boxes by 9.30 a.m.

   Blankets will be dumped at a spot to be selected by Sgt. Blayney, who will refuse any not properly tied.

   Ammunition, bombs and tools (less S.A.A., K, or KR) (picks and small tools) will be exchanged with the 2/4th. Oxford and Bucks. Regt.

4. 2nd. Lieut. G. G. FARMER with 6 O.R. of Headquarter Company will report at the Huts MARTINSART WOOD at 9.30 a.m. to take over.
   Lieut. F. W. BLANCHARD and 8 O.R. of Headquarter Coy. will act as Rear Party and not leave the Camp until it is thoroughly clean and all our Stores have been despatched.

5. The Camp will be ready for inspection by 10 a.m. The usual certificates that all Huts and surroundings have been thoroughly cleaned, will be handed to the Adjutant at the starting point.

6. Watches will be synchronised by Despatch Rider sent to companies about 8 a.m.

7. The usual falling-out states and other particulars will be forwarded to the Orderly Room immediately upon arrival.

Issued at 12 noon.
  Copy No. 1 to "H.Q" Coy.
  Copy No. 2 to "H.Q" Mess.   No. 10 War Diary.
      No. 3 to "A" Coy.   No. 11 File.
      No. 4 to "B" Coy.
      No. 5 to "C" Coy.
      No. 6 to "D" Coy.
      No. 7 to Transport Officer
      No. 8 to Quartermaster.
      No. 9 to Billeting Officer.

J. Chuzzlehouse
Captain
for Lieut.-Col.
Comdg. 2/5. R. Warwick. Regt.

Vol 9

Confidential

War Diary
of
1/5th Bn. Royal Warwickshire Regt.

From June 1st 1917 to June 30th 1917.

WAR DIARY
or
INTELLIGENCE SUMMARY. JMC

Army Form C. 2118.

(Erase heading not required.)

Instructions regarding War Diaries and Intelligence Summaries are contained in F. S. Regs., Part II. and the Staff Manual respectively. Title pages will be prepared in manuscript.

Place	Date	Hour	Summary of Events and Information	Remarks and references to Appendices
MARTINSART	1/1/17	—	Working Parties.	JMC
"	2/1/17	—	" "	JMC
"	3/1/17	—	" "	JMC
"	4/1/17	—	" "	JMC
"	5/1/17	—	" "	JMC
"	6/1/17	—	Battⁿ Relieved 2/8ᵗʰ WORCESTER R. in MOUQUET FARM Left Subsection. Relief complete at 9.10 pm.	JMC appendix
MOUQUET FARM	7/1/17	—	Battⁿ holding Left subsection MOUQUET FARM AREA.	JMC
"	8/1/17	—	" "	JMC
"	9/1/17	—	" "	JMC
"	10/1/17	—	" "	JMC
"	11/1/17	—	Battⁿ relieved in Left subsection MOUQUET FARM area by 7ᵗʰ WARWICKS & moved into Left support. Relief complete at 10.10 pm.	JMC appendix
"	12/1/17	—	Battⁿ in Left support	JMC
"	13/1/17	—	" "	JMC
"	14/1/17	—	" "	JMC
"	15/1/17	—	" "	JMC
"	16/1/17	—	Battⁿ relieved in support by 1/2ᵗʰ MIDDLESEX. R. (Relief complete at 9pm) & proceeded by motor bus to billets at VAL de MAISON arriving 12.30 am 17ᵗʰ inst.	JMC appendix

Army Form C. 2118.

WAR DIARY
or
INTELLIGENCE SUMMARY. 1/6

(Erase heading not required.)

Instructions regarding War Diaries and Intelligence Summaries are contained in F. S. Regs., Part II. and the Staff Manual respectively. Title pages will be prepared in manuscript.

Place	Date	Hour	Summary of Events and Information	Remarks and references to Appendices
VAL M. MAISON	17/1/17	—	Battn marched to billets in FIENVILLERS arriving 4.30 p.m.	WD appendix 1
FIENVILLERS	18/1/17	—	Battn marched to billets in COULONVILLERS arriving 12 noon	WD appendix 5
COULONVILLERS	19/1/17	—	Battn marched to billets in LAMOTTE-BULEUX arriving 12.45 p.m.	WD appendix 6
LAMOTTE-BULEUX	20/1/17	—	Company Training	WD.
"	21/1/17	—	"	WD.
"	22/1/17	—	"	WD.
"	23/1/17	—	Platoon Training	WD.
"	24/1/17	—	"	WD.
"	25/1/17	—	"	WD.
"	26/1/17	—	"	WD.
"	27/1/17	—	"	WD.
"	28/1/17	3 p.m.	Church Parade	WD.
"	29/1/17	—	Company Training	WD.
"	30/1/17	—	"	WD.
"	31/1/17	—	"	WD.

M Coulton Lt Col
Comdg 12th Manch R
1/2/17

SECRET.

Appendix 1

RED SQUARE OPERATION ORDER, No. 42.   Copy No. 11
Reference – Map 57 D. S.E.   January 5th 1916.

---

1. The 182nd. Infantry Brigade will relieve the 183rd.
   Infantry Brigade in the line on the night 6/7th. inst.
   The Battalion will relieve the 2/4th. Gloucester Regt.
   in accordance with the following relief table.

   "A" Coy. plus 5 Lewis Guns will relief "D" Coy.
   Gloucester Regt. Five guides at GRAVEL PIT at 5.30 p.m.
   "C" Coy. plus 3 Lewis Guns will relieve "C" Coy.
   Gloucester Regt. Four guides at GRAVEL PIT at 6.0 p.m.
   "B" Coy. plus 1 Lewis Gun will relieve "A" Coy.
   Gloucester Regt. Three guides at GRAVEL PIT at 6.30 pm.
   "D" Coy. plus 1 Lewis Gun will relieve "B" Coy.
   Gloucester Regt. Two guides at GRAVEL PIT at 7.0 p.m.

   One guide for Headquarter Staff at GRAVEL PIT at
   8.30 p.m.
   Parties will be organised ready for loading into
   the trenches before leaving MARTINSART. From
   MARTINSART to Rest position (where men will be fed with
   a hot meal) companies my move closed up, from thence
   onwards with 150 yards between platoons.

2. Dinner will be served before leaving MARTINSART Camp.
   "B" and "D" companies will each detail one platoon, not
   less than 20 men to report to 2nd. Lieut. G. G. FARMER
   at GRAVEL PIT for carrying parties.
   Platoons will be commanded by Sergeants.
   Men will not be allowed to proceed into GRAVEL PIT on
   marching into relief nor must they stand about the
   vicinity.
   Lewis Guns are to march in front of their Platoons and
   to set the pace. Remainder of days rations will be
   carried into the trenches by the men. Water-bottles are
   to be filled and men warned not to give water to
   outgoing troops.

3. One Officer per company and one N.C.O. per platoon of
   the front line companies will proceed to the line today,
   and one Officer per company and one N.C.O. per platoon
   of the support companies will proceed to the line
   tomorrow to take over Stores in daylight.
   Sniping Sergeant and eight snipers will be attached
   to "A" Coy. and Sniping Sergeant will report at Battalion
   Headquarters, ZOLLERN REDOUBT at 2.30 p.m. for
   information from Sniping Officer of Gloucester Regt. *The*
   Snipers will march in with "A" Company. *Remainder of snipers will be attached to Bn HQrs*

4. Two runners per company and linesmen will go into the
   line tonight, the runners to complete at least one
   journey from Battalion Headquarters to each Company
   Headquarters before daylight.
   Signallers will report at Headquarters and Reserve
   Company Headquarters at 2.30 p.m. tomorrow.
   Party for GRAVEL PIT (under 2nd. Lieut. G.G.FARMER)
   consisting of two platoons detailed; Police and Pioneers
   under 2nd/Lt. G.G. Farmer, will complete relief by 2.6

- 2 -

5. The Quartermaster will arrange for rations to be
delivered by the Transport personnel at the GRAVEL PIT
daily at 4 p.m.
They must be there on day of relief in time for the
rations carrying parties to follow their platoon into
the trenches during relief.

6. Dress. Marching order, less packs, which are to be
labelled, packed in sacks and labelled by platoons,
and collected by the Transport at 9 a.m. at WELLINGTON
MARTINSART Camp, and from "B" Coy. at WELLINGTON HUTS
and stored by the Quartermaster.

7. All blankets to be tightly rolled in 10s, tied in two
places, and will be collected by transport not later
than 9 a.m. on the morning of the 6th.
Officers' Kits and Mess Boxes will be stored in the
Shoemaker's Hut in rear of Church Army Hut, MARTINSART
Camp.
Transport Officer will arrange for sufficient
transport to carry 700 pairs Gum Boots (100 pair per
limbered wagon) from CRUCIFIX CORNER to Rest Position
where the Gum Boots will be fitted.
Ankle boots with puttees securely fastened in them
and labelled, packed in sacks and again labelled by
platoons, and brought back to be stored by the
Quartermaster.
2nd. Lieut. J.H.P.DARWIN will be responsible for
this and will give signature for gum boots taken from
CRUCIFIX CORNER, and will obtain signature for excess
gum boots returned.

8. Companies will report relief complete by code word.
The Confidential Box and Stationery Boxes will be
removed by Orderly Room Staff (less Sergt. Simpson
who will proceed to the trenches) to space allotted by
the 2/6th. R. Warwick.Regt. in Warwick Huts.
Transport Officer to provide limber space for the
above material, to be moved up with the rations for
the 7th.
Company Commanders will be responsible that Lewis
Guns and ammunition as detailed by the Lewis Gun Officer
move up with their men.

W.P.Churchouse
Capt. & Adjt.
2/6th.Bn.R.Warwick.Regt.

Issued at 4 p.m.
Copy No. 1 to H.Q. Coy.
     2 to H.Q. Mess.
     3 to A. Coy.
     4 to B. Coy.
     5 to C. Coy.
     6 to D. Coy.
     7 to Quartermaster.
     8 to Transport Officer.
     9 to Lewis Gun Officer.
    10 to 2nd. Lieut. G.G.Farmer.
    11   War Diary.
    12   File.

SECRET.

RED SQUARE OPERATION ORDER, No. 43.　　　　　Copy No.
Reference - Sheet 57 D, S.E.　　　　　　　　January 10th.1917.

----

1. The Battalion will be relieved tomorrow by the 2/6th.Bn.R.Warwick.Regt., and will proceed as follows, "H.Q", "A" and "C" Coys. to WARWICK HUTS, "B" Coy. to Dugouts at X.2.a.2.2., "D" Coy. to Dugouts at R.26.a.& b. Usual distances will be kept.

2. Guides will be sent by companies to the GRAVEL PIT as follows:-

    "A" Coy. - 4 guides for "D" Coy. 2/6th.R.Warwick.Regt.
    　　　　　　　　　　　　　　　　　　　　　at 4.45 p.m.
    "C" Coy. - 4 guides for "A" Coy. 2/6th.R.Warwick.Regt.
    　　　　　　　　　　　　　　　　　　　　　at 5.15 p.m.
    "D" Coy. - 3 guides for "C" Coy. 2/6th.R.Warwick.Regt.
    　　　　　　　　　　　　　　　　　　　　　at 5.45 p.m.
    "B" Coy. - 3 guides for "B" Coy. 2/6th.R.Warwick.Regt.
    　　　　　　　　　　　　　　　　　　　　　at 6.15 p.m.
    GRAVEL PIT Staff will be relieved about 1 p.m.
    "H.Q" Staff at ZOLLERN and H.Qrs., "B" and "D" Signals by daylight.

3. One N.C.O. per company will be sent out to take over new quarters tomorrow morning, 2nd. Lieut. G.G.FARMER arriving at WARWICK HUTS at 2 p.m.
Guides for "D" Coy. will be at the GRAVEL PIT at 7.30 p.m.
2/6th.R.Warwick.Regt. are sending Officers and N.C.O's to take over to front line companies tonight and to support companies to take over by daylight tomorrow. No guides required.

4. Transport Officer will take "A", "B" and "C" Coys. Cookers to ground on opposite side of road to WARWICK HUTS, also all Officers' Kits, Mess boxes, blankets and packs for "H.Q", "A" and "C" Coys. to WARWICK HUTS by 2.pp.m.
Mess, Medical Carts and 1 limber will be sent to the junction of NAB VALLEY ROAD and MOUQUET FARM-THIEPVAL ROAD by 3 p.m. If it is not possible to get so far the Transport Officer will bring a carrying party of 10 O.R. of Transport Section to ZOLLERN REDOUBT by 2.30pm. Two limbers will be at the junction of roads as above at 7 p.m., and will not move back without an order from L/Sgt.FELLOWS.

5. Cooks will be sent out ahead to prepare a hot meal. "D" Company's cooks remain at the GRAVEL PIT.

6. Trench Store Lists will be rendered to Battalion Headquarters by 12 noon tomorrow. Gum Boots will not be handed over but will be taken out with the men. Tactical Progress Reports to time of relief will reach Battalion Headquarters not later than 7 p.m.

7. The usual code word for "relief complete" will be sent.

　　　　　　　　　　　　　　　　　　　　Lieut.-Col.

Issued at 6 p.m.
Copy No. 1. to H.Q. Coy.
2. to A. Coy.
3. to B. Coy.
4. to C. Coy.
5. to D. Coy.
6. to Transport Officer.
7. to Quartermaster.
8 to 2/6th.R.Warwick.Regt.
9   War Diary.
10   File.

SECRET.

RED SQUARE OPERATION ORDER, No. 44.   Copy No. 10
Reference — Map 57 D, S.E.   January 15th. 1917.

1. The Brigade will be relieved on the 15th. and 16th. inst. by the 54th. Infantry Brigade, and will move to the RUBEMPRE — LA VICOGNE area.

2. The Battalion will be relieved by the 12th. Middlesex Regiment, and will move to RUBEMPRE by Motor Buses from AVELUY. *tomorrow*
    Companies will march to AVELUY arriving there at times as follows:—

"H.Q" Coy.	2.40 p.m.
"B" Coy.	2.50 p.m.
"A" Coy.	3.0 p.m.
"C" Coy.	3.10 p.m.
"D" Coy.	3.15 p.m.

    usual distances between platoon will be kept.

    Each man will carry his two blankets strapped on top of the pack.

    "D" Coy. will pick up blankets, packs and any ankle boots at WARWICK HUTS and will move off in sufficient time to deposit their gum boots at CRUCIFIX Corner before the buses leave.

3. Billeting party consisting of Captain C.F.L.GIBSON and one N.C.O. and one man per company, will proceed today with the Machine Gun Coy., to which unit they will be attached for tonight.

4. Four loaded limber wagons under 2nd. Lieut. J.R.B.DARWIN will proceed to RUBEMPRE today leaving MARTINSART at 12 noon. Remainder of Transport will proceed tomorrow under orders to be issued by Lieut. C.H.JERMYN.
    Officers' Kits, mess boxes and other stores (other than those at MARTINSART) will be taken to WARWICK HUTS ready for loading up by 9 a.m. tomorrow.

5. A cold meat ration will be issued for the mid-day meal tomorrow. O's C. companies will detail cooks, who will march with the cookers proceeding with the Transport, so that a hot meal will be ready for the men upon arrival at RUBEMPRE.

6. Dugouts and huts will be thoroughly cleaned ready for inspection half-an-hour before each company moves off and certificates that they are thoroughly clean will be handed to the Adjutant at AVELUY.

7. Watches will be synchronised by telephone about 12 noon.

Lieut.-Col.
Comdg.2/5th.R.Warwick.Regt.

Issued at 1.0 p.m.
Copy No. 1 to H.Q. Coy.
        2 to H.Q. Mess.
        3 to A. Coy.
        4 to B. Coy.
        5 to C. Coy.
        6 to D. Coy.
        7 to Quartermaster.
        8 to Transport Officer.
        9 to Billeting Officer.
        10   War Diary.
        11   File.

SECRET.

RED SQUARE OPERATION ORDER, No. 45. January, 16th. 1917.
Reference — LENS Sheet 1/100000. Copy No.

Appendix H

1. The Brigade marches to the CANDAS area tomorrow, and the Battalion will be billetted for the night in FIENVILLERS.

    Route:— Fne de ROSEL — Cross roads just S. of last "E" in ANCn. Min de VALHEUREUX — CANDAS.

2. Companies will march in the following order, the head of the Column passing the Starting Point (cross roads 200 yards E. of "N" in VAL de MAISON) at 12.37 p.m:—

    "H.Q" Company.
    "A" Company.
    "B" Company.
    "C" Company.
    "D" Company.
    Transport.

and the normal halts will be observed.

3. Billeting Parties will meet the Staff Captain at CANDAS CHURCH tomorrow at 11.0 a.m.

4. Transport Officer will arrange to collect Officers' Mess Boxes, Officers' Kits and blankets from Company Headquarters.
    Blankets will be tightly rolled in bundles of ten. All Stores will be ready for collection by 11.0 a.m. Baggage wagons will accompany the unit.

5. Billets will be ready for inspection by 12.0 noon and the usual certificates that they are thoroughly clean will be handed to the Adjutant at the Starting Point.

6. Watches will be synchronised by Despatch Rider sent to companies about 9 a.m.

Churchouse
bur Major, Captain
Comdg. 2/5th. Bn. R. Warwick. Regt.

Issued at 6 p.m.
Copy No. 1. to H.Q. Coy.
    2. to H.Q. Mess.
    3. to A. Coy.
    4. to B. Coy.
    5. to C. Coy.
    6. to D. Coy.
    7. to Quartermaster.
    8. to Transport Officer.
    9. to Billeting Officer.
    10.   War Diary.
    11.   File.

SECRET.

RED SQUARE OPERATION ORDER, No. 46.
Reference — LENS Sheet, 1/100000.

Appendix 5

Copy No. 10
January, 17th. 1917.

1. The Brigade marches to the CRAMONT area tomorrow. The Battalion will be billetted for the night in COULONVILLERS.
   Route:— BERNAVILLE — BEAUMETZ.

2. Companies will march in the following order, the head of the Column passing the starting point (cross-roads ¼ mile North of second "l" in FIENVILLERS) at 8.15 a.m:—

    "A" Company.
    "B" Company.
    "C" Company.
    "D" Company.
    "H.Q". Compy.
    Transport.

    Distances of 200 yards between companies and Transport, and 500 yards between Battalions will be maintained. Cookers will march with their companies.

3. The Billeting Party will meet the Staff Captain at CRAMONT CHURCH at 10 a.m.
    Captain C.F.L.GIBSON will detail one of the Billeting Party to meet the Supply Wagons and guide them to the Quartermaster's Stores. Time for guide to meet wagons will be notified by Staff Captain.

4. Transport Officer will arrange to collect Officers' Kits and blankets from Company Headquarters at 7.0 a.m. Blankets to be tightly rolled in bundles of ten.
    Officers' Mess Boxes will be collected at 7.30 a.m. Baggage wagons will accompany the Unit.

5. Billets will be ready for inspection by 7.45 a.m., and the usual certificates that they are thoroughly clean will be handed to the Adjutant at the starting point.

6. Watches will be synchronised by Despatch Rider sent to companies about 7 a.m.

for Major, Capt adjt
Comdg.2/5th.Bn.R.Warwick.R.

Issued at 6.30 p.m.
Copy No. 1. to H.Q. Coy.
        2. to H.Q. Mess.
        3. to A. Coy.
        4. to B. Coy.
        5. to C. Coy.
        6. to D. Coy.
        7. to Quartermaster.
        8. to Transport Officer.
        9. to Billeting Officer.
       10.   War Diary.
       11.   File.

SECRET.

RED SQUARE OPERATION ORDER, NO. 47. Copy No. 11
Reference – Abbeville 14, 1/100000 January 18th 1917

1. The Brigade marches to the CANCHY area tomorrow. The Battalion will proceed to billets at LAMOTTE BULEUX. Route:- ST.RIQUIER – NEUILLY L'Hopital.

2. Companies will march in the following order:- "B", "C", "D", H.Qrs. "A" and Transport, the head of the column passing the Starting Point (road junction 1/6 mile west of COULONVILLERS CHURCH) at 8.40 a.m. Distances of 200 yards between companies and Transport and 500 yards between battalions will be maintained. Coomrs will march with their companies.

3. The Billeting party will meet the Staff Captain at CANCHY CHURCH at 10.0 a.m. Capt. C.W.L.GIBSON will detail one of the billeting party to meet the supply wagons and guide them to the Quartermaster's stores. Time for guide to meet wagons will be notified by Staff Captain.

4. Officers' kits will be brought to the wagon park (in the GRAND PLACE) ready for loading at 7.45 a.m. The Transport Officer will arrange to collect blankets from Company headquarters at 7.30 a.m. Blankets to be tightly rolled in bundles of ten. Officers' mess boxes will be collected at 8.0 a.m. Baggage wagons will accompany the unit.

5. Billets will be ready for inspection at 8.15 a.m. and the usual certificates that they are thoroughly clean will be handed to the Adjutant at the Starting Point.

6. Watches will be synchronised by Despatch Rider sent to Companies at 7.30 a.m.

W.P. Churchouse
Capt. & Adjt.

Issued at 5.0 p.m.
Copy No. 1 to H.Q.Coy.
        2 to H.Q.Mess
        3 to A. Coy.
        4 to B. Coy.
        5 to C. Coy.
        6 to D. Coy.
        7 to Quartermaster
        8 to Transport Officer
        9 to Billeting Officer
       10   War Diary
       11   File

Confidential

War Diary
of
2/5th Bn. Royal Warwickshire Regt.

From 1/5/17 to 28/7/17

WAR DIARY
or
INTELLIGENCE SUMMARY. JMC

(Erase heading not required.)

Army Form C. 2118.

Instructions regarding War Diaries and Intelligence Summaries are contained in F. S. Regs., Part II. and the Staff Manual respectively. Title pages will be prepared in manuscript.

Place	Date	Hour	Summary of Events and Information	Remarks and references to Appendices
LAHOUSSOYE-BUSSY	1/7/17	—	Company Training.	JMC
"	2/7/17	—	" "	JMC
"	3/7/17	—	Battalion Training. Attack Practice.	JMC
"	4/7/17	12 noon	Church parade	JMC
"	5/7/17	—	16th INF BDE marched to billets in BELLANCOURT area. The Battn. proceeded to VAUCHELLES-LES-QUESNOY arriving 12.30 p.m.	JMC appendix 1
VAUCHELLES-LES-QUESNOY	6/7/17	—	Company Training	JMC
"	7/7/17	—	" "	JMC
"	8/7/17	—	" "	JMC
"	9/7/17	—	" "	JMC
"	10/7/17	—	" "	JMC
"	11/7/17	12 noon	Church Parade.	JMC
"	12/7/17	9.30 a.m.	Battn. in attack practice. 2.30 p.m. Battalion muster parade.	JMC
"	13/7/17	9.30 a.m.	Battn. muster parade. Transport proceeded via BELLANCOURT- AILLY-FLIXECOURT- to ST SAVEUR.	JMC appendix 2
"	14/7/17	10 a.m.	Battn muster parade. Transport proceeded via ARGOEUVES to AVRIGNY.	JMC ditto.
"	15/7/17	—	Transport proceeded via VILLERS-BRETONNEUX to "C" Staging area. Battn marched to PONT REMY & entrained at 10.15 a.m. for "C" Staging area, detraining at MARCELCAVE at 1.30 p.m.	JMC ditto. appendix 3

WAR DIARY
or
INTELLIGENCE SUMMARY.

Army Form C. 2118.

Place	Date	Hour	Summary of Events and Information	Remarks and references to Appendices
MARCELCAVE	16/2/17	10 a.m.	Bath. Muster Parade. Company Training.	IPC
"	17/2/17	10 a.m.	" " " "	IPC
"	18/2/17	—	Company Training	IPC
"	19/2/17	8.35 a.m.	18-11/6 Bn. marched to HARBONNIÈRES area to train preceding to billets at VAUVILLERS arriving 11.30 a.m.	IPC appendix 4
VAUVILLERS	20/2/17	—	Company Training	IPC
"	21/2/17	—	" "	IPC
"	22/2/17	—	" "	IPC
"	23/2/17	—	" "	IPC
"	24/2/17	—	" "	IPC
"	25/2/17	—	Bath. relieved 2/8 Worcesters R. in KRATZ section in Relief complete at 2.30 a.m. 26/2/17 (AMBERG subsection)	IPC appendix 5
ERMENONVILLERS	26/2/17	—	Batt. holding KRATZ sector in (AMBERG subsection)	IPC
"	27/2/17	—	" " " "	IPC
"	28/2/17	—	" " " "	IPC

M Coates
Lieut. Col.
Cmdg 1/1st R. War. R.
28/2/17

Appendix

SECRET.

RED SQUARE OPERATION ORDER, NO.48   Copy No. 10
Reference - Sheet ABBEVILLE 14, 1/100000   February 4th 1917.

1. The Brigade marches to the BELLANCOURT Area tomorrow. The Battalion will proceed to billets at VAUCHELLES-LES-QUESNOY. Route:- Cross roads at U in NEUILLY-L'HOPITAL - LE PLESSIEL - ABBEVILLE.

2. Companies will march in the following order:- H. Qrs. "A", "B", "C" and "D" Companies and Transport. The head of the column will pass the Starting Point (cross roads on the NEUILLY road 700 yards S. of the M in LAMOTTE-BULEUX) at 8.53 a.m. Field Kitchens and Lewis Gun handcarts will march with their companies. Baggage wagons will proceed with the Transport. Distances of 200 yards between companies and 500 yards between Battalions will be maintained.

3. The Billeting party (1 N.C.O. per company) will meet Sec.Lieut. W.CLEGG at the church VAUCHELLES-LES-QUESNOY at 9.30 a.m. Sec.Lieut. Clegg will detail one of this party to meet the supply wagons outside the billeting area and guide to the Quartermaster's Stores.

4. Officers' kits, blankets tightly rolled in bundles of ten and labelled, and palliasses with straw, will be brought to the Quartermaster's Stores ready for collection by 7.30 a.m. Mess boxes will be ready for collection at 8.15 a.m. Lewis Guns will be loaded at the Transport by 7.30 a.m.

5. Billets will be ready for inspection at 8.0 a.m. The usual certificates that they are thoroughly clean will be handed to the Adjutant at the Starting Point.

6. Watches will be synchronised by Despatch Rider sent to Companies about 7.30 a.m.

7. The usual Falling-Out states and other returns will be rendered to the Orderly Room immediately upon arrival.

                         Churchouse
                         Capt. & Adjt.

Issued at 11.0 a.m.
Copy No. 1 to H.Q. Coy.
         2 to H.Q. Mess
         3 to A. Coy.
         4 to B. Coy.
         5 to C. Coy.
         6 to D. Coy.
         7 to Quartermaster
         8 to Transport Officer
         9 to Billeting Officer
        10   War Diary
        11   File

SECRET.

RED SQUARE OPERATION ORDER, NO. 49.   Copy No.
Reference – Maps 1/100000 LENS, AMIENS, ABBEVILLE.   12th Feb. 1917.

1. The 182nd Infantry Brigade Group Transport will move to the C. STAGIN area on 13th, 14th & 15th February.
   Route:– BELLANCOURT – AILLY – FLIXECOURT – ST.SAVEUR – AUBIGNY – VILLERS – BRETONNEUX.

2. The daily Starting Points, Times and Destinations for the Transport section are as follows:–

   Feb.13th. Cross roads ¼ mile S.W. of the B in BELLANCOURT at 8.35 a.m. to ST.SAVEUR.
   Feb.14th. Cross roads in ARGOEUVES at 10.0 a.m. to AUBIGNY.

   Feb.15th. Details to be issued later.

   Distances of 200 yards will be maintained between the Transports of units.

3. All kit, equipment, stores and necessaries with the exception of the following will be carried by the Transport on the march:–
   2 Blankets per man
   Camp kettles for cooking
   1 Valise per Officer (35 lbs.)
   Officers' mess boxes

4. No.6304, Cpl. J.BINNES, "D" Coy. is detailed to billet the Transport section while on the march, and will report to an Officer of the 2/6th R. War.Regt. at the main main entrance to FLIXECOURT STATION at 10.0 a.m. on the 13th inst. mounted on a bicycle.

5. Three days rations and fuel for men and horses will be taken. On the 13th inst. the column will halt between 12.30 p.m. and 1.15 p.m. to water and feed.

6. Transport billets and stables will be thoroughly cleaned before moving off and a certificate to that effect rendered to the Adjutant.

                                        Capt. & Adjt.

Issued at 6.0 p.m.
Copy No. 1 to TRANSPORT OFFICER,
        2   WAR DIARY,
        3   FILE.
        4 to QUARTERMASTER,
        5 to A. Coy.
        6 to B. Coy.
        7 to C. Coy.
        8 to D. Coy.
        9 to H.Q. Coy.

SECRET.

Appendix

RED SQUARE OPERATION ORDER, NO.50   Copy No. 8
Reference — Maps 1/100000 ABBEVILLE   Feb. 14th 1917.
                       AMIENS.

---

1. The 182nd Brigade Group personnel will proceed by train from PONT REMY Station at 10.15 a.m. tomorrow to the "C. STAGING" area, detraining at MARCELCAVE.

2. The battalion will march to PONT REMY Station with companies in the following order, H.Qrs. A. B. C and D Coys. the head of the column passing the Starting Point (road junction ½ mile S.S.W. of V. in VAUCHELLES-D-s-QUESNOY) at 7.30 a.m. Lewis Gun handcarts will march independently under LIEUT. THIRLWELL, arriving at PONT REMY Station at 8.30 a.m. Haversack rations will be carried. Food for hot meal, to be prepared immediately upon arrival in new area, will be carried by companies in camp kettles.

3. Officers' kits, Officers' mess boxes, blankets and paillasses tightly rolled and properly labelled, camp kettles and Orderly Room boxes will be ready for collection by 6.45 a.m. A. C and D Coys. will dump these stores at D. Coy's Headquarters. The Quartermaster will arrange to collect the above from Headquarter Mess "B" Coy. and "D" Coy's headquarters. Paillasse straw will be dumped at one billet in each company area and billetor informed thereof. Motor lorries will arrive at the station by 8.30 a.m. The Quartermaster will be responsible for loading of baggage and rations for the 16th inst. on to the train. Fuel will be drawn at MARCELCAVE Station.

4. SERGT. BLAYREY will detail one Policeman to report to the Brigade Major at PONT REMY Station at 8.45 a.m.

5. Billets will be ready for inspection at 7.0 a.m. Certificates that they have been thoroughly cleaned will be handed to the Adjutant at the Starting Point.

6. Marching Out states will be rendered to the Orderly Room by 7.0 p.m. today, any alteration after that hour being handed to the Adjutant at the Starting Point.

7. Falling Out states and other returns will be rendered to the Orderly Room immediately upon arrival.

                                        W Churchouse
                                        Capt. & Adjt.

Issued at 5.30 p.m.

Copy No. 1 to H.Q. Coy.
         2 to H.Q. Mess
         3 to A. Coy.
         4 to B. Coy.
         5 to C. Coy.
         6 to D. Coy.
         7 to Quartermaster.
         8   War Diary
         9   File

SECRET.

RED SQUARE OPERATION ORDER, NO.51.　　　　　　Copy No. 9
Reference - Sheet AMIENS 17, 1/100000　　　　　February 18th 1917.

1. The Brigade marches to the HARBONNIERES area tomorrow.
   The Battalion will proceed to billets at VAUVILLERS.
   Route:- WIENCOURT - GUILLAUCOURT - HARBONNIERES.

2. Companies will march in the following order:- B, C, D, A
   Coys. and Transport (H.Qr. Coy. marching with B. Coy.).
   The head of the column will pass the Starting Point (cross
   roads 200 yards N.N.E. of MARCELCAVE CHURCH) at 8.25 a.m.
   Field Kitchens and Lewis Gun handcarts will march with
   companies. Distances of 200 yards between companies
   and Transport and 500 yards between battalions will be
   maintained.

3. Officers' kits, blankets and paillasses tightly rolled in
   bundles and labelled will be ready for collection at A.
   Coy's. billet at 7.30 a.m. The Transport Officer will
   arrange to collect Officers' mess boxes at 8.0 a.m.

4. Billets will be ready for inspection at 8.0 a.m. Each
   Company will detail one Officer to meet MAJOR FOSTER at
   their billets and accompany him on the inspection. The
   usual certificates that billets have been thoroughly cleaned
   will be handed to the Adjutant at the Starting Point.

5. Watches will be synchronised by Despatch Rider sent to
   Companies about 7.30 a.m.

6 The usual Falling out states and other returns will be
   rendered to the Orderly Room immediately upon arrival.

　　　　　　　　　　　　　　　　　　　　　　Capt. & Adjt.

Issued at 2.0 p.m.

Copy No. 1 to H.Q. Coy.
         2 to H.Q. Mess
         3 to A. Coy.
         4 to B. Coy.
         5 to C. Coy.
         6 to D. Coy.
         7 to Quartermaster.
         8 to Transport Officer.
         9   War Diary
        10   File

SECRET.

RED SQUARE OPERATION ORDER, NO.52.　　　　　Copy No. 14
Reference - ROSIERES Map 1/40000　　　　　　February 24th 1917.

1. The Brigade relieves the 183rd Brigade in the KRATZ SECTION tomorrow, the Battalion relieving the 2/8th Worcesters in the AMBERG Sub-section.   Route:- X.20.b.5.6 and LIHONS.   Movement will be by platoons at 200 yards interval.   During daylight vehicles will move at 200 yards distance and after dark in columns of not more than four.

2. <u>Dispositions</u>.
   　　　　In Front Line - Right, A. Coy. Left, C. Coy.
   　　　　GUILLAME TRENCH　　　　D. Coy.
   　　　　East of LIHONS　　　　　　B. Coy.
   Guides will meet Companies at the entrance to BOYAU CAIN (S.26.c.2.8.) as follows:-
   　　6.0 p.m. Two guides per platoon for C. Coy. from
   　　　　　　　B. Coy. 2/8th Worcesters.
   　　6.30 p.m. Two guides per platoon for A. Coy. from
   　　　　　　　A. Coy. 2/8th Worcesters.   Two guides for
   　　　　　　　Headquarters.
   　　7.0 p.m. Two guides per platoon for D. Coy. from
   　　　　　　　C. Coy. 2/8th Worcesters.
   　　　　　　　No guides will be provided for B. Coy.

3. Company cookers will proceed with companies not further than LIHONS, returning to VAUVILLERS after companies have had a hot meal.   B. Coy's cooker will wait to take back any surplus gum boots.   The unconsumed portion of the day's rations will be carried on the man.   B. Coy. will take with them on their cooker, and will carry into the trenches, *all* dixies and stores and the following day's rations.

4. The Transport Officer will detail 18 Pack Mules to proceed to HERLEVILLE Church first thing tomorrow morning where they will remain with their drivers.   Rations and stores for Headquarters and for all companies except B. Coy. will be sent by transport via X.20.b.5.5. - X.21.d.8.1 X.6.c.4.2. to VERMANDOVILLERS where they will be loaded upon the pack mules at point 85.   Guides for these pack mules will meet them at S.22.a.1.9. at 7.30 ~~each evening~~ p.m. Rations for B. Coy. will proceed via X.20.b.5.5. and LIHONS the rations being carried by hand from S.26.c.2.8. (entrance to BOYAU CAIN).   The Water Carts will proceed to and remain at S.26.a.0.0.   B. Coy. will provide all water carrying parties.

5. The Transport Officer will collect from No.7 Billet, Rue Harbonnieres, FRAMERVILLE, first thing tomorrow morning, sufficient new dry gum boots for the trench strength of the battalion, these being dumped at the west entrance to LIHONS.   SERGT. BLAYNEY will be in charge of the dump. He will remain there and load any surplus gum boots upon B. Coy's cooker.

- 2 -

6. Packs, blankets, surplus stores and Officers' kits will be taken to the Quartermaster's Stores by 10.0 a.m. tomorrow. Service Dress caps will be placed in the packs.

7. Duplicate Trench Store receipts and Disposition sketches will be sent to Battalion Headquarters by 12 noon, 26th inst. A. & C. Companies will take over two stretchers each and A. C. & D. Companies will take over 20 filled Lewis Gun drums per gun from the 2/8th Worcesters. Corresponding articles will be left in the Quartermaster's Stores to be handed over to the 2/8th Worcesters on production of the companies' official receipts.

8. Companies will report "Relief complete" by the usual code word.

9. Twenty-two runners went into the line last night and the following personnel today:- 1 Officer per Company, 1 N.C.O. per platoon, 6 signallers and 3 men of each front line Lewis Gun teams with guns.

            Capt. & Adjt.
           2/5th R. Warwick. Regt.

Issued at 8.0 p.m.
Copies to:-
  No. 1. A. Coy.
    2 B. Coy.
    3 C. Coy.
    4 D. Coy.
    5 Signalling Officer
    6 Transport Officer
    7 Quartermaster
    8 C.O.
    9 Second-in-Command
   10 Adjutant
   11 2/8th Worcesters
   12 182nd Infantry Brigade
   13 Medical Officer
   14 War Diary
   15 File

Vol XI 182/61

Confidential

War Diary

of

2/5th Bn. Royal Warwickshire Regt.

From March 1st 1917 to March 31st 1917.

WAR DIARY
or
INTELLIGENCE-SUMMARY. JMG

Army Form C. 2118.

Place	Date	Hour	Summary of Events and Information	Remarks and references to Appendices
VERMANDOVILLERS	1/3/17	—	Batt. holding the AMBERG subsection of the KRATZ section.	JMG
"	2/3/17	—	"	JMG
"	3/3/17	—	Batt. relieved in the AMBERG subsection by 2/6th WARWICKS & moved into Brigade Support at VERMANDOVILLERS and CARRÉE PARSON. Relief complete at 10.15 pm.	JMG appendix 1
"	4/3/17	—	Battn. in Brigade Support. Working Parties.	JMG
"	5/3/17	—	"	JMG
"	6/3/17	—	"	JMG
"	7/3/17	—	"	JMG
"	8/3/17	—	Battn. relieved by 1/4th GLOUCESTER R. & proceeded into reserve at HARGONNIERES. Relief complete at 7.30 pm.	JMG appendix 2
HARGONNIERES	9/3/17	—	Company Training. Cleaning up.	JMG
"	10/3/17	—	"	JMG
"	11/3/17	—	"	JMG
"	12/3/17	—	"	JMG
"	13/3/17	—	"	JMG
"	14/3/17	—	"	JMG
"	15/3/17	1.15 pm	Battn. relieved 1/5th GLOUCESTERS at RAINECOURT. Relief completed at 3 pm. Battn. in Brigade Reserve.	JMG appendix 3
RAINECOURT	16/3/17	—	Company Training	JMG

Army Form C. 2118.

WAR DIARY
or
INTELLIGENCE SUMMARY.

(Erase heading not required.)

Place	Date	Hour	Summary of Events and Information	Remarks and references to Appendices
RAINECOURT	17/3/17	—	Company Training. Battn moved up to DEMUICOURT. Area & walked billets at the CASINO (M12.a.93) by RESERVES Stationary	M.C.
DEMUICOURT	18/3/17	—	Battn moved into trenches at ASSAINYCOURT. Battn in Brigade Reserve.	M.C.
ASSAINYCOURT	19/3/17	—	Battn moved into billets at MATCRIÉLEPOT, arriving 7.15pm. Battn in Brigade Reserve.	M.C.
MARCRELET	2/3/17	—	Battn in Brigade Reserve. Road mending.	M.C.
" "	21/3/17	—	"	M.C.
" "	22/3/17	—	"	M.C.
" "	23/3/17	5.30am	Battn marched to billets at EPENANCOURT, arriving 10.15am. Battn commenced to dig outpost line.	M.C. appendix 4
EPENANCOURT	24/3/17	—	Battn in Brigade Reserve. Digging series of strong points H.g. EPENANCOURT.	M.C.
" "	25/3/17	—	Battn retaining EPENANCOURT — FALVY ROAD. A Coy marched to POEUILLY + came under orders of 9.O.C. UMBALLA CAVALRY BRIGADE	M.C.
" "	26/3/17	—	Battn in Brigade Reserve. Battn retaining EPENANCOURT—FALVY ROAD. A Coy detached with UMBALLA CAVALRY BDE.	M.C.
" "	27/3/17	—	Battn moved to MONTECOURT arriving 10.30 p.m.	M.C. appendix 5
" "	28/3/17	—	Battn moved to POEUILLY at 7.30 pm + entrenched E of POEUILLY	M.C. appendix 6
MONTECOURT	29/3/17	—	Battn holding left subsection. A Coy withdrawn + moved to billets at MEERAUCOURT.	M.C.
POEUILLY	30/3/17	—	"	M.C.
" "	31/3/17	—	Battn returned to billets at MONTECOURT, arriving 4 p.m.	M.C.

W. Crallikind. Col.
3/3/17
Comdg 2/5th Bn. R. Warwick. Regt.

SECRET

RED SQUARE OPERATION ORDER NO.59   Copy No. 9
Reference - ROSIERES Map 1/40000   March 2nd 1917.

1. The Battalion will be relieved in the AMBERG Subsection by the 2/6th R. War. Regt. on the night of 3rd/4th inst. A. & C. Coys. will proceed to dug-outs at the QUARRIES (X.24.a.0.4), H.Q. B. & D. Companies to dug-outs at VERMANDOVILLERS (Lieut. FARMER arranging for guides to meet them at Cross Roads S.9.d.2½.4). Usual distances will be observed. The Battalion will be in Brigade support and be ready to turn out at 10 minutes notice.

2. D. Coy. will be relieved by A. Coy. 2/6th Warwicks - 3 guides at S.21.b.9½.8 (junction of tape and road) at 7.0 p.m. B. Coy. will be relieved by B. Coy. 2/6th Warwicks - 3 guides at same place as for D. Coy. at 8.0 p.m. C. Coy. will be relieved by C. Coy. 2/6th Warwicks, who will probably arrive about 7.30 p.m. - no guides required. A. Coy. will be relieved by D. Coy. 2/6th Warwicks, who will probably arrive about 6.30 p.m. - No guides required. One guide for Battn. Headquarters at same place as for B. Coy. at 8.0 p.m. They will move behind B. Coy. 2/6th Warwicks. The companies of 2/6th Warwicks are 3 platoons strong only.

3. The 2/6th Warwicks will send into the line tonight, one Officer per company, one N.C.O. per platoon and three O.R. for special patrol duty for each front line company, and one Officer & one N.C.O. per company for rear companies, runners, one signaller per company & Battn. Headquarters. The following advance parties from this unit will be sent out of the line tomorrow to take over:-
    1 N.C.O. each from A. & C. Coys. to the QUARRIES by daylight.
    1 N.C.O. each from B. & D. Coys. to VERMANDOVILLERS at dawn.
    Lieut. FARMER and 2 signallers to VERMANDOVILLERS by daylight.

4. Twenty filled drums per Lewis Gun will be handed over to the 2/6th Warwicks. These are to be thoroughly cleaned beforehand. The same number being taken over on arrival at new quarters. Any surplus will be taken out to the Q.M. Stores, notification of the number being returned being sent to the Orderly Room.
Two stretchers per front line company will be handed over and same number taken over on arrival at new quarters. Bomb buckets & 5 bombs per man of bombing sections will be taken out and will remain with companies while in support. All gum boots will be taken out. The Transport Officer will arrange to withdraw the pack mules from HERLEVILLE to VAUVILLERS on arrival of the animals from 2/6th Warwicks and to hand the 16 pack saddles over to them obtaining receipt.

5. O.C. "A" Coy. will collect 97 petrol tins and deliver to water duty men at LIHONS tomorrow morning. These will be filled, 30 being taken to the QUARRIES with one water cart and 45 to VERMANDOVILLERS with the other. The horses for the water cart at the QUARRIES will remain

water being drawn from LIHONS daily. The other water cart will proceed daily from VAUVILLERS to VERMANDOVILLERS with filled petrol tins which will be carried by the transport to companies. Cooking water only is to be obtained at VERMANDOVILLERS.

6. The Q.M. will arrange for Sunday's rations to be delivered at new quarters tomorrow. The transport will carry rations daily from the limbers at the cross roads (S.9.d.2½.4) to companies.

7. L/Sgt. BIRD will arrange to take a limber of canteen stores to the new billets daily (unless wet) for sale between the hours of 2.0 p.m. and 4.0 p.m. On Sunday, Tuesday and Thursday it will go to the Quarries and on Monday and Wednesday to the cross roads VERMANDOVILLERS.

8. Trench Store lists to be sent in to the Orderly Room by 12.0 noon tomorrow.

9. Reliefs complete to be notified by the usual code word.

Capt. & Adjt.
2/5th R. Warwick. Regt.

Copy No. 1 to A. Coy.
      2 to B. Coy.
      3 to C. Coy.
      4 to D. Coy.
      5 to H.Q.
      6 to T.O. & Q.M.
      7 to 2/6th Warwicks
      8 to Adjutant
      9   War Diary
    10   File

SECRET

RED SQUARE OPERATION ORDER NO.60　　　　Copy No. 9
Reference – ROSIERES Map 1/400000　　　　March 7th 1917.

1. The Brigade will be relieved by the 183rd Brigade tomorrow, the battalion being relieved by the 2/6th Gloucesters and moving to HARBONNIERES occupying the quarters vacated by the 2/7th Worcesters.

2. Companies will be relieved by opposite numbers of the 2/6th Gloucesters, and will move independently to new quarters on relief. Route:- A. & C. Companies via X.17.c.4.8 and X.21.d.8.1. Headquarters, B. and D. Companies via Point 90 and X.21.d.8.1. Distances of 200 yards will be observed between platoons (B. & D. Companies will also observe 100 yards between sections until passing point 90).

3. No guides will be provided by 2/5th R.War.R. but 2/6th Gloucesters will send in one Officer per Company and one N.C.O. per platoon for B. & D. Companies and make their own arrangements for guides and take over billets and stores. A. & C. Companies 2/6th Glosters will take over on arrival.

4. A. & C. Companies will have dinner and B. & D. Companies tea before moving off. Cookers will then be sent on and have a hot meal ready for the men on arrival at HARBONNIERES.

5. The Transport Officer will provide horses and transport to remove Water carts, Officers' valises, mess boxes, Lewis Guns, bomb buckets and bombs and company dixies, at 1.0 p.m. at the GRAVEL PITS and 6.0 p.m. at D. Company's Headquarters. All material for transport from B. & D. Companies and Headquarters will be dumped at D. Company's headquarters and left in charge of Sergt. Blayney, between the hours of 4.30 p.m. and 6.0 p.m.

6. Filled magazines for Lewis Guns to the number of 20 magazines per gun will be handed over to the 2/6th Glosters, a receipt being obtained. The Q.M. will draw an equivalent number from the Quartermaster's Stores, 2/6th Gloucesters, FRAMERVILLE, on the 9th inst. delivering them to companies, who will at once unload, clean and reload magazines. All petrol tins taken over in present billets are to be left, receipts being obtained, the remainder being taken to the watercarts for return to the Quartermaster's Stores.

7. Trench Store lists will be handed in to the Orderly Room not later than 3.0 p.m. tomorrow.

8. The usual billeting parties have been sent on and the Quartermaster instructed to forward Company blankets and packs to new billets at HARBONNIERES.

- 2 -

9. Companies will report relief complete by the usual code word.

[signature]
Capt. & Adjt.
2/5th R. Warwick. Regt.

Issued at 5.0 p.m.

Copy No. 1 to A. Coy.
        2 to B. Coy.
        3 to C. Coy.
        4 to D. Coy.
        5 to Headquarters
        6 to Transport Officer
        7 to Quartermaster.
        8 to 2/6th Gloucesters
        9   War Diary
      10   File

SECRET.

RED SQUARE OPERATION ORDER, NO.61   Copy No. 10
Reference - ROSIERES Map 1/40000   March 14th 1915.

1. The 182nd Infantry Brigade will take over the ABLAINCOURT SECTION from the 184th Infantry Brigade on the night of the 15th/16th inst. the 2/5th R. War. Regt. relieving the 2/5th Gloucesters in Brigade Reserve at RAINECOURT. The billets now occupied by this unit will be taken over by the 4th Royal Berks. The Transport lines & Q.M.Stores of 2/5th Glosters in RAINECOURT will be taken over by this unit.

2. On marching from HARBONNIERES the battalion will come under the orders of the G.O.C. 184th Brigade until the G.O.C. 182nd Brigade takes over the line. The battalion will march in the following order:- H.Q. A, B, C & D Coys, the head of the column passing the Starting Point (HARBONNIERES CHURCH) at 1.15 p.m. Lewis Gun handcarts and cookers will march with their companies. Distances of 200 yards between companies will be observed. Route:- HARBONNIERES - VAUVILLERS Road to X.15.d.2.9 - VAUVILLERS - FRAMERVILLE. The Transport will move independently under the Transport Officer.

3. Officers' kits and blankets rolled in bundles of 10, will be ready in one place in each Company billets by 8.30 a.m. Officers' mess boxes will be ready for collection at 1.30 p.m.

4. The usual billeting parties will report to LIEUT. BLANCHARD at Battalion Headquarters at 9.0 a.m.

5. Area stores will be handed over to relieving units. Trench Store lists and Disposition sketches to be in the Orderly Room by 7.30 p.m. tomorrow.

6. Water carts will be kept filled at RAINECOURT ready to move up in case of emergency.

7. Billets to be ready for inspection not later than 10.30 a.m. One Officer from each company will report to Orderly Room when billets are ready for inspection and accompany the inspecting Officer round billets.

8. Watches will be synchronised by Despatch Rider sent to companies about 10.0 a.m.

9. The usual Falling Out states and other returns will be rendered to the Orderly Room immediately upon arrival.

10. Relief complete will be notified by the usual code word.

                                    Capt. & Adjt.
                                    2/5th R. Warwick. Regt.

Issued at 6.0 p.m.

Copy No. 1 to H.Q.   Copy No. 6 to D. Coy.
        2 to H.Q.Mess   7 to Quartermaster
        3 to A. Coy.   8 to Transport Officer
        4 to B. Coy.   9 to Billeting Officer
        5 to C. Coy.   10.   War Diary
                                       11.   File

SECRET.

RED SQUARE OPERATION ORDER, NO.62.

Appendix 4

Copy No. 10
March 22nd 1917.

1. The Battalion moves to EPENANCOURT tomorrow.

2. Headquarters will march at 8.30 a.m. followed by companies in the following order:- B, D, A & C Companies all at 200 yards distance. Cookers and Lewis Gun handcarts will proceed with companies. One pack mule will proceed with each company for the purpose of carrying surplus stores and the other four will be allotted to Battalion Headquarters.

3. The Quartermaster's Stores and Transport will move to MARCHELEPOT tomorrow.

4. Cpl. WHEELER will send a limber to each company headquarters for Officers' mess boxes which are to be ready by 8.0 a.m. He will also arrange for all Lewis guns etc. not loaded on handcarts and all tools, ammunition and bombs to proceed with the rear company. Tools and Lewis Guns must proceed with the column, a second journey being made for any ammunition and bombs left behind.

Capt. & Adjt.
2/5th R. Warwick. Regt.

Issued at 10.0 p.m.

Copy No. 1 to H.Q.
2 to A. Coy.
3 to B. Coy.
4 to C. Coy.
5 to D. Coy.
6 to Quartermaster
7 to Transport Officer
8 to Billeting Officer
9 to Cpl. Wheeler.
10   War Diary
11   File

SECRET.

RED SQUARE OPERATION ORDER, NO.63   Copy No. 9
Reference - Sheet 66D. 1/40000   March 27th 1917.
            Sheet 62C. 1/40000

Appendix 5

1. The Battalion (less A Coy) will march to MONTECOURT today and billet for the night there. Route:- FALVY (cross roads C.5.a.5.0) ENNEMAIN - FOURQUES - DEVISE.

2. Headquarters will pass the Starting Point (EPENANCOURT BRIDGE) at 7.30 p.m. followed by D, B & C Companies and Transport, all at 100 yards distance. D. Company will provide an advance guard of one platoon. Field Kitchens, Lewis Gun handcarts and pack mules will proceed with companies. Dress - Marching order steel helmets being worn.

3. Mess boxes and Officers' valises will be taken to the Quartermaster's stores by 6.45 p.m. and loaded straight on to the Mess Cart and baggage wagon respectively. Rations for tomorrow will be carried on the Field Kitchens. Ammunition, wiring material, Very Lights and sandbags will be taken with the battalion tonight. Forty empty petrol tins to be carried on each water cart.

4. Troops must conceal themselves as much as possible tomorrow. Movement is to be reduced to a minimum.

5. All billets are to be thoroughly cleaned and a certificate to that effect handed to the Adjutant at the Starting point.

6. Watches will be synchronised by Despatch Rider sent to Companies about 6.0 p.m.

7. Disposition sketch maps and falling out returns to be sent to the Orderly Room immediately upon arrival.

                                          Capt. & Adjt.

Issued at 5.45 p.m.

Copy No. 1 to H.Q.
        2 to A. Coy.
        3 to B. Coy.
        4 to C. Coy.
        5 to D. Coy.
        6 to Quartermaster,
        7 to Transport Officer,
        8 to Officer i/c Advance Guard,
        9   War Diary
       10   File

SECRET.

RED SQUARE OPERATION ORDER, NO.84   Copy No. 11
Reference - Sheet 62.C. S.E. 1/20000   March 28th 1917.

appendix 6

1. The enemy in our immediate front has established posts on the line SOYECOURT – VERMAND, with machine guns commanding the valley running through Q.24. and Q.29.

2. The battalion will move forward tonight to the line Q.29.c.1.4½ exclusive to Q.23 central. The 2/7th Warwicks will be on the right and the 59th Division on the left. Upon this line, a line of resistance will be dug with a support line behind it, connected by Communication Trenches, if possible, the work (including wiring) to be completed before dawn on the 29th inst.

3. Dispositions.
   RIGHT – C. Coy. with a front line trench joining up two existing Lewis Gun posts behind the hedge at Q.29.a.4½.2 and Q.29.a.6½.4. A Lewis Gun post also exists at Q.29.a.2½.1. and it is proposed to put another Lewis Gun post at Q.29.c.2.7½. These two posts may be occupied or not at the discretion of the Company Commander.
   CENTRE. B. Coy. with a front line trench about Q.23.c.9.2. the existing German communication trench about 100 yards behind this being converted into a support trench.
   LEFT – D. Coy. with a front line trench about Q.23 central, and a support trench (dug by A. Coy.) about 100 yards behind.
   SUPPORT A. Coy. After digging the support trench for D.Coy. they will occupy VRAIGNES WOOD at dawn on the 29th inst.

   Each front and support trench should be about 100 yards long, with eight bays, fire trench and traverse in each.
   The Quartermaster's stores and remainder of the Transport will remain in MONTECOURT.

4. D, B & C Coys. (in that order) will move via MERAUCOURT, P.30.d.6.5½. and thence due east to Q.28.c.7.5. where two guides (provided by A. Coy.) will meet them to guide them to the dumps of tools and barbed wire, thence to the tasks which have been taped out by the R.E. Starting Point – Road fork at V.11.b.2.2. at 7.30 p.m. Distances of 100 yards between platoons will be observed.

5. Dress – March order, with steel helmets. Each man will also carry three sandbags and will wear a white arm band on the right arm which must be fixed before leaving MONTECOURT. One extra bandolier of S.A.A. per man will also be carried.

6. The Transport Officer will arrange for 5 limbers, pack mules and water carts to be loaded as follows, and ready to move from MONTECOURT at 5.45 p.m.

       For C. Coy. – 1 limber with 80 shovels, 15 picks, screw stakes and barbed wire.
       For B. Coy. – 1 limber with 90 shovels, 15 picks and screw stakes only.
       For D. Coy. – 1 limber with 80 shovels, 15 picks, screw stakes and barbed wire.

For C. & D.   1 limber with 50 shovels for A. Coy.
Companies   and filled up with barbed wire.

For H.Qrs.   -   1 limber, empty, and pack mules loaded
                 with ammunition.

The three Field Kitchens for B, C & D. Coys. will proceed to the north eastern edge of VRAIGNES WOOD immediately after C. Coy. via MERAUCOURT, P.30.d.6.5½. leaving the road at Q.26.d.2.5.

Rations and water will be sent to battalion headquarters unless otherwise ordered.

7. As the whole operation is to be one of surprise to the enemy, and for the safety of the troops engaged, no noise must be made during the operation. During the occupation of the position, no smoking will be allowed at night and no fires by night or day unless in properly made stoves which cannot be seen. O.C. Companies will be held personally responsible that this order is carried out.

8. No Very Lights will be fired until further orders. Front line companies will carry in with them the S.O.S. rifle grenades.

9. Four machine guns of 182nd Machine Gun Coy. are allotted as follows:-
   One for C. Coy. & one for D. Coy. 6½.2
   One will also be placed at Q.22.d.5½.3 and
   One in Q.22.a. or b.

The Signalling Sergeant will run telephone wires to B, C & D. companies from battalion headquarters at Q.27.b.4.4.

                Capt. & Adjt.
                2/5th R. Warwick. Regt.

Issued at 4.0 p.m.

Copy No. 1 to H.Q.
      2 to A. Coy.
      3 to B. Coy.
      4 to C. Coy.
      5 to D. Coy.
      6 to Quartermaster,
      7 to Transport Officer,
      8 to 182nd Machine Gun Coy.
      9 to Section 476th Coy. R.E.
    10   War Diary
    11   File

CONFIDENTIAL.

Vol 12

War Diary.

of

2/5th Bn Royal Warwickshire Regt.

from April 1st to April 30th 1917.

Army Form C. 2118.

WAR DIARY
or
INTELLIGENCE SUMMARY. JMC

(Erase heading not required.)

Instructions regarding War Diaries and Intelligence Summaries are contained in F. S. Regs. Part II. and the Staff Manual respectively. Title pages will be prepared in manuscript.

Place	Date	Hour	Summary of Events and Information	Remarks and references to Appendices
MONTECOURT	1/4/17	—	Battn employed on road mending. Strength of Battn 674.	JMC.
"	2/4/17	—	" " " "	JMC.
"	3/4/17	—	" " " and afterwards moved to billets in MONCHY LAGACHE.	JMC.
MONCHY LAGACHE	4/4/17	—	Battn employed on road mending.	JMC.
"	5/4/17	—	" " " "	JMC.
"	6/4/17	—	" " " and bivouaced for the night at MARTEVILLE.	JMC.
MARTEVILLE	7/4/17	—	Battn relieved 2/1st Worcesters in shelters at MARTEVILLE. Relief complete at 12 noon.	JMC.
"	8/4/17	—	Battn in Brigade support. Working parties.	JMC.
"	9/4/17	—	Battn relieved 2/7th WARWICKS in FRESNOY-LE-PETIT. Relief complete 10.40 pm.	JMC.
FRESNOY-LE-PETIT	10/4/17	—	Battn holding FRESNOY-LE-PETIT (night outposts).	JMC.
"	11/4/17	—	Battn relieved in FRESNOY-LE-PETIT (night outposts) by 17th LANCS FUSILIERS. (Relief complete at 10.45 pm) & moved into support at MARTEVILLE.	JMC. appendix 2
MARTEVILLE	12/4/17	—	Battn relieved in support by 18th LANCS FUSILIERS (relief complete at 11 pm) & marched to billets at QUIVIERES arriving	JMC. appendix 3
QUIVIERES	13/4/17	—	Bathing, cleaning & refitting.	JMC.
"	14/4/17	—	Working parties. Inspection of Companies.	JMC.
"	15/4/17	—	" "	JMC.

WAR DIARY or INTELLIGENCE SUMMARY.

Army Form C. 2118.

(Erase heading not required.)

Place	Date	Hour	Summary of Events and Information	Remarks and references to Appendices
OUVIERE S.	16/4/17	—	Working parties. Inspection of companies	App.6
"	17/4/17	—	" " "	App.6
"	18/4/17	—	" " "	App.6
"	19/4/17	—	Battn. marches parade at 8.45 a.m.	App.6
"	20/4/17	—	" " "	App.6
"	21/4/17	—	185 INF BDE relieved 1st INF BDE in right sector. Battn marched to SAVY.	App.6 appendix 4
SAVY.	22/4/17	—	Battn. in Brigade Reserve. Carrying parties from AMB Cage to outpost Battn (2/6th Warwicks) with wiring materials.	App.6
"	23/4/17	—	Working parties on ponds. Wells. Carrying parties to outpost battn.	App.6
"	24/4/17	—	Working parties. Battn. relieved 2/6 R.WAR.R. in left sub-section BROWN LINE. Relief complete at 11.45 p.m.	App.6 appendix 5
BROWN LINE (ST QUENTIN SECTOR)	25/4/17	—	Battn. holding BROWN LINE, left subsection. Wiring & improvements to lines.	App.6
"	26/4/17	—	"	App.6
"	27/4/17	—	"	App.6
"	28/4/17	—	"	App.6
"	29/4/17	—	"	App.6
"	30/4/17	—	Battn. relieved in BROWN LINE by 2/6th Warwicks (relief complete at 10 pm) left subsection & covenant 2/6th Warwicks (relief complete at 11.59 pm)	App.6
—	—	—	and took over Outpost line from 2/6th Warwicks. Relief complete at 11.59 pm. Strength of Battn. 690. Drafts received during month. 47. Casualties 31.	appendix 6

1/5/17 M. Crofton, Col.
Cmdg 2/5th R. Warwick R.

Appendix 1

9

RED SQUARE OPERATION ORDER NO. 64.   Copy No
Reference - Sheet 62C S.E. and 62B. S.W. 1/20000   April 9th 1917.

1. The Battalion will relieve the 2/7th R.War.Regt. in the right Sub-section tonight.

2. Dispositions as follows:-
   Left front   -   A. Coy.
   Right "   B. Coy.
   In Support,
   in Quarry   D. Coy.
   In Reserve   -   C. Coy.

One guide per platoon will meet companies at battalion battle headquarters (M.32.d.2.5) at times shown below:-
   C. Coy.   5.30 p.m.
   D. Coy.   6.0 p.m.
   B. Coy.   7.30 p.m.
   A. Coy.   8.0 p.m.

Dress, marching order. C. Coy's dispositions will be three platoons at M.32.d. and one platoon in front line trench M.33.b. The three platoons in M.32.d. will be available for carrying parties, for rations and material, all of which will be carried from the crater near M.26.d.4.2. Cookers will not be taken, but the Transport Officer will provide transport for oval dixies. All cooking will be done at the second crater where the dump for rations and matr material will be. The Transport Officer will supervise loading carefully so that limbers are always approximately about half loaded. At least six limbers must be available for work throughout the night.

3. Work of consolidation will be carried on by A. & B. Coys. and platoon of C.Coy. in M.33.b.

4. Battalion Headquarters will be at KEEPER'S LODGE. Companies will point out position of Battalion Headquarters as they march past to their company runners.

                                    Capt. & Adjt.
                                    2/5th R. Warwick. Regt.

Issued at 5.0 p.m.

Copy No. 1 to H.Q.
        2 to A. Coy.
        3 to B. Coy.
        4 to C. Coy.
        5 to D. Coy.
        6 to Quartermaster,
        7 to Transport Officer,
        8 to 2/7th Warwicks.
        9   War Diary
        10   File

appendix 2

SECRET.

RED SQUARE OPERATION ORDER, NO.65.　　　　　　　Copy No. 1
Reference - Sheet 62B. S.W. 1/20000　　　　　　　11th April 1917.
　　　　　　Sheet 62C. S.E. 1/20000

1. The Battalion will be relieved by the 17th Lancashire Fusiliers tonight. On completion of relief, companies will proceed to old quarters at MARTEVILLE.

2. A. Coy. will be relieved by　　— 4 guides at C.Coy's H.Q.
   Y. Coy. 17th Lancs. Fusiliers　　at 8.30 p.m.

   B. Coy. will be relieved by　　— 4 guides at C.Coy's H.Q.
   W. Coy. 17th Lancs. Fusiliers　　at 8.50 p.m.

   D. Coy. will be relieved by　　— 4 guides at C.Coy's H.Q.
   Z. Coy. 17th Lancs. Fusiliers　　at 9.10 p.m.

   C. Coy. will be relieved by　　— No guides required. Relieving
   X. Coy. 17th Lancs. Fusiliers　　Company will arrive about
   　　　　　　　　　　　　　　　　　9.30 p.m.

3. Twenty filled Lewis Gun drums per gun will be handed over, a similar number being taken over by LIEUT.FARMER from the 17th Lancs. Fusiliers. All drums to be thoroughly cleaned. All English pattern tools will be handed over, each company making one dump. French pattern tools will be taken by companies to the QUARRY, O.C. "D" Coy. collecting same and loading on our limbers tonight. Ammunition, grenades, (including S.O.S. grenades) Very Lights, Red Flares etc. and trench shelters will be handed over, receipts being obtained. All petrol tins will be taken out with the Battalion, care being taken that all are collected.

4. The Transport Officer will send 2 limbers, mess cart and horses for Maltese cart to Battn. H.Q. at 6.0 p.m. - 4 limbers to collect all stores and Lewis Guns and horses for the water carts to the QUARRY (M.27.c.1.5) at 8.0 p.m. Headquarters Officers' chargers to be at KEEPER'S HOUSE at 9.30 p.m.

5. Duplicate trench store lists will be sent to the Orderly Room by 3.0 p.m. today.

6. Relief complete will be notified by the usual code word.

　　　　　　　　　　　　　　　　　　　Capt. & Adjt.
　　　　　　　　　　　　　　　　2/5th R Warwick. Regt.

Issued at 12.30 p.m.

Copy No. 1 to H.Q.　　　　　　　Copy No. 6 to Transport Officer.
　　　　2 to A. Coy.　　　　　　　　　　 7 to Quartermaster
　　　　3 to B. Coy.　　　　　　　　　　 8 to 17th Lancs. Fusiliers
　　　　4 to C. Coy.　　　　　　　　　　 9　 War Diary
　　　　5 to D. Coy.　　　　　　　　　　10　 File

SECRET.

RED SQUARE OPERATION ORDER, NO.66   Copy No. 9
Reference – Sheets 62O. 1/20000   11th April 1917.
                66D. 1/20000

Appendix B

1. The Battalion will be relieved in support tomorrow and on completion of relief will march to billets at QUIVIERES. Route:– VILLEVEQUE – BEAUVOIS – LANCHY.

2. Companies will march in the following order, the leading company passing the Starting Point (cross roads at X.2.b.6½.7) at zero which will be somewhere about 12.0 noon and will be notified tomorrow morning:– H.Qrs. A. C. B. D. & A. Coys. and Transport (that portion which is at MARTEVILLE). Lewis Gun handcarts and Field Kitchens will march with companies. Distances of 200 yards between companies will be observed. The remainder of the Transport and Quartermaster's Stores which is at TREFCON will proceed to QUIVIERES independently.

3. Billeting parties consisting of 1 N.C.O & 1 man per Coy. will report to LIEUT. FARMER at Battalion H.Q. at 9.0 a.m.

4. The Transport Officer will arrange for 4 limbers to be at Battalion H.Q. at 10.0 a.m. Two limbers are for Lewis guns which must be loaded by companies by 10.30 a.m. and two for Headquarters. Mess boxes will be ready for collection at 11.45 a.m.

5. Billets will be thoroughly cleaned and ready for inspection by 11.30 a.m. The usual certificates will be handed to the Adjutant at the Starting Point.

6. Watches will be synchronised by Despatch rider sent to companies about 11.0 a.m.

7. The usual falling out states and other returns will be forwarded to the Orderly Room immediately upon arrival.

                                            Capt. & Adjt.
                                            2/5th R Warwick. Regt.

Issued at 12.0 p.m.

Copy No. 1 to H.Q.
         2 to A. Coy.
         3 to B. Coy
         4 to C. Coy.
         5 to D. Coy.
         6 to Quartermaster,
         7 to Transport Officer,
         8 to Lieut. Farmer,
         9   War Diary
        10   File

appendix 4

SECRET.

RED SQUARE OPERATION ORDER, NO. 67 Copy No. 11
Reference — Sheet 62.c. 1/20000   April 20th 1917.
          Sheet 66.d. 1/20000

1. The 182nd Infantry Brigade will relieve the 14th Infantry Brigade in the right sector tomorrow. The Battalion will march to billets in SAVY, relieving the 2/6th Warwicks, and will be in Brigade Reserve. Route:— UGNY — LANCHY — BEAUVOIS — VAUX — ETRIELLERS — SAVY. Quartermaster's Stores and Transport lines will move to GERMAINE, taking over from the 2nd Battalion Manchester Regiment.

2. Companies will march in the following order, H.Q. A, C, B, and D Companies and Transport, the head of the Column passing the Starting Point (cross roads at D.6.a.2.1) at 7.15 p.m. Field Kitchens and Lewis Gun handcarts will march with companies. Two hundred yards distance between companies will be observed as far as ETRIELLERS. From there onwards, 100 yards between platoons. Dress, Marching Order.

3. Billeting parties consisting of 1 N.C.O. & 1 man per company will report to Sec.Lieut. FARMER at Battalion H.Q. at 9.0 a.m.

4. Limbers for Lewis Guns, mobilisation tools, S.A.A. and bombs, 1 baggage wagon, water carts, Mess and Maltese carts will accompany the Battalion. The remainder of the Transport and Q.M.Stores will move to GERMAINE independently. Officers' valises will be taken to the Q.M.Stores ready for loading at 3.0 p.m. Mess boxes will be ready for collection at 6.30 p.m. Lewis Guns will be loaded on limbers at the Transport lines by 6.0 p.m.

5. Billets will be thoroughly cleaned and ready for inspection by 6.30 p.m. The usual certificates will be handed to the Adjutant at the Starting Point.

6. Watches will be synchronised by Despatch Rider sent to companies about 6.0 p.m.

7. The usual falling out states and other returns will be rendered to the Orderly Room immediately upon arrival.

Capt. & Adjt.
2/5th R. Warwick. Regt.

Issued at 8.0 p.m.

Copy No. 1 to H.Q.
         2 to A. Coy.
         3 to B. Coy.
         4 to C. Coy.
         5 to D. Coy.
         6 to Quartermaster,
         7 to Transport Officer,
         8 to Sec.Lieut. FARMER,
         9 to 2/6th Warwicks
        10 to 2nd Manchesters
        11   War Diary
        12   File

SECRET.

Appendix 5

RED SQUARE OPERATION ORDER, NO.68   Copy No. 10
Reference - Sheet 62.c. 1/40000   April 24th 1917.
           Sheet 62.b. S.W. 1/20000

1. The Battalion will relieve the 2/6th R.War.Regt. in the left Subsection of the Brown Line tonight.   Dispositions:-
         D. Coy. in Brown Line - Right front
         C. Coy.   -do-   Left front
         B. Coy. in SAVY WOOD - Right Support
         A. Coy.   -do-   Left Support.

2. Guides will meet companies at junction of track and the SAVY-ROUPON road (X.18.d.7.4) as follows:-
         D. Coy. - 10.0 p.m.
         C. Coy. - 10.10 p.m.
         B. Coy. - 10.20 p.m.
         A. Coy. - 10.30 p.m.
      Battalion H.Q. - 10.30 p.m.
   Distances of 100 yards between platoons will be observed. One officer per company and one N.C.O. per platoon will be sent up to take over the line before dusk. Signallers and runners will take over by daylight.

3. During hours of daylight movement above ground in the Brown Line is to be reduced to an absolute minumum.

4. The Transport Officer will send two limbers to Battalion H.Q. and one limber to each company at 8.30 p.m. for the collection of Officers' kits and mess boxes, Lewis Guns, Dixies, etc. Officers' valises of A. & B. Coys. may be taken up if desired.
       Lieut. FARMER will arrange for a guide to meet the ration limbers, Maltese cart, H.Q. limbers and water carts at Battalion H.Q. at 9.30 p.m. and guide them to the Railway embankment at S.20.a.1.9. where the water carts will remain, the remainder of the transport returning to GERMAINE.
       Twenty filled Lewis Gun magazines per gun only will be taken into the line, the remainder being dumped at Battalion H.Q. by 8.0 p.m.
       The Transport Officer will arrange to collect at Battn. H.Q. picks, bombs, surplus Lewis Gun drums, Orderly Room boxes, Officers' valises of C. & D. Coys. for return to the Q.M. Stores.   Field Kitchens will be withdrawn to GERMAINE.

5. C. Coy. will take with them into the line the 30 shovels they are using on the working party tonight.   A. & D. Coys. will each draw 30 shovels and B. Coy. 20 shovels and take in with them.

6. Trench Store lists to be sent to the Orderly Room by 12.0 noon tomorrow.   Disposition sketches to accompany tomorrow's T.F.R.

7. Billets to be thoroughly cleaned and ready for inspection by 8.0 p.m.

8. Watches will be synchronised by Despatch rider sent to companies about 8.0 p.m.

9. The usual code word for "Relief complete" will be sent.

Copies To:-
1   HQrs   6   QM
2   A Coy   7   TO
3   B "   8   McCormick
4   C "   9   Asst.
5   D "   10   War Diary

                                  Capt. & Adjt.

SECRET.

Appendix 6

RED SQUARE OPERATION ORDER, NO.69   Copy No. 10
Reference - Sheet 62.b.S.W. 1/20000   April 29th 1917.

1. The Battalion will be relieved by the 2/6th Warwicks tomorrow. Upon relief it will take over the Outpost line from the 2/7th Warwicks. Dispositions:-
   RIGHT, A.Coy; LEFT, B.Coy; SUPPORT, C.Coy.
   D.Coy. ~~(less 2 Lewis guns with half gun teams)~~ will proceed to billets in SAVY.

2. Two guides from C.Coy. will be sent to the Railway crossing over the SAVY-HOLNON road (S.13.) for the 2/6th Warwicks at 9.15 p.m. tomorrow and two guides from D.Coy. at 9.45 p.m. No guides will be required from A. or B. Coys.

3. Guides will be at the road and track crossing at S.15.d.1.6 as follows:-
   9.30 p.m. 4 guides from B.Coy. 2/7th Warwicks for A.Coy. 2/5th Warwicks.
   10.0 p.m. 2 guides from C.Coy. 2/7th Warwicks for B.Coy. 2/5th Warwicks.
   10.30 p.m. 2 guides from A.Coy. 2/7th Warwicks for C.Coy. 2/5th Warwicks.
   Headquarters ~~(plus 2 Lewis guns with half gun teams from D.Coy.)~~ will follow behind C.Coy.

4. An extra 50 rounds of ammunition will be carried by each man. This surplus will not be brought out on relief by another battalion. Companies will take in with them their own S.O.S. signals. All tools in the present line will be handed over to the 2/6th Warwicks and all tools and Lewis Gun drums in the new line will be handed over by the 2/7th Warwicks.

5. All Lewis Gun drums (properly cleaned), Officers' valises and surplus stores will be handed to SERGT. BLAYNEY at A.Coy's headquarters before moving off. The Transport Officer will arrange to transport all these articles to GERMAINE with the exception of the Lewis Gun drums, which will be handed over to the 2/7th Warwicks in SAVY. The Quartermaster will arrange to collect all shovels from the 2/6th Warwicks in SAVY and dump them at the Canteen.

6. In daylight, no movement of any kind is allowed between posts in the Outpost Line, or between company and Battalion headquarters, or Battalion headquarters and Brigade without a written pass signed by the Adjutant. In order to avoid hostile shelling, every effort must be made to ensure perfect concealment.

7. Two N.C.O's and two runners per company and 4 runners for Battalion headquarters will go into the line tonight, arriving at the new Battalion headquarters at 9.0 p.m.

8. Trench Store lists and Disposition sketches of the old line will be sent to Battalion headquarters by 3.0 p.m. tomorrow. Trench Store lists and Disposition sketches of the new line will be sent to new Battalion headquarters as soon as possible after relief.

9. Companies will report "Relief complete" by usual code word.

Vol 13

CONFIDENTIAL.

War Diary.

of

2/5th Bn. The Royal Warwickshire Regt.

from May 1st to May 31st 1919.

Army Form C. 2118.

WAR DIARY
or
INTELLIGENCE SUMMARY. *MC*

(Erase heading not required.)

Instructions regarding War Diaries and Intelligence Summaries are contained in F. S. Regs., Part II. and the Staff Manual respectively. Title pages will be prepared in manuscript.

Place	Date	Hour	Summary of Events and Information	Remarks and references to Appendices
ST. QUENTIN SECTOR	1/5/17	—	Battn holding OUTPOST LINE, left section. Strength of Battn. 32 officers. 696 other ranks.	HQC.
"	2/5/17	—	" night	MC.
"	3/5/17	—	Battn relieved in OUTPOST LINE by 7/8th WARWICKS & moved into Brigade Reserve. Relief completed at 11:55 pm.	HQC appendix 1
"	4/5/17	—	Battn in Brigade Reserve at SAVY. Reserve	2/C
"	5/5/17	—	Battn in Brigade Reserve.	2/C
"	6/5/17	—	Battn relieved in Bde Reserve by 7/8th WARWICKS & relieved 2/6 WARWICKS on left subsection BROWN LINE. Relief complete at 11:15pm.	2/C appendix 2
"	7/5/17	—	Battn in support in left subsection BROWN LINE	2/C
"	8/5/17	—	"	2/C
"	9/5/17	—	"	2/C
"	10/5/17	—	"	2/C
"	11/5/17	—	"	2/C
"	12/5/17	—	"	2/C
"	13/5/17	—	"	2/C
"	14/5/17	—	"	2/C
"	15/5/17	—	Battn relieved in support line by 121st FRENCH Regt and moved into billets at BEAUVOIS. Relief complete at 12:30am	MC appendix 3
"	16/5/17	—	Battn in billets at BEAUVOIS. Battn marched to billets at BRANCOURT arriving at 11:45am.	2/C appendix 4

WAR DIARY
INTELLIGENCE SUMMARY. /nc

Army Form C. 2118.

(Erase heading not required.)

Instructions regarding War Diaries and Intelligence Summaries are contained in F. S. Regs., Part II. and the Staff Manual respectively. Title pages will be prepared in manuscript.

Place	Date	Hour	Summary of Events and Information	Remarks and references to Appendices
BULANCOURT	17/5/17	—	Battn entrained at NESLE at 4.15pm, detrained at LONGEAU & marched to billets at FLESSELLES arriving 11.45pm	/nc appendix
FLESSELLES	18/5/17	—	Company Training.	/nc 5 appx /nc
" —	19/5/17	—	" "	/nc
" —	20/5/17	—	Church parade at 6.30 p.m.	/nc
" —	21/5/17	—	Battn marched to billets at GEZAINCOURT arriving 10.45am. Capt H.P. Churchman {London Gazette. Sanctioned in Reparation. + 2ndLt H.P. Churchman → 2ndLt C.S.M. W.Rgle. }	/nc appendix 6
GEZAINCOURT	22/5/17	—	Battn muster parade at 10.30am. Inspection by G.O.C. 182 INF. BDE.	/nc
" —	23/5/17	—	Battn marched to billets at BEAUDRICOURT arriving 10.30am.	/nc appendix 7
BEAUDRICOURT	24/5/17	—	Battn entrained at BEAUDRICOURT, detrained at KARBRET & marched to BERNEVILLE arriving at 2.45 p.m.	/nc appendix 8
BERNEVILLE	25/5/17	—	Company Training.	/nc
" —	26/5/17	—	Battn musketry parade at 4.30pm. Company Training Attack practice.	/nc
" —	27/5/17	—	Battalion in Attack practice.	/nc
" —	28/5/17	—	Company Training. Musketry Practice	/nc
" —	29/5/17	—	" "	/nc
" —	30/5/17	—	" "	/nc
" —	31/5/17	—	Brigade in Attack practice. Inspection of billets & Transport by G.O.C. 182 INF. BDE.	/nc

Strength of Battn. 34 officers. 688 other ranks. Drafts. 3 off. 45 other ranks during month. Casualties. 1 off. 53 other ranks.

A6913   Wt. W14422/M1160   350,000   12/16   D. D. & I.   Forms/C./2118/14.

R Coates. Lieut. Col.
Comdg. 2/5 R. War. R.

Secret.
Appendix 1
Red Square Operation Order No. 69.   Copy No. 10.
Reference, sheet 62 B. N.W. 1/20000   May 3rd/17.
          sheet 62 c. 1/40000
_____

1. The Battn. will be relieved in the Outpost Line, ST QUENTIN Sector, on the night 3rd/4th May by 2/8 Warwicks. On relief the Battn. will be in Brigade Reserve at SAVY and companies will proceed direct to former billets there.

2. B. Coy will be relieved by B. Coy 2/8 Warwicks Left Front
   A. Coy   "   "   "   "   C. Coy 2/8 Warwicks Right Front
   C. Coy   "   "   "   "   D. Coy 2/8 Warwicks In support
   D. Coy   "   "   "   "   A. Coy 2/8 Warwicks In SAVY

Guides will be sent to Battn. H.Q. tomorrow as follows:-
B. Coy. 5 guides (1 for Coy HQ and one for each post) at 9.45pm
A. Coy. 5 guides (do   ) at 10.5pm.
C. Coy. 2 guides at 10.25pm.
D. Coy. no guides required.

3. Advance parties from 2/8 Warwicks have already been sent up to take over stores etc. One Officer per Coy will also be sent up during daylight today.

4. All Disposition maps, tools, S.A.A. Bombs, Gas Alarm rockets, Strombos Horns and other Trench Stores will be handed over. Certificates of receipt to be in the Orderly Room by 8.45pm. Lewis Gun magazines & S.O.S. Grenades will not be handed over.

5. Lewis guns, magazines, dixies, petrol tins and other stores not being handed over, will be dumped in the SUNKEN ROAD at L.15.d.6.4. by Coys. as they pass. R.S.M. Hedges will detail 1 N.C.O. and 1 man to take charge of all stores at this dump and to supervise loading. The Transport Officer will arrange for 3 limbers to collect the above stores at 12.0 midnight. These limbers will be loaded

with barbed wire and screw pickets at R.E
dump SAVY on way up and will dump it
in the SUNKEN ROAD at usual place

6. Major F. W. Foster, M.C. will proceed to SAVY today
and will take over billets from 2/7 Warwicks
Coy QM Sergt. will go with him.

The Transport Officer will arrange for Officers
~~valises~~ mess boxes, Field Kitchens, water carts,
~~medical~~ ~~This~~ cart to be taken to SAVY today
Each Coy will send cooks out of the line at
dusk to prepare a hot meal for the men on
arrival at SAVY.

7. Relief complete will be notified by the usual
code word

Whitehouse
Capt & Adjt
2/5th R. Warwick Regt.

Issued at 3.0 am
Copy No 1. to A. Coy
    2 . B. Coy
    3 . C. Coy
    4 . D. Coy
    5 . H.Q.
    6 . Major Foster, M.C.
    7 . Quartermaster
    8 . Transport Officer
    9 . 2/8 Warwicks
  10. War Diary
  11 File

appendix 2

SECRET.
RED SQUARE OPERATION ORDER, NO.70   Copy No. 9
Reference - Sheet 62.c.1/40000   May 6th 1917.
            Sheet 62.b.S.W. 1/200000

1. The Battalion will relieve the 2/6th Warwicks in the left
   Subsection of the BROWN LINE tonight. Dispositions:-
       D.Coy. 2/5th. relieve⎫
       C.Coy. 2/6th.   ⎬ Left front at 10.50 p.m.
       C.Coy. 2/5th. relieve⎫
       D.Coy. 2/6th.   ⎬ Right front at 9.50 p.m.
       B.Coy. 2/5th. relieve⎫
       A.Coy. 2/6th.   ⎬ Left Support at 10.00 p.m.
       A.Coy. 2/5th. relieve⎫
       B.Coy. 2/6th.   ⎬ Right Support at 10.10 p.m.
   Battalion Headquarters will follow A.Company.
   No guides will be required. 1 Officer per company & 1 N.C.O.
   per platoon will be sent up to take over before dusk. Signallers
   and runners will take over by daylight. Distances of 100
   yards between platoons will be observed.

2. During hours of daylight, movement above ground in the BROWN LINE
   is to be reduced to an absolute minimum. Work in hand by 2/6th
   WARWICKS. will be taken over and continued immediately after
   relief.

3. The Transport Officer will send 2 limbers to Battn. H.Q. and 1
   limber to each Coy. at 8.30 p.m. for the collection of Officers'
   kits, mess boxes, Lewis guns, dixies etc. Officers' valises
   may be taken up if desired. A guide will be at SAVY CHURCH
   at 9.30 p.m. to meet ration limbers & H.Q. limbers & guide them
   to the dump at S.20.central. Water Carts will be sent to
   S.20.a.1.9 as before, the remainder of the Transport returning
   to GERMAINE. Rations for all Coys. except D.Coy. will be
   dumped on the road at S.20.Central. Those for D.Coy. will be
   taken to S.14.d.3.8 (Coy. H.Q.). Coys. will provide their own
   carrying parties. The Transport Officer will arrange to collect
   at Battalion H.Q. Orderly Room boxes and Officers' valises for
   return to the Q.M.Stores. Field Kitchens will be withdrawn to
   GERMAINE.

4. All Lewis Gun magazines will be taken into the line filled.
   Coys. will take in with them their own S.O.S. Grenades and
   will take over from the Coy. they relieve all "Golden Rain"
   rockets and tools.

5. Trench Store Lists to be sent to the Orderly Room by 12.0 noon
   tomorrow. Disposition sketches to accompany tomorrow's T.P.R.

6. Billets to be cleaned and ready for inspection by 8.0 p.m.

7. Watches will be synchronised by D.R. sent to Coys. about 8.0 p.m.

8. The usual code word for "Relief complete" will be sent.

                                         Gilbert G. Farmer
                                       Sec.Lieut. & Actg.Adjt.
Issued at 4.15 p.m.   2/5th R. Warwick. Regt.

Copy No. 1 to H.Q.   Copy No. 6 to Quartermaster,
        2 to A.Coy.   7 to Transport Officer
        3 to B.Coy.   8 to 2/6th Warwicks
        4 to C. Coy.   9   War Diary
        5 to D. Coy.   10   File

SECRET.

RED SQUARE OPERATION ORDER, NO. 71   Copy No. 9
Reference — Sheet 62.c. 1/40000   May 13th 1917.

appendix 3

1. The 3rd Battalion of the 121st French Regiment relieves the 2/5th and 2/8th WARWICKS in the BROWN LINE on the night of the 14th/15th May 1917. The machine gun company of this Battalion will be placed in position tonight (13th/14th) the guns of the 182nd Machine Gun Company remaining for 24 hours afterwards.

2. Battalion H.Q. will detail 7 guides under Sec.Lieut. J.E.TARVIN, to meet the incoming Battalion at X.29.c.6.2. at 8.45 p.m. on the 14th May.

3. Strombos horns, latrine seats and R.E.Stores will be handed over, particulars being forwarded to Battalion H.Q. by 5.0 p.m. Fullerphones, gas rockets, stands & sticks, tools, S.O.S. Grenades and any other remaining stores will be brought out upon relief. All printed maps 1/40000 and 1/100000 will be retained. All 1/10000 and 1/20000 printed maps and all cyclostyle maps will be sent to Battalion H.Q. by 5.0 p.m.

4. Upon relief the Battalion will be billeted in BEAUVOIS. East of ETREILLERS all movement will be by platoons at 200 yards distance and West of ETREILLERS by companies at 200 yards distance. Men undergoing Bombing Course under Sec.Lieut. J.DONALDSON, will march direct to BEAUVOIS on completion of days instruction.

5. Billeting parties will report to Sec.Lieut. S.C.SQUIRES at Battalion H.Q. at 8.0 a.m. tomorrow.

6. Limbers for "C" Coy. will be sent to the Quarry, for "D" Coy. to Company H.Q. and for remainder of the Battalion at "A" Coy's old H.Q. Dumps are to be ready for collection by 9.0 p.m.

7. An Officer from each company will personally report "Relief complete" at Battalion H.Q.

           Lieut. Col.
           Comdg. 2/5th R. Warwick. Regt.

Issued at 6.30 p.m.

Copy No. 1 to H.Q.
       2 to A. Coy.
       3 to B. Coy.
       4 to C. Coy.
       5 to D. Coy.
       6 to Quartermaster,
       7 to Transport Officer,
       8 to Billeting Officer,
       9 to War Diary
     10   File

appendix 4

SECRET.

RED SQUARE OPERATION ORDER, NO. 72   Copy No. 9
Reference — AMIENS MAP, 1/100000   May 15th 1917.
           ST.QUENTIN Map, 1/100000

1. The Battalion moves to BILLANCOURT tomorrow. Route:-
FORESTE — DOUILLY — MATIGNY — VOYENNES.

2. Order of march — H.Q. A, B, C & D Coys. the head of the column passing the Starting Point (road junction 400 yards S. of BEAUVOIS CHURCH) at 5.40 a.m. The Transport will join the column at FORESTE cross roads. Distances of 200 yards between companies and Transport will be maintained during the march.

3. Billeting parties will report to Lieut. F.W. BLANCHARD at Battalion H.Q. at 5.30 a.m.

4. Officers' valises will be ready for collection at 4.30 a.m. and mess boxes by 5.0 a.m.

5. O.C. Companies will be responsible that a good hot breakfast is provided before starting and haversack rations are carried.

6. Billets will be ready for inspection by 5.15 a.m.

7. Watches will be synchronised by Despatch Rider sent to companies about 4.30 a.m.

8. The usual Falling out states and other returns will be rendered to the Orderly Room immediately upon arrival.

           P. Coates,
           Lieut. Col.
      Comdg. 2/5th R. Warwick. Regt.

Issued at 3.0 p.m.

Copy No. 1 to H.Q.
        2 to A. Coy.
        3 to B. Coy.
        4 to C. Coy.
        5 to D. Coy.
        6 to Quartermaster,
        7 to Transport Officer,
        8 to Billeting Officer,
        9   War Diary
      10   File

SECRET.

RED SQUARE OPERATION ORDER, NO. 73.   Copy No. 9
Reference – AMIENS Map 1/100000   May 16th 1917.
           LENS Map 1/100000

appendix 5

1. The Battalion entrains at NESLE tomorrow for LONGUEAU, from thence marching to FLESSELLES. Order of march, H.Qrs. D, C, B & A. Coys. the head of the column passing the Starting Point (road junction 200 yards N.N.W. of BILLANCOURT cross roads) at 2.0 p.m. The Transport will move by road under orders to be issued by Major FOSTER, M.C.

2. Lieut. F.W.BLANCHARD, and L/Sgt. W.R.BENNETT, will report to the R.T.O. at NESLE Station at 5.30 a.m. tomorrow for entraining duties.

3. The only stores to be taken by train will be Lewis Guns, Officers' mess boxes, dixies and necessary H.Q. office stores. These will be kept down to the absolute minimum and will be ready for collection at 1.0 p.m. Officers' valises and other stores will be loaded on the Transport and will be ready for collection at 7.30 a.m. The remainder of the day's rations will be carried on the man.

4. One platoon of B.Coy. under Sec.Lieut. S. GRANT, will arrive at NESLE Station at 2.30 p.m. as loading party. They will also act as unloading party on arrival at destination.

5. Billets will be ready for inspection at 1.30 p.m.

6. Watches will be synchronised by Despatch rider sent to companies about 12.0 noon.

7. The usual Falling-out states and other returns will be rendered to the Orderly Room immediately upon arrival.

                                                Lieut. Col.
                                   Comdg. 2/5th R. Warwick. Regt.

Issued at 7.30 p.m.

Copy No. 1 to H.Q.
        2 to A. Coy.
        3 to B. Coy.
        4 to C. Coy.
        5 to D. Coy.
        6 to Lt. Blanchard,
        7 to Quartermaster,
        8 to Transport Officer,
        9   War Diary
       10   File

Secret
Red Square Operation Order No. 75.74   Copy No 8
Reference - LENS Map 1/100000   May 20/17

Appendix 6

1. The Battalion marches to GEZAINCOURT tomorrow, via TALMAS and BEAUVAL.

2. Order of march H.Qrs B. D. C. & A. Coys & Transport, the head of the column passing the Starting Point (road junction just S of the F in FLESELLES) at 5.3 a.m. and moving in rear of Brigade H.Qrs. Steel helmets will be worn and service dress caps slung on the waist belt by the chin strap.

3. The stores which were brought on the train will be sent to the Q.M. Stores, ready for collection before moving off.

4. Companies will arrange for tea and a light meal to be served before starting. There will be one hour's halt for breakfast at 6.50 A.M.

5. Railhead for the 22nd inst will be ROSEL and the refilling point and fuel dump for the Brigade Group at 8 a.m. at the road junction N. of the H in HAMENCOURT.

6. Billets will be ready for inspection at 4.45 a.m.

7. Watches will be synchronised by Despatch Rider sent to Coys about 4.30 A.M.

8. The usual falling out states and other returns will be forwarded to the Orderly Room immediately upon arrival.

F.W. Blanchard
Lieut & Actg. Adjt

Issued at 9.0 p.m.
Copy No 1 to H.Q.
     2   A Coy.
     3   B Coy.
     4   C Coy.
     5   D Coy.
     6   Quartermaster
     7   Transport Officer
     8   War Diary
     9   File

Secret.
Red Square Operation Order No. 75.
Reference - LENS Map 1/100,000.

Appendix 7
Copy No.
May 22/17.

1. The 182nd Infantry Brigade marches to the IVERGNY area tomorrow the 23rd inst., the Battalion proceeding to billets at BEAUDRICOURT. Route:- BRETEL - DOULLENS - BOUQUEMAISONS - LE SOUICH - IVERGNY.

2. Coys will march in the following order, HQrs. C.B. A & D Coys & Transport, the head of the column passing the starting point (road junction 250 yards N.N.W. of GEZAINCOURT Church) at 6·7 am and moving in rear of Brigade H.Q. There will not be more than 10 yards distance between Coys & Transport. 500 yards will be maintained between units. Field Kitchens will march with the Transport. The Transport will not pull out from the Transport field until it is ready to take its place in the column.

3. Coys will arrange for a hot breakfast to be served before moving off.

4. Lewis guns will be loaded on the limbers tonight. Officers valises, Orderly Room boxes & HQ cooking utensils will be ready for collection at 5·15 am, those of HQrs, C & D Coys being dumped at the QM Stores and A & B Coys at B Coys HQrs. Mess boxes will be ready for collection at 5·45 am.

5. Billets will be ready for inspection at 5·45 am. The usual certificates that they have been thoroughly cleaned will be handed to the Adjutant at the Starting Point. Major F.W. Foster will remain behind & collect any claims.

6. Watches will be synchronised by D.R. sent to Coys about 5 am.

7. The usual falling out states & other returns will be forwarded to the Orderly Room immediately upon arrival.

H.P. Churchman
Capt & Adjt.

Issued at 8·30 pm
Copy No 1 to HQ
   2 to A Coy
   3 to B Coy
   4 to C. Coy
   5 to D. Coy

Copy No 6 to Quartermaster
   7 to Transport Officer
   8 to War Diary
   9 to File.

Secret
Red Square Operation Order No 76.
Reference LENS map 1/100000

Appendix 8   Copy No 8
May 23/17

1. The 182nd Infantry Brigade proceeds to the BERNEVILLE area by Bus + march route tomorrow. The Battn. will be billeted in BERNEVILLE. The Battn. will embus at BEAUDRICOURT, de-bussing on the main DOULLENS-ARRAS road near LARBRET and march from there via the main DOULLENS-ARRAS road - BAUMETZ - LES LOGES. Distances of 100 yards between coys + 250 yards between Battalions will be maintained.

2. Coys will march to the embussing point in the following order, H.Q., A, B, C + D Coys., the head of the column passing the starting point (cross roads 100 yds S. of BEAUDRICOURT Church) at 7.15 am., where they will be split up into parties of 25 ready for embussing (Officers + N.C.O.'s being evenly allotted to the parties) On arrival at the embussing point the Battn will be formed up in groups of 25 on the west side of the road + opposite the motor busses. Haversack rations will be carried by all parties.

3. The Transport will proceed by road as per orders issued separately to the Transport Officer. Signallers with bicycles will proceed with the Transport. Lewis guns will be loaded on the transport tonight. Officers' kits, mess boxes, Orderly Room boxes, HQ cooking utensils and other stores will be dumped at Battn HQ ready for collection by the Transport at 7am. Riding horses under Lieut. F.W. BLANCHARD will proceed to LARBRET by road + await, (keeping clear of the main road,) the arrival of the Battalion about 10 am.

4. Billets + Horse lines will be thoroughly cleaned + ready for inspection at 7am, certificates to that effect being handed to the Adjutant at the starting point. Major F.W. FOSTER will obtain a certificate from the Area Officer that the billets have been left in a satisfactory condition.

5. Watches will be synchronised by D.R. sent to Coys about 6am

6. The usual falling-out states and other returns will be sent to the Orderly Room immediately on arrival.

Capt & Adjt.

Issued at 9 pm.
Copy No 1 to HQ
    2 to A Coy
    3 to B Coy
    4 to C Coy
    5 to D Coy

Copy No 6 to Quartermaster
    7 to Transport Officer
    8 to War Diary
    9 to File.

Confidential.

War Diary.

of

2/5th Bn. The Royal Warwickshire Regt.

from 1/6/17 to 30/6/17

WAR DIARY
or
INTELLIGENCE SUMMARY. 11016

(Erase heading not required.)

Army Form C. 2118.

Place	Date	Hour	Summary of Events and Information	Remarks and references to Appendices
BERNEVILLE	1/6/17	9.70 am	Battn marched to billets at ACHICOURT, arriving at 11.30 am. In Divisional reserve. Strength of Battn. Offrs. 37. O.R. 688.	11016 appendix 1
ACHICOURT	2/6/17	—	Company Training. Cleaning of billets.	11016
"	3/6/17	11.0 am	Church parade.	11016
"	4/6/17	—	Company Training. Batting.	11016
"	5/6/17	—	" " "	11016
"	6/6/17	—	Company in Attack practice.	11016
"	7/6/17	—	" " " "	11016
"	8/6/17	—	Range practice	11016
"	9/6/17	—	Battn. on Exercise with Tanks at WAILLY.	11016
"	10/6/17	11.0 am	Church parade. B Coy attached for work at 'Q' dump. ARRAS (9.16 & 1.11 ref sheet 51.G.4000)	11016
"	11/6/17	5.30 am	Battn marched to billets at DAINVILLE, arriving at 6.30 am. Working parties.	11016 appendix 2
DAINVILLE	12/6/17	—	Working party. Specialist Training.	11016
"	13/6/17	—	" " "	11016
"	14/6/17	—	" " "	11016
"	15/6/17	—	" " "	11016
"	16/6/17	—	" " "	11016

Army Form C. 2118.

WAR DIARY
or
INTELLIGENCE SUMMARY.

(Erase heading not required.)

Instructions regarding War Diaries and Intelligence Summaries are contained in F. S. Regs., Part II. and the Staff Manual respectively. Title pages will be prepared in manuscript.

Place	Date	Hour	Summary of Events and Information	Remarks and references to Appendices
AIRVILLE	17/6/17	9.30am	Church parade. Tactical Exercise without troops at WARLUS.	1916
"	18/6/17	—	Battn in Attack Scheme arranged by Bde. Bathing parade.	1916
"	19/6/17	—	Brigade Horse Show.	1916
"	20/6/17	—	Company Training. Attack practice.	1916
"	21/6/17	—	Company Training & Range firing.	1916
"	22/6/17	—	Company Training. Transport proceeded by road to ERQUIÈRES.	1916
"	23/6/17	—	Rd INF BDE moved to new area; its battalion proceeded by bus to billets at JACQUERIETTE (HQrs, A & C Coys) and ERQUIÈRES (B & D Coys & Transport) arriving 3pm.	1916 Appendix 3
JACQUERIETTE & ERQUIÈRES	24/6/17	—	Company Inspection. 6.30pm Church Service.	1916
"	25/6/17	—	Company & Specialist Training.	1916
"	26/6/17	—	" "	1916
"	27/6/17	—	data	1916
"	28/6/17	—	Battalion with Brigade in Brigade Scheme. Continues on a outpost manning etc.	1916
"	29/6/17	—	Battn in Wood Fighting Scheme. Companies in outpost in evening.	1916
"	30/6/17	—	Company Training. Range practice.	1916

Strength of Battn. 35 off. 672 o.r. { Drafts received during month. 2 off. 11 o.r. }
{ Casualties " 1 off. 27 o.r. Comdg 27st R.War R. }

A.J. Coates Lt Col
1/7/17

appendix 1

SECRET.

RED SQUARE OPERATION ORDER, No.76.   Copy No. 10
Reference – Sheet 51.c. 1/40000   May 31st 1917.
            Sheet 51.b. 1/40000

1. The 182nd Infantry Brigade marches to the ARRAS area tomorrow, and will be in Divisional Reserve. The Battn. will proceed to billets in ACHICOURT. Route:– BAC DU NORD and cross roads at L.35.b.5.7.

2. Companies will march in the following order, H.Qrs. D. C. B. & A.Coys. and Transport, the head of the column passing the Starting Point (cross roads R.1.c.9½.6) at 9.22 a.m. 100 yards will be maintained between companies and between last company and Transport. Field Kitchens will march with companies; baggage wagons with the Transport. The road through ACHICOURT is to be kept clear for the passage of units proceeding to ARRAS.

3. Lewis Guns are to be loaded by Companies on the limbers in the Transport field before 8.0 a.m. tomorrow. Officers' kits, Orderly Room boxes, H.Q. cooking utensils and other stores will be ready for collection at 8.0 a.m. Mess boxes will be ready for collection at 9.0 a.m. The Transport Officer will arrange for their collection.

4. Billets will be ready for inspection at 8.30 a.m. and the usual certificates that they have been thoroughly cleaned will be handed to the Adjutant at the Starting Point. B.Coy. will detail 1 Sergt. & 6 O.R. as "Cleaning up" party, who will report at Battn. H.Q. at 9.15 a.m. where MAJOR FOSTER will hand them written instructions as to any billets which require further cleaning. On completion of their work, they will report to an Officer of the 2/7th R.War.R. and will be marched by him to ACHICOURT.

5. Watches will be synchronised by Despatch Rider sent to companies about 8.0 a.m.

6. The usual falling-out states, condition of billets when taken over and other returns will be forwarded to the Orderly Room immediately upon arrival.

                                          Capt. & Adjt.
                                          2/5th R. Warwick. Regt.

Issued at 6.0 p.m.
Copy No. 1 to C.O.
         2 to Adjutant
         3 to A.Coy.
         4 to B.Coy.
         5 to C.Coy.
         6 to D.Coy.
         7 to Quartermaster
         8 to H.Q.
         9 to Transport Officer,
        10   War Diary
              File

TO:-

Reference attached Operation Order.
All times mentioned therein are put forward ½ hour, i.e. Para. 2. read 5.30 a.m. for time of passing Starting Point. Para. 3. read 4.30 a.m. and 5.0 a.m. Time for Lewis Guns to be loaded stands. Para. 5. read 5.0 a.m. and 5.30 a.m. Para. 6. read 4.30 a.m.

[signature]
Capt. & Adjt.
2/5th R. Warwick. Regt.

10/6/17.

SECRET.
RED SQUARE OPERATION ORDER, NO. 77   Copy No. 8
Reference — LENS Sheet 1/100000   June 10th 1917.

Appendix X

1. The 182nd Infantry Brigade marches to the DAINVILLE area tomorrow, the 11th inst. The Battalion (less B.Coy.) will proceed to billets at DAINVILLE. Route:— ACHICOURT — DAINVILLE ROAD.

2. Companies will march in the following order, H.Qrs. D. A. & C. Coys. and Transport, the head of the column passing the Starting Point (cross roads ½ mile due S. of the 2nd E. in Citadelle) at 6.0 a.m. Field Kitchens will march with the Transport. Distances of 100 yards will be observed between companies and between the last company and Transport.

3. Officers' kits, Orderly Room boxes, H.Qrs. cooking utensils and other stores will be dumped at the Q.M.Stores ready for collection by the Transport at 5.0 a.m. Messboxes will be ready for collection at 5.30 a.m. Lewis Guns will be loaded at the Transport Lines by 8.0 p.m. tonight.

4. The Quartermaster's Stores will move to DAINVILLE this afternoon under orders to be issued by the Quartermaster.

5. Billets will be ready for inspection at 5.30 a.m. and certificates handed to the Adjutant at the Starting Point. Sec.Lieut. H.G.SENIOR and 10 O.R. of "D" Coy. will remain behind as "cleaning up" party and will report at 6.0 a.m. at Battalion H.Q. to Capt. S.C.MILLS, who will hand them written instructions as to any billets which require further cleaning. Before leaving ACHICOURT, Sec.Lieut. SENIOR will obtain a certificate that the billets have been left in a clean and sanitary condition from the Town Major.

6. Watches will be synchronised by Despatch Rider sent to companies about 5.0 a.m.

7. Falling out States, report on condition of billets when taken over and other returns will be sent to the Orderly Room immediately upon arrival.

                                                Capt. & Adjt.
                                                2/5th R. Warwick. Regt.

Issued at 2.0 p.m.
Copy No. 1 to H.Q.
        2 to A. Coy.
        3 to B. Coy.
        4 to C. Coy.
        5 to D. Coy.
        6 to Quartermaster,
        7 to Transport Officer,
        8   War Diary
        9   File

SECRET.

RED SQUARE OPERATION ORDER, NO. 78.   Copy No. 7
Reference — Sheet 51.c. 1/40000   June 22nd 1917.
            LENS Sheet 11, 1/100000

appendix 3

1. The dismounted personnel of the 182nd Infantry Brigade moves to the WAIL Area tomorrow. The Battalion will proceed by bus to billets at VACQUERIETTE and ERQUIERES.

2. Companies will march to the embussing point (85 yards E. of L.32.a.1.1½ on the DAINVILLE—WARLUS road) in the following order, H.Q. A. C. D. & B. Coys. the head of the column passing the Starting Point (main entrance of Camp at L.28.a.9.2) at 7.22 a.m. 100 yards distance will be observed between companies. On arrival at the embussing point, the Battalion will be drawn up on the right of the road in parties of 25 opposite the buses. The Battalion will de-bus at ERQUIERES. Dress:- Marching Order. Haversack rations will be carried by all ranks.

3. Officers' kits, mess boxes, company cooking utensils, Orderly Room boxes and other stores will be taken to the Q.M.Stores before moving off. Lewis Guns will be taken by the troops on the buses.

4. The Camp will be ready for inspection by Capt. C.F.L.GIBSON at 7.0 a.m. Certificates of cleanliness will be handed to the Adjutant at the Starting Point.

5. Watches will be synchronised by Despatch Rider sent to companies about 6.30 a.m.

6. "Condition of billets when taken over" and other returns will be sent to the Orderly Room as soon as possible after arrival in the new area.

                                    Capt. & Adjt.
                                    2/5th R. Warwick. Regt.

Issued at 9.30 p.m.

Copy No. 1 to H.Q.
         2 to A.Coy.
         3 to B.Coy.
         4 to C.Coy.
         5 to D.Coy.
         6 to Quartermaster,
         7   War Diary
         8   File.

Vol 15

Confidential.

War Diary
of
2/5th Bn. The Royal Warwickshire Regt.

from 1/7/17 to 31/7/17.

WAR DIARY
or
INTELLIGENCE SUMMARY.
(Erase heading not required.)

Army Form C. 2118.

Instructions regarding War Diaries and Intelligence Summaries are contained in F. S. Regs., Part II. and the Staff Manual respectively. Title pages will be prepared in manuscript.

Place	Date	Hour	Summary of Events and Information	Remarks and references to Appendices
VACQUERIETTE and ERQUIERES	1/7/17	9.45am	Church parade. Strength of Battalion. 35 off. 672 other ranks.	
	2/7/17	9am	Battn. muster parade. Inter platoon competition. Range practice.	
	3/7/17	9am	Inter platoon competition. Platoon tactical exercise (Advance Guard 3½ miles S of Q in QUATREVAUX.)	
	4/7/17	9am	Batta. inspected in Wood fighting by G.O.C. 165 INF BDE. in NAIL Training Area	
	5/7/17	9am	Battn. muster parade. Range practice.	
	6/7/17	8.30am	D'Coy in Brigade Inter-company Tactical Scheme. Company Training. Range practice	
	7/7/17	9am	Battn. muster parade. Demonstration of "Platoon in Attack" near QUATREVAUX.	
	8/7/17	11am	Brigade Church Parade at ERQUIERES. Draft of 56 o.r. from Monmouth R. reported for duty.	
	9/7/17	9am	Battn. muster parade. Collection of Lewis Gun firing of 5 platoon competition	
	10/7/17	—	Divisional Sports.	
	11/7/17	9am	Battn. muster parade. Inspection in "Open Warfare Attack" at NAIL by G.O.C. 165 INF BDE	
	12/7/17	9am	" Range Practice. Platoons in attack on objective (½ mile S of Q in QUATREVAUX at 1.25 pts /700. mos)	
	13/7/17	9am	" Bomb Throwing Competition. Tactical exercise without troops at QUATREVAUX at 2.30pm.	
	14/7/17	9am	Battn. muster parade. Rifle Grenadier Competition. Company Training.	
	15/7/17	6pm	Church Parade. Draft of 160 O.R. (including 10 Cannocks) arrived.	
	16/7/17	7.30am	Battn. Route March. Route BAIAMETZ - FIEVRES - HAUT MAISNIL - QUOEUX - FONTAINE - ERQUIERES - Officers Tactical Exercise on the BAIAMETZ - ERQUIERES ROAD	

WAR DIARY
or
INTELLIGENCE SUMMARY

Army Form C. 2118.

(Erase heading not required.)

Place	Date	Hour	Summary of Events and Information	Remarks and references to Appendices
VACOGNERIETTE and ERQUIÈRES	17/7/17	6 a.m.	Brigade Scheme to Launch Assault Scheme. (S. of recent U in QUATREVAUX) ref sheet LENS 1/100,000	JMG
	18/7/17	9 a.m.	Battn. muster parade. Range Practice.	JMG
	19/7/17	6 a.m.	Battn. march to Launch Assault Practice. (S. of Sector U in QUATREVAUX ref sheet LENS 1/100,000) Night Patrol Scheme for NCO's of "D" Coy.	JMG
	20/7/17	10 a.m.	Battn. Inspected by G.O.C. 162 INF BDE in marching order on Sports Ground, ERQUIÈRES. Range practice. Night Patrol Scheme for NCO's of "B" Coy.	JMG
	21/7/17	7.30 a.m.	Route march. ERQUIÈRES – QUŒUX – FONTAINE – CHÉRIENNE – FREMBEAUCOURT – LE QUESNOY – VACOGNERIETTE.	JMG
		8 a.m.	Practical Exercise without troops for Subaltern officers. (Near recent E in ERQUIÈRES, ref sheet LENS 1/100,000.	JMG
	22/7/17	11.30	Church parade on Sports Ground. ERQUIÈRES.	JMG
	23/7/17	9 a.m.	Battn. muster parade. Company Training.	JMG
	24/7/17	6.20 a.m.	162 INF BDE. marched to PREVENT from where the battalion proceeded to billets at FORTEL arriving at 10.20 a.m.	JMG appendix 1
FORTEL	25/7/17	—	Company Training	JMG
"	26/7/17	-	162 INF BDE moved to the RUBROUCK area, the battn entrained at FREVENT, detrained at CASSEL marched to billets at RUBROUCK, arriving at 3.40 pm	JMG appendix 2
RUBROUCK	27/7/17	-	Company Training. Draft of 143 o.r. arrived	JMG
"	28/7/17	12 noon	Church parade. G.O.C. 162 INF BDE inspected draft at 11.30 a.m.	JMG
"	29/7/17	-	Company Training. (route marches) Draft of 25 o.r. arrived.	JMG
"	30/7/17	-	Company Training. Inspection of draft by G.O.C. 162 INF BDE.	JMG
"	31/7/17	10 a.m.	Battn. march to Launch Assault Practice. (Sq b, G6b & H1c ref sheet 27NW 1/20,000) Strength of Battn. 37 off. 938 o.r. Distinguished during month off. 303. off. 37 Casualties — 1 —	JMG

J.C. Reid, Col
Cmdg 7/R. Irish.

SECRET.

RED SQUARE OPERATION ORDER, NO. 79.　　　Copy No. 11?
Reference - LENS Sheet, Edition 2, 1/100000　　July 23rd 1917.

---

1. The 182nd Infantry Brigade moves to the PREVENT Area tomorrow, the Battalion proceeding to billets in FORTEL. Route:- QUOEUX, HARAVESNES, BACHIMONT, ROUGEFAY, VACQUERIE-le-BOUCQ, FORTEL.

2. Companies will march in the following order, Battn. H.Q. D. B. C. & A. Coys. and Transport, the head of the column passing the Starting Point (road junction immediately N. of the I. in ERQUIERES) at 6.20 a.m. Ten yards distance between companies and between the rear company and Transport will be observed. Field Kitchens and Lewis Gun limbers will march with the Transport. Breakfast will be served before moving off.

3. Billeting Party under Sec.Lieut. S.C.SQUIRES will proceed to FORTEL this afternoon to take over billets.

4. Officers' Kits (at Coy. H.Q.) Orderly Room boxes and H.Qrs. cooking utensils will be ready for collection by the Transport at 5.0 a.m. Lewis Gun limbers will join the Transport Column at a time to be arranged by the Transport Officer. Field Kitchens will march with companies to the Starting Point where they will join the Transport. The Transport Officer will arrange for the Mess Cart to collect the Canteen stores and H.Qrs. mess boxes.

5. Billets and the area occupied will be cleaned and ready for inspection by Capt. C.D.L.GIBSON at 5.30 a.m. All open latrines are to be filled in before moving off. Lieut. F.W.BLANCHARD will remain behind until 6.0 p.m. to deal with any claims.

6. Certificates as to cleanliness of billets and parade states will be handed to the Adjutant at the Starting Point. "Condition of billets when taken over" and other returns will be sent to the Orderly Room as soon as possible after arrival in the new area.

7. Watches will be synchronised by D.R. sent to Companies about 5.0 p.m.

8. ACKNOWLEDGE.

　　　　　　　　　　　　　　　　　　　　　Lieut. & Adjt.
　　　　　　　　　　　　　　　　　　　　　2/8th R. Warwick. Regt.

Issued at 12.0 noon.
Copy No. 1 to C.O.
　　　　　2 to Adjutant,
　　　　　3 to A.Coy.
　　　　　4 to B.Coy.
　　　　　5 to C.Coy.
　　　　　6 to D.Coy.
　　　　　7 to H.Q.
　　　　　8 to Quartermaster,
　　　　　9 to Transport Officer,
　　　　　10 to Billeting Officer,
　　　　　11　　War Diary

SECRET.

RED SQUARE OPERATION ORDER, NO.80.   Copy No.
Reference - Maps LENS 11, Edn. 2, 1/100000   July 24th 1917.
            HAZEBROUCK 5a. "   2, 1/100000

1. The 182nd Infantry Brigade will move by march and train
   route from the PREVENT Area to the RUBROUCK Area on the
   25th/26th inst. entraining at PREVENT and detraining at
   CASSEL. On the march to the entraining station, 10 yards
   distance between companies and between rear company and
   Transport will be observed; from the detraining station to
   the new area, 200 yards distance will be observed.

2. The Battalion will move in two sections:-
   Section No. 1. "A" Coy. with field kitchen and team, by
                   No. 11 train leaving PREVENT station at 2.20 a.m.
                   on the 26th inst. under orders to be issued by the
                   O.C. "A" Coy. Transport to arrive at the station
                   three hours before departure of the train; personnel
                   1½ hours before departure of the train.

   Section No. 2. Battalion and Transport (less "A" Coy. and
                   field kitchen) by No. 14 train, leaving PREVENT
                   at 6.20 a.m. on the 26th inst. Transport to arrive
                   at the station at 3.20 a.m. under orders to be
                   issued by the Transport Officer.
   Companies will march to the entraining station via cross
   roads 500 yards N. of the second E. in BONNIERES, in the
   following order:- H.Qrs. C. B. & D. Coys. the head of the
   column passing the Starting Point (road junction 600 yards
   N. of the O. in FORTEL) at 3.27 a.m.

3. Officers' kits will be ready for collection at Company H.Q.
   at 9.0 p.m. on the 25th inst; company Lewis Gun limbers at
   12.0 midnight. The mess cart will collect Orderly Room
   boxes, H.Q. cooking utensils and H.Q. mess boxes at 12.0
   midnight.

4. Lieut. F.W.BLANCHARD is detailed as Battalion Entraining
   Officer. He will report to the R.T.O. PREVENT station
   for instructions at 11.0 p.m. on the 25th inst. and will
   travel on the second train. Loading and unloading parties
   are being found from other units. The Transport Officer
   will provide a horse holder for each animal (drawing men
   from companies if necessary) also drag ropes for use as
   breast lines in the covered trucks. Strict silence is to
   be maintained during the entrainment and detrainment.
   No lights are to be lit in any train after dark. Fires
   will be withdrawn from field kitchens before entrainment.
   Water carts and water bottles must be full on entrainment

5. Breakfast will be served before moving off, companies
   arranging for camp kettles to be carried to the station
   by the men. Sufficient rations will be carried on company
   field kitchens to enable a hot meal to be prepared on
   arrival in the new area. The remainder of the rations
   will be carried on the man.

6. Billets will be cleaned and ready for inspection at 3.0 a.m.
   Two sanitary men of each company will report to the
   Inspecting Officer at their company H.Q. (those of A.Coy.
   travelling on the second train with Battalion H.Q.)

- 2 -

7. Certificates that billets have been left clean and parade states will be handed to the Adjutant at the Starting Point (with the exception of those of A.Coy. and Transport, who will send them in to the Orderly Room before moving off).

8. Watches will be synchronised by Despatch Rider sent to companies about 10.0 p.m. on the 25th inst.

9. ACKNOWLEDGE.

                                  Lieut. & Adjt.
                              2/5th R. Warwick. Regt.

Issued at 9.0 p.m.

Copy No. 1 to C.O.
        2 to Adjutant,
        3 to A.Coy.
        4 to B.Coy.
        5 to C.Coy.
        6 to D.Coy.
        7 to H.Q.
        8 to Transport Officer
        9 to Quartermaster,
      10 to Lieut. F.W.BLANCHARD,
      11   War Diary
      12   File.

Vol 16

Confidential

War Diary.

of

The 1/5th Bn. The Royal Warwickshire Regt.

from Aug 1st to Aug 31st 1917

WAR DIARY
or
INTELLIGENCE SUMMARY.

(Erase heading not required.)

Army Form C. 2118.

Place	Date	Hour	Summary of Events and Information	Remarks and references to Appendices
RUBROUCK	1/8/17	—	Company Training. Strength of Battn. Off- O.R. 27. 936	JMC
"	2/8/17	—	" "	JMC
"	3/8/17	—	" "	JMC
"	4/8/17	—	Inspection of B Coy by G.O.C. 61st Div at 9:30am	JMC
"	5/8/17	—	" "	JMC
"	6/8/17	—	Church Parade Service 12 noon	JMC
"	6/8/17	—	Brigade Trench to Trench Assault Practice. RUBROUCK Training Area.	JMC
"	7/8/17	—	Company Training. Intensive digging. Off & Sgt to 5th Army Range for Lewis Gun firing	JMC
"	8/8/17	—	Officers Tactical Ride.	JMC
"	9/8/17	—	Brigade Trench to Trench Assault. BROXEELE Training Area	JMC
"	10/8/17	6:30am	Route march by Companies & Transport. 8:30am Revolver practice for all Officers. Mass Demonstration to Officers & Platoons on attacks on Strong Points. 2:30pm Platoons practice Attacks on Strong Points.	JMC
"	11/8/17	—	Route march by Companies. Platoons practice "Attack on Strong Point"	JMC
"	12/8/17	12noon	Church parade. 2:30pm Battalion Sports	JMC
"	13/8/17	6am	Route march (Postn) by Companies. Platoons practice Attack on Strong Point. Range Practice	JMC
"	14/8/17	—	Route march (Postn) by Companies	JMC

Army Form C. 2118.

WAR DIARY
or
INTELLIGENCE SUMMARY.
(Erase heading not required.)

Instructions regarding War Diaries and Intelligence Summaries are contained in F. S. Regs., Part II. and the Staff Manual respectively. Title pages will be prepared in manuscript.

Place	Date	Hour	Summary of Events and Information	Remarks and references to Appendices
RUBROUCK	15/8/17	8:30am	Inspection of A Coy in "Fighting Order" by G.O.C. R.S. Inf. BDE. Company Training.	M6
"	16/8/17	4:10am	Batt'n marched to RENEKE entraining at 6:35am arriving at NOEWTRE at 7:55am, marched to BRANDHOEK No.1 Area arriving at 11:30am	M6 appendix 1
BRANDHOEK	17/8/17	—	Specialist Training. Revolver practice.	M6
"	18/8/17	—	" " "	M6
"	19/8/17	—	Revolver practice.	M6
"	20/8/17	—	Coy Comdrs, platoon Off'rs & platoon Sgts attended demonstration of Attack on Machine Gun in a concrete emplacement at GUEMY.	M6
"	21/8/17	—	Specialist Training. Range practice.	M6
"	22/8/17	—	" " " "	M6
"	23/8/17	—	" " " "	M6
"	24/8/17	—	Range practice.	M6
"	25/8/17	—	Batt'n marched to YPRES, N., relieving 2/5th GLOUCESTERS, arriving at "E" Camp (H.12.a.0.3. ref sheet 28 NW (5000)) at 9:30am	M6 appendix 2
YPRES, N.	26/8/17	—	Batt'n relieved 2/4th GLOUCESTERS in left support WIELTJE & came under orders of 183 INF BDE. Relief complete at 11:30am DT.	M6 appendix 3
WIELTJE	27/8/17	—	Batt'n in left support to 183 INF BDE. Batt'n HQ moved from WIELTJE FM to GARH FARM.	M6
"	28/8/17	—	Batt'n withdrawn from support & returned to Camp at GOLDFISH CHATEAU, VLAMERTINGHE, arriving at 3:45pm	M6
GOLDFISH CH AU. VLAMERTINGHE	29/8/17	—	Company Inspections & bathing	M6

Army Form C. 2118.

WAR DIARY
or
INTELLIGENCE SUMMARY.
(Erase heading not required.)

Instructions regarding War Diaries and Intelligence Summaries are contained in F. S. Regs., Part II. and the Staff Manual respectively. Title pages will be prepared in manuscript.

Place	Date	Hour	Summary of Events and Information	Remarks and references to Appendices
GOLDFISH CHATEAU	30/8/17	—	Battn. took over front line (SOMME – HULL35 roads) from 9th YORKSHRS, 7/K ROS & 7th YHLI. Relief complete a/c 12.20 a.m. 31st.	Att. appending App.
BRICK FARM	31/8/17	—	Battn. holding front line (SOMME – HULL35 road). Strength of Battn. Offs. 34. OR. 939. Drafts received. 1. 35. Casualties. 4. 32.	

A/Lieut. Col.
Comdg. 7/5 R.Wan.R.
7/9/17

SECRET.
RED SQUARE OPERATION ORDER, NO. 80.   Copy No. 10
Reference — Sheets 27 & 28, 1/40000   August 15th 1917.
           Sheet HAZEBROUCK 5a. 1/100000

1. The 182nd Infantry Brigade will move from the RUBROUCK area
   to the BRANDHOEK No. 1 area tomorrow the 16th inst. Dismounted personnel will move by train, entraining at ARNEKE
   and detraining at HOPOUTRE. The Transport will move by
   road under orders which have been issued separately.

2. The Battalion will march to the entraining Station in the
   following order:— H.Qrs. A. C. D. & B. Coys. the head of the
   column passing the Starting Point (road junction at
   H.14.C.8.9) at 4.10 a.m. Route:— DOORNAERT — MIN DUYVELINNE.
   Distances of 10 yards between companies will be observed.
   On the march from the detraining Station to BRANDHOEK, 200
   yards distance between companies will be observed. Mounted
   officers will ride their horses to ARNEKE, from where they
   will be sent forward under No. 201127, Cpl. R.MORRIS, to
   join the Transport Column at L'ERKELSBRUGGE.

3. Lieut. F.W.BLANCHARD is detailed as entraining and detraining
   officer and will report to the R.T.O. ARNEKE, at 4.25 a.m.
   Special instructions will be issued to him separately.

4. MEALS. Breakfast will be served before moving off. Haversack
   rations and filled water bottles will be carried. Camp
   kettles containing remainder of days rations, one cook and
   one officers' mess box per company will be sent forward
   by motor lorry and must be at the Q.M.Stores ready for
   collection before the Battalion moves off. A hot meal will
   be prepared for the men on arrival in the new area.

5. Officers' mess boxes (except one per company), Officers' kits
   Orderly Room boxes, Lewis Gun limbers and field kitchens will
   be ready for collection by the Transport at 9.0 p.m. tonight,
   at company headquarters.

6. Billets and Transport Lines will be cleaned and ready for
   inspection by Capt. S.C.MILLS at 3.30 a.m. Each company
   will detail a rear party consisting of three men, who will
   report to the Inspecting Officer at their company H.Q. and
   will march to the station under orders to be issued by him.
   The usual certificates will be handed to the Adjutant at
   the Starting Point.

7. Watches will be synchronised by D.R. sent to companies
   about 10.0 p.m. this evening.

8. Falling out states, "Condition of billets when taken over"
   and other returns will be sent in to the Orderly Room as
   soon as possible after arrival in the new area.

9. Acknowledge.

                                        Capt. & Adjt.
                                        2/5th R. Warwick. Regt.

Issued at 8.0 p.m.
Copy No. 1 to C.O.   Copy No. 7 to Lieut. BLANCHARD
        2 to Adjutant.   8 to Transport Officer.
        3 to A.Coy.   9 to Quartermaster.
        4 to B.Coy.   10   War Diary
        5 to C.Coy.   11   File
        6 to D.Coy.   12   Batt. H.Qrs.

SECRET.

RED SQUARE OPERATION ORDER, NO. 81.
Reference — Sheet 28 N.W. 1/20000

Copy No.
August 24th 1917.

1. The 182nd Infantry Brigade relieves the 184th Infantry Brigade tomorrow at YPRES (North). The Battalion will proceed to E. Camp, GOLDFISH CHATEAU, in H.11.a. in relief of the 2/5th Glosters.

2. Dismounted personnel will move by Track No. 1. Distances of 200 yards between platoons will be observed. Battalion H.Q. will march as two platoons. Companies will pass the Starting Point (junction of Track No. 1 and Light Railway 200 yards S. of the Camp) at the undermentioned times:—

    Battalion H.Q.   7.0 a.m.
    A. Company   7.5 a.m.
    C. Company   7.17 a.m.
    B. Company   7.29 a.m.
    D. Company   7.41 a.m

   Dress, Marching Order, steel helmets to be worn. The Transport Section will move by the main POPERINGHE — YPRES road, leaving the Transport lines at 8.30 a.m. and will be under the command of the Brigade Transport Officer. It will be divided equally into two echelons which will march at 200 yards distance.

3. Officers' kits, officers' mess boxes, A.Coy's and Battalion H.Qrs. cooking utensils and Orderly Room boxes will be dumped on the side of the road near the Company Officers' lines ready for collection by the Transport at 7.0 a.m. Field Kitchens and Lewis Gun limbers will be ready loaded at the same time. The Regt. Sergt. Major will detail a rear party of 1 N.C.O. and 6 men from the Drummers to guard all stores etc. until collected by the Transport and to carry out any cleaning up the Inspecting Officer may think necessary.

4. Company and Transport lines will be cleaned and ready for inspection by Capt. F.J. BREEDEN before moving off. The usual certificates will be handed to the Adjutant at the Starting Point.

5. Watches will be synchronised by Despatch Rider sent to companies about 6.0 a.m.

6. Falling Out, Condition of billets when taken over, and other returns will be sent to the Orderly Room as soon as possible after arrival in the new area.

7. ACKNOWLEDGE.

Capt. & Adjt.

Issued at 8.30 p.m.
Copy No. 1 to C.O.
      2 to Adjutant,
      3 to A. Company
      4 to B. Company
      5 to C. Company.
      6 to D. Company.
      7 to H.Qrs.
      8 to Lieut. Blanchard,
      9 to Quartermaster,
     10 to Transport Officer
     11   War Diary

Copy No. 12 to File.

SECRET.
Appendix 3

RED SQUARE OPERATION ORDER, NO. 82.
Reference — FREZENBURG Map, Edn. 3. 1/10000   Copy No. 11
        Sheet 28 N.W. 1/20000.   August 26th 1917.

1. The Battalion will move to WIELTJE today, relieving the 2/4th Glosters, and will be in left support to the 183rd Infantry Brigade. Companies will relieve corresponding companies of the 2/4th Glosters. Route — Wooden track — SALVATION CORNER — CANAL BANK — TRACK NO. 6.

2. Companies will leave the camp at times shewn below. Distances of 200 yards will be maintained between platoons:—

B. Coy.	7.30 p.m.
A. Coy.	7.40 p.m.
Batt. H.Q.	7.50 p.m.
C. Coy.	7.53 p.m.
D. Coy.	8.3 p.m.

   Dress, Fighting Kit. Each man will carry three days rations and two filled water bottles.

3. An advance party, consisting of 1 Officer and 2 N.C.O's per company and 1 Officer and 1 N.C.O. for Battalion H.Q. will go forward this morning to take over. They will arrange for their companies to be met on Track No. 6, West of WIELTJE, and guided to their positions.

4. Officers' kits, Officers' mess boxes, surplus Orderly Room boxes, Canteen Stores, Sandbags (which must be properly marked with the owner's name) containing personal belongings and haversack; great coat and entrenching tool (with carrier) and other stores will be dumped in company dumps ready for collection by the Transport at 7.0 p.m. Guards will be detailed from the personel left out of the line to take charge of these dumps. The Transport Officer will also arrange for Field Kitchens and Lewis Gun limbers to be withdrawn to the Transport lines and for two pack animals to report at Battalion H.Q. at 6.30 p.m. to carry stores to the line.

5. Personnel left out of the line will clean the camp as soon as companies have marched out, and will afterwards be marched under an Officer or the senior N.C.O. to the Transport lines, reporting there to Sec.Lieut. J.E.TARVIN. Sec.Lieut. TARVIN will be responsible that the camp is left thoroughly clean and that all stores are removed.

6. Watches will be synchronised by Despatch Rider sent to companies about 6.0 p.m.

7. Relief complete will be reported by the usual code word.

8. ACKNOWLEDGE.

Issued at 10.30 a.m.
                                        Capt. & Adjt.
                                        2/5th R. Warwick. Regt.

Copy No. 1 to C.O.   Copy No. 7 to D. Coy.
        2 to Adjutant,   8 to Transport Officer,
        3 to H.Q.   9 to Quartermaster,
        4 to A. Coy.   10 to 2/4th Glosters
        5 to B. Coy.   11   War Diary
        6 to C. Coy.   12   File.

SECRET.
RED SQUARE OPERATION ORDER, NO. 82.   Appendix 4   Copy No. 11
Reference — FREZENBURG Map, 1/10000.   August 29th 1917.

1. The Battalion takes over the line from D.19.a.6½.1 to D.13.c.3.5. with posts on HILL 35 and in front of SOMME on the night of 30th/31st inst. Approximate dispositions as per attached sketch map.

2. Guides will meet companies as follows:—
   5 guides from 7/8th K.O.S.B. for "B" Coy. 2/5th R.War.R. at MILL COTT (I.5.a.0.6) at 9.0 p.m.

   2 guides from 7/8th K.O.S.B. and 3 guides from 10/11th H.L.I. for "D" Coy. 2/5th R.War.R. at MILL COTT at 9.15 p.m.

   4 guides from 2/8th Worcesters for "A" Coy. 2/5th R.War.R. at the junction of No. 5 Track and OXFORD ROAD (C.28) at 8.30 p.m.

   5 guides from 2/8th Worcesters for "C" Coy. 2/5th R.War.R. at the same place at 8.45 p.m.

   1 guide for Battalion H.Q. (just S. of the K. in BANK FM.) at the same place at 9.0 p.m.

   Guides will be provided with chits as per attached list.

3. All companies will send in to arrive not later than 6 p.m. tomorrow, 1 Officer and 5 N.C.O's, these being dribbled in pairs over the open at long intervals. They will proceed, if possible, to the places to be occupied by their platoons later on. Battalion H.Q. will also send two signallers to just S. of the K. in BANK FM. by the same time.

4. Lewis Guns and any stores companies want to take in will be taken by limbers to the junction of No. 5 Track and OXFORD ROAD for H.Q. A. & C. Coys. and to MILL COTT for B. & D. Coys. from which places they will be carried in by the men. Each man will carry into the line 2 days preserved rations, 1 barrage ration, Iron rations, 3 days' supply of Solidified Alcohol and 2 filled water bottles as far as they will go. Rum and water will be dumped nightly at the junction of No. 5 Track and OXFORD ROAD, from which spot they will be carried forward by the Transport personnel to Coy. H.Q. for "C" Coy. and as far as BANK FM. for the remainder of the Battalion. Returning Transport personnel will carry back salvage.

5. Relief complete will be notified by the usual code word to Battalion H.Q.

6. Watches will be synchronised by Despatch Rider sent to companies about 12.0 noon.

7. ACKNOWLEDGE.

                                          P/ Coates,
                                          Lieut. Col.
Issued at 8.0 p.m.   Comdg. 2/5th R.Warwick.Regt.

Copy No. 1 to A.Coy.   Copy No. 7 to Quartermaster,
         2 to B.Coy.   8 to 2/8th Worcesters.
         3 to C.Coy.   9 to 7/8th K.O.S.B.
         4 to D.Coy.   10 to 10/11th H.L.I.
         5 to H.Q.   11   War Diary
         6 to Transport Officer,   12   File.

2/5 Bn ROYAL WARWICKSHIRE REGIMENT

WAR DIARY — SEPTEMBER 1917

MDsh. Major
Comdg 2/5 Bn Royal Warwickshire Regt.

30.9.17

Army Form C. 2118.

WAR DIARY
or
INTELLIGENCE SUMMARY.

(Erase heading not required.)

Instructions regarding War Diaries and Intelligence Summaries are contained in F. S. Regs., Part II. and the Staff Manual respectively. Title pages will be prepared in manuscript.

Place	Date	Hour	Summary of Events and Information	Remarks and references to Appendices
			Strength of Battn. Offrs. 34 O.R. 939	
BANK FARM	1/9/17	—	Battn. holding front line (SOMME – HILL 35 area). Unsuccessful attempt by 1 platoon of B Coy to reach HILL 35 at 4 a.m.	J.M.C.
	2/9/17	—	Unsuccessful attempt by 2 platoons of D Coy to reach HILL 35, at 11 p.m.	J.M.C.
WIELTJE	3/9/17	—	Battn. relieved in front line by 1/5th WARWICKS. Relief completed at midnight. Battn moved back into right support at WIELTJE.	appendix 1 J.M.C.
	4/9/17	—	Battn. in right support.	J.M.C.
	5/9/17	—	Battn. + 1 company 7/8 WARWICKS relieved 7/6th WARWICKS in front system (SOMME – HILL 35 area). Relief completed at 2.20 a.m. (6th).	J.M.C. appendix 2.
BANK FARM.	6/9/17	—	Battn. unsuccessfully attacked HILL 35 at 7.30 p.m. Reorganised + again attacked at 9 p.m. unsuccessfully. 1/2 companies of 1/5th R. Warks R. + 1 company of 1/6 R. War R. came up to hold the line during second attack.	J.M.C. appendix 2
	7/9/17	—	Battn. relieved in front line by 1/1st BUCKS + moved to RED ROSE CAMP, BRANDHOEK. Relief completed at 12.20 p.m. (8th)	J.M.C. appendix 3
BRANDHOEK	8/9/17	—	Reorganisation + refitting	J.M.C.
	9/9/17	—	" "	J.M.C.
	10/9/17	—	Specialist Training	J.M.C.
	11/9/17	—	" "	J.M.C.
	12/9/17	—	" "	J.M.C.
	13/9/17	—	" "	J.M.C.
	14/9/17	9.21 a.m.	Battn. moved to TAY CAMP, WATOU N°1 area, arriving at 12.30 p.m.	J.M.C. appendix 4

Army Form C. 2118.

WAR DIARY
or
INTELLIGENCE SUMMARY.
(Erase heading not required.)

Instructions regarding War Diaries and Intelligence Summaries are contained in F. S. Regs., Part II. and the Staff Manual respectively. Title pages will be prepared in manuscript.

Place	Date	Hour	Summary of Events and Information	Remarks and references to Appendices
TAY CAMP MORT WATOU	15/9/17	—	Specialist Training. Inspection of Transport by G.O.C. 152 INF BDE at 12 noon	M.6
	16/9/17	9.30am	Battn Muster parade. 11.30am Church parade.	M.6
	17/9/17	7.15am	Battn moved to the EECKE Arer, arriving in billets at ST SILVESTRE CAPPEL at 11.45am	M.6 appendix 3
ST. SILVESTRE CAPPEL	18/9/17	3pm	Battn entrained at CAESTRE at 3pm returned to ARRAS at 9.45pm. Marched to billets at NARLUS arriving at 12 noon	M.6 appendix 6
NARLUS	19/9/17	—	Company Training.	M.6
	20/9/17	—	" "	M.6
	21/9/17	—	Bathing - Medical Inspection.	F.W.B.
	22/9/17	—	Battn Muster parade 3pm.	F.W.B. appendix
HULL CAMP ST NICHOLAS	23/9/17	—	Battn relieved the 9 West Ridings at HULL CAMP ST NICHOLAS area ARRAS. relief complete 1pm	F.W.B.
	—	—	Battn relieved 8 South Staffs Reg in Left Sub-sect. GAVRELLE SMITCH relief complete 9.45pm	F.W.B.
RT NICHOLAS LINE	24/9/17	—	In Support	F.W.B.
	25/9/17	—	" "	F.W.B.
	26/9/17	—	" "	F.W.B.
	27/9/17	—	" "	F.W.B.
	28/9/17	—	" "	F.W.B.
CHEMICAL WORKS	29/9/17	—	Battn relieved R.2/f R.War.R. Right Sub section. Chemical Works	F.W.B. appendix 9
	30/9/17	—	Right Sub section. Strength of Battn 27 off. 625 OR Casualties 7 Off. 255 OR Reinforcements — 1 —	F.W.B.

SECRET.

RED SQUARE OPERATION ORDER NO. 83.　　　　　Copy No. 9
Reference — FREZENBURG Map, 1/10000　　　　　September 2nd 1917.

Appendix 1

1. The Battalion will be relieved tonight (2nd/3rd Sept.) by the 2/6th R.War.R. the Battalion taking their place in right support.

2. The following guides (in order of entry) will be at the junction of No. 5 Track and OXFORD ROAD at 7.30 p.m. this evening:—

   4 guides from B.Coy. 2/5th R.War.R. for C.Coy. 2/6th R.War.R.

   4 guides from A.Coy. 2/5th R.War.R. for D.Coy. 2/6th R.War.R.

   5 guides from D.Coy. 2/5th R.War.R. for A.Coy. 2/6th R.War.R.

   1 guide from Batt. H.Q. 2/5th R.War.R. for Batt. H.Q. 2/6th War.

   4 guides from C.Coy. 2/6th R.War.R. for B.Coy. 2/6th R.War.R.

   All guides will be picked men who know the exact dispositions of their own company as at 2.0 p.m. yesterday (1st inst.)

3. Companies will send out by daylight today, 1 Officer per company and 1 N.C.O. per platoon to arrange dispositions in support, A. B. C. & D. Coys. taking over from A. B. C. & D. Coys. 2/6th R.War.R. respectively.

4. Trench Stores (including S.O.S. rockets) will be handed over and receipts obtained. Trench Store lists will be sent to Battalion H.Q. by 6.0 p.m. today. The second water bottle per man will be taken out together with all possible equipment of casualties. The second water bottle per man will afterwards be dumped at the junction of No. 5 Track and OXFORD ROAD by daylight tomorrow, Batt. H.Q. providing a guard pending their removal by the Transport Officer. All available petrol tins will also be carried out and dumped with the water bottles.

5. Rations, water, camp kettles and fuel will be dumped by the Transport Officer at the junction of No. 5 Track and OXFORD ROAD at 2.0 a.m. companies providing their own carrying parties.

6. All movement by day will be in pairs at long intervals and by night by platoons at 200 yards interval.

7. Relief of three front line companies only will be notified to Battn. H.Q. by the usual code word.

8. ACKNOWLEDGE.

　　　　　　　　　　　　　　　　　　　　　　　Capt. & Adjt.

Issued at 11.0 a.m.
Copy No. 1 to A.Coy.　　　　Copy No. 6 to 2/6th R.War.R.
       2 to B.Coy.　　　　　　　 7 t Transport Officer
       3 to C.Coy.　　　　　　　 8 to Quartermaster.
       4 to D.Coy.　　　　　　　 9   War Diary
       5 to Battn. H.Q.　　　　 10   File

SECRET.

appendix 2

RED SQUARE OPERATION ORDER, NO. 84.   Copy No. 11
Reference — FREZENBURG Map, 1/10000   Sept. 5th 1917.

1. The Battalion (plus one company of the 2/8th Warwicks) will be ready any time after midnight 5th/6th inst. to relieve the 2/6th Warwicks on the line POMMERN CASTLE — SOMME, and at Zero tomorrow attack the gun emplacements on HILL 35, in conjunction with troops on our right flank only, whose objective is IBERIAN.

2. DISPOSITIONS.
D. Coy. 2/8th Warwicks — from D.13.c.6.0 to D.13.c.2½.5¼: with two platoons in the front line and two platoons in support in CAPRICORN TRENCH and BANK FM. Four guides from A. Coy. 2/5th Warwicks will report to them tonight.

B. Coy. 2/5th Warwicks will take over their old area in D.19.a. but without occupying the forward post at D.19.a.9½.9. They will be ready to occupy the two assembly trenches used by A. and C. Coys. after they have moved forward and will be ready, if necessary, to support the attack.

D. Coy. 2/5th Warwicks will take over their former area, with dispositions approximately as before.

Battalion Headquarters will be near BANK FM.

The Regimental Aid Post will be at PLUM FM.

One company of the 2/6th Warwicks will be at PLUM FM. and UHLAN FM. They will get into touch with the Artillery lamp there and on receipt of the code word "COME" from Battalion H.Q. will move the two platoons from PLUM FM. to DUST TRENCH, the Coy. H.Qrs. and one platoon at UHLAN FM. taking their place at PLUM FM.

3. The assault on HILL 35 will be carried out by C. Coy. supported by A. Coy. C. Coy. will assemble in the trench between D.19.a.6½.5 and D.19.a.5¾.7. A. Coy. will assemble in the trench between D.19.a.5.4 and D.19.a.4½.7. One guide for each company from B. Coy. will report to them tonight.

4. Companies will assault on a frontage of one platoon to cover the whole front of about 120 yards, each platoon being in two lines. Distance between lines, 25 yards; between waves 75 yards. A. Coy. will move in columns of sections if possible. Extensions should be about 8 paces.

5. The positions will be at once consolidated and a line dug in front of it. Patrols of Lewis Guns will be pushed forward towards GALLIPOLI to cover consolidation. Connection will be established with the troops taking IBERIAN on the right and a party detailed to clear the line of shell holes towards IBERIAN. B. Coy. will arrange to fill any gap on the left and D. Coy. on the right.

6. COMMUNICATIONS.
   (a) Red flares will be lit when called for by contact aeroplane.
   (b) Immediately the objective has been taken, the Signalling Officer will run out a triple line with telephone to HILL 35 and will also establish visual communication both

\- 2 -

with Battalion H.Q. and BRIDGE HO. B. & D. Companies will also be connected by telephone and by visual.

7. Sketch Map "A" shows position of our latest trenches and of derelict tanks.

8. The Artillery barrage will be as per attached sketch map "B". and C.Company will be in position to go with it when it moves.

9. All dugouts and enemy dead are to be carefully searched by parties detailed from A.Coy. and documents forwarded in sandbags to Battalion H.Q. at once.

10. Watches will be synchronised under arrangements to be made by the Signalling Officer. Zero will be at 7.30 a.m. unless corrected.

11. The code word for the move into position will be "PENINSULA", when companies will move at once.

12. ACKNOWLEDGE.

P.J. Coates,
Lieut. Col.
Comdg. 2/5th R. Warwick. Regt.

Issued at 6.0 p.m.

Copy No. 1 to A.Coy.
   2 to B.Coy.
   3 to C.Coy.
   4 to D.Coy.
   5 to Batt. H.Q
   6 to Coy. 2/6th Warwicks.
   7 to D.Coy. 2/8th Warwicks.
   8 to 2/7th Warwicks.
   9 to Transport Officer.
   10. to Quartermaster,
   11. War Diary
   12. File.

SPECIAL RELIEF ORDERS.

(a) All sketch maps and trench stores will be taken over and a list sent to Battalion H.Q. by 10.0 p.m. tomorrow.

(b) Rum and water will be dumped at the junction of No. 5 Track and OXFORD ROAD as before. The Transport Officer will arrange for the pack loaders to be accommodated in the forward area and to carry the stores for H.Qrs. A. C. & D. Coys. to BANK FM. B. Company will carry their own supplies.

(c) Relief complete will be notified to Battalion H.Q. by the usual code word.

SECRET.

RED SQUARE OPERATION ORDER, NO. 85.   Copy No. 9
Reference — FREZENBURG Map, 1/10000   Sept. 7th 1917.

---

1. The Battalion will be relieved tonight (7th/8th inst.) by the 2/1st Bucks. and will proceed on relief to RED ROSE CAMP, BRANDHOEK. Bus or train will probably convey the personnel from ST. JEAN, but details will follow.

2. Prior to the relief all troops within the rectangle D.19.a.9½.2 D.19.a.5.½ – D.19.a.½.8 – D.13.c.6.2½ will be withdrawn in order to allow for the heavy bombardment of HILL 35 tomorrow.

3. At 8.45 p.m. the following troops will move out without waiting for relief. On no account is movement to commence earlier:-

   C. Coy. 2/6th R.War.R. to camp at G.6.a.8.1
   A. B. & C. Coys. 2/5th R.War.R. (all four companies to go to entraining point).

4. At 8.45 p.m. the following troops will take up new positions as follows:-

   D. Coy. 2/5th R.War.R. to DUST TRENCH.

   2 Platoons, B. Coy. 2/8th R.War.R. to hollow about C.24.b.6.5

   D. Coy 2/8th R.War.R. will retain present positions except that any troops just south of SOMME will be withdrawn to BANK FM.

5. The troops mentioned in para. 4 will wait for relief by 2/1st Bucks before moving off, all troops of 2/8th R.War.R. proceeding and reporting to their own unit which is remaining in support as before. Guides will be sent to the junction of OXFORD ROAD and Nos. 4 & 5 Tracks at 8.15 p.m. tonight:-

   By Battn. H.Q. 1 guide for Battn. H.Q. 2/1st Bucks.
      D. Coy. 2/8th R.War.R. 3 guides for Left Coy. 2/1st Bucks.
      D. Coy. 2/5th   –do–   3   "   " Right "   –do–
      Battn. H.Q.   –do–   3   "   " Centre Coy.   –do–
      C. Coy. 2/5th R.War.R. 3   "   " Reserve "   –do–

   The last mentioned will be proceeding to PLUM and UHLAN FMS. All guides will be picked men and will report to Battn. H.Q. at 7.15 p.m. for chits.

6. All movement will be by platoons at 200 yards interval.

7. Care is to be taken that all men carry out packs, arms, Lewis Guns and other stores, together with all possible arms and equipment of casualties. All Lewis Guns and salvaged kits will be dumped at the corner of No. 4 Track and OXFORD ROAD, Battn. H.Q. providing a guard until the limbers arrive and depart with them. Men will carry their own packs right back to Camp.

- 2 -

8. Trench Stores will be handed over and receipts obtained by D.Coy. 2/5th R.War.R. and D.Coy. 2/8th R.War.R. and forwarded to Battn. H.Q. before moving off.   D.Coy. 2/5th and D.Coy. 2/8th R.War.R. will hand over Lewis Gun positions.

9. O's.C. all companies moving out will report personally to Battalion H.Q. on their way out.

10. ACKNOWLEDGE.

[signature]
Captain
for Lieut. Col.
Comdg. 2/5th R. Warwick. Regt.

Issued at 5.45 p.m.

Copies to:-
No. 1 to A.Coy.
    2   B.Coy.
    3   C.Coy.
    4   D.Coy.
    5   Battn. H.Q.
    6   C.Coy. 2/6th R.War.R.
    7   B.Coy. 2/8th R.War.R.
    8   D.Coy. 2/8th R.War.R.
    9   War Diary
   10   File

SECRET.

RED SQUARE OPERATION ORDER, NO. 86.   Copy No. 11
Reference, Sheet 27, 1/40000   September 13th 1917.
          " 28, 1/40000.

1. The 182nd Infantry Brigade moves to the WATOU No. 1 Area tomorrow the 14th inst. the Battalion proceeding to TAY Camp L.15.b.4.6. Route:- No. 1 Track to G.5.d.8.8 - cross roads G.5.d.0.2 - cross roads G.4.d.3.3 - road junction G.15.c.0.9 - cross roads G.20.a.4.4 - level crossing in L.17.d - road junction L.17.b.3.1. - road junction L.22.a.8.8.

2. Companies will march in the following order:- H.Qrs. & A. B. C. & D. Coys. and Transport, the head of the column passing the Starting Point (No. 1 Track at H.1.d.6.8) at 9.21 a.m. Dress, Marching Order, steel helmets to be worn. The Transport section will join the column at the road junction at G.5.c.6.4, keeping clear of the main road in the meantime. Field Kitchens and Company Lewis Gun Limbers will march with the Transport. Distances of 200 yards will be maintained between companies and between the rear company and Transport, east of POPERINGHE; 10 yards distance west of POPERINGHE. No halts will take place on the main YPRES - POPERINGHE road.

3. Officers' kits, Orderly Room boxes, Canteen Stores and H.Qrs. cooking utensils will be dumped by the side of the road near the Officers' lines ready for collection by the Transport at 8.0 a.m. Field Kitchens and Company Lewis Gun limbers will be ready loaded at the same time. Officers' mess boxes will be ready for collection at 8.30 a.m.

4. The camp will be cleaned and ready for inspection by Major F.W.FOSTER, M.C. at 9.0 a.m. No. 200944. Sergt. A.J.VERNON and 3 men per company will report to Major FOSTER at Battalion H.Qrs. at 9.15 a.m. as rear party. Certificates that company lines have been thoroughly cleaned will be handed to the Adjutant at the Starting Point.

5. Watches will be synchronised by Despatch Rider sent to companies about 8.0 a.m.

6. Condition of billets when taken over, falling out state and other returns will be sent to the Orderly Room as soon as possible after arrival in the new area.

7. ACKNOWLEDGE.

                                            Capt. & Adjt.

Issued at 2.30 p.m.
Copy No. 1 to C.O.
         2 to Adjutant.
         3 to H.Q.
         4 to A.Coy.
         5 to B.Coy.
         6 to C.Coy.
         7 to D.Coy.
         8 to Sec.Lieut. FARMER,
         9 to Quartermaster,
        10 to Transport Officer,
        11   War Diary
        12   File

SECRET.

RED SQUARE OPERATION ORDER, NO. 87.   Copy No. 10
Reference, Sheet 27, 1/40000   September 16th 1917.

Appendix 5

1. The Battalion will move tomorrow the 17th inst. to the EECKE Area. Route:— Road junction L.22.a.8.8 — HILHOEK — ABEELZE — STEENVOORDE.

2. Companies will march in the following order, H.Qrs. & B. C. D. and A. Coys. and Transport, the head of the column passing the Starting Point (cross roads at L.15.b.6.4) at 7.13 a.m. Dress, Marching order, steel helmets to be worn. Ten yards distance will be observed between companies and between the rear company and Transport. Field Kitchens and company Lewis Gun limbers will march with the Transport.

3. Company Lewis Gun limbers will be loaded at 7.0 p.m. tonight under the supervision of a Transport N.C.O. Officers' kits, Orderly Room boxes, H.Q. cooking utensils, Canteen Stores and Field Kitchens will be ready for collection by the Transport at 6.15 a.m. Officers' mess boxes will be ready for collection at 6.45 a.m.

4. The camp will be cleaned and tent flies rolled up ready for inspection by Major F.W.FOSTER, M.C. at 7.0 a.m. Each company will detail 3 O.R's as a rear party to report to Major FOSTER at Battalion H.Q. at 7.0 a.m. Certificates that company lines have been left thoroughly clean will be handed to the Adjutant at the Starting Point. Major FOSTER will hand over all tents to the Area Commandant or his representative and also obtain a signature for clean camp.

5. Watches will be synchronised by Despatch Rider sent to companies about 6.30 a.m.

6. Condition of billets when taken over, Falling out state and other returns will be sent to the Orderly Room as soon as possible after arrival in the new area.

7. ACKNOWLEDGE.

                                                    Capt. & Adjt.

Issued at 3.0 p.m.

Copy No. 1 to C.O.
        2 to Adjutant,
        3 to A.Coy.
        4 to B.Coy.
        5 to C.Coy.
        6 to D.Coy.
        7 to H.Qrs.
        8 to Transport Officer,
        9 to Quartermaster,
      10   War Diary
      11   File

SECRET.
RED SQUARE OPERATION ORDER, NO. 88.   Copy No. 9   Appendix 6
Reference — Sheet 27, 1/40000   September 17th 1917.
          LENS Sheet, 1/100000

1. The 61st Division is being transferred to the Third Army. The Battalion will proceed by train from CAESTRE Station at 3.0 p.m. tomorrow the 18th inst. detraining at ARRAS.

2. The Transport will arrive at CAESTRE Station at 12.0 noon under orders to be issued by the Transport Officer.
   Companies will march to the Station in the following order:- H.Qrs. D. A. B. & C. Coys. the head of the column passing the Starting Point (road junction at P.30.a.6.1) at 12.58 p.m. Dress, Marching Order. Ten yards distance will be observed between companies.
   Dinners will be served in time for Field Kitchens to be collected by the Transport Officer at 10.45 a.m. Haversack rations will be carried and men instructed that they will probably not have another meal until early on the morning of the 19th inst. Rations for the 19th inst. will be carried on the Field Kitchens.

3. Capt. L.T.V.BARNES will report to the R.T.O. at CAESTRE Station at 11.30 a.m. tomorrow and will act as entraining officer for the Battalion. The Transport Officer will provide a horse holder for each animal, also drag ropes for use as breast lines in the covered trucks. No lights will be lit in the train after dark. Fires of cookers will be drawn before entrainment. Water carts and water bottles will be full on entrainment.
   Sec.Lieut. A.E.PALMER and Sec.Lieut. F.DANIELS, M.C. will report to the R.T.O. at ARRAS Station on arrival, and will act as detraining officers for the Brigade group, as per instructions issued separately.
   "D" Coy. plus one platoon of "C" Coy. with Officer, (minimum total strength 150 O.R's) under Capt. F.J.BREEDEN, is detailed as unloading party for the Brigade group and will report to the R.T.O. at ARRAS Station immediately on arrival for work until the last train has been unloaded. The Q.M. will arrange for "D" Coy's field kitchen and rations for the whole party up to and including the 20th inst. to be handed to "D" Coy. at the detraining station.

4. Officers' kits, Officers' mess boxes (except one per company), Orderly Room boxes and H.Qrs. cooking utensils will be ready for collection by the Transport Officer at 10.0 a.m. H.Qrs. A. B. & C. Coys. will dump at Battalion H.Qrs. and D.Coy. at their own H.Q. One mess box per company may be kept back and dumped at the Q.M.Stores at 12.0 noon, when they will be taken to the Station by motor lorry.

5. Billets will be cleaned ready for inspection by Major F.W. FOSTER, M.C. at 12.15 p.m. Each company will detail a rear party of 1 N.C.O. and 2 men to report to Major FOSTER at their Coy. H.Q. Certificates that billets have been left thoroughly clean will be handed to the Adjutant at the Starting Point.

6. Watches will be synchronised by Despatch Rider sent to companies about 11.0 a.m.

7. Condition of billets when taken over, Falling-out states and other returns will be handed in to the Orderly Room as soon as possible after arrival in the new area.

8. ACKNOWLEDGE.

Issued at 7.0 p.m.

Copy No. 1 to C.O.
2 to H.Qrs.
3 to A.Coy.
4 to B.Coy.
5 to C.Coy.
6 to D.Coy.
7 to Quartermaster,
8 to Transport Officer,
9 War Diary
10 File

SECRET.

RED SQUARE OPERATION ORDER, NO. 89   Copy No. 10 Appendix 4
Reference — Sheet 51.C. 1/40000   September 21st 1917.
         "   51.B. 1/40000

1. The Battalion will move tomorrow the 22nd inst. to the ST. NICHOLAS Area, taking over from the 9th West Ridings at HULL CAMP at G.10.b.9.8. On arrival in the ST.NICHOLAS Area the Brigade will come under the orders of the G.O.C. 17th Division until the G.O.C. 61st Division assumes command at 10.0 a.m. on the 25th inst. Route:— DAINVILLE — road junction G.25.b.5.3 — cross roads G.20.d.0.4 — forked roads G.20.b.1.7 — G.21.a.3.6 — G.16.c.5.6 — G.10.b.9.8.

2. Companies will march in the following order:— H.Qrs. C. D. A. & B. Coys. and Transport (the latter being divided into two portions at 200 yards interval), the head of the column passing the Starting Point (road junction L.31.c.3.9) at 9.35 a.m. Dress, Marching Order, steel helmets to be worn. 200 yards distance will be observed between companies and between the rear company and Transport and 400 yards distance between Battalions. Owing to the shortage of maps, the leading company will be provided with maps and the remaining companies must maintain touch by connecting files thrown out where necessary. Field kitchens and company Lewis Gun limbers will march with the Transport.

3. Company Lewis Gun limbers will be loaded by 7.0 a.m. under the supervision of a Transport N.C.O. Officers' kits, Officers' mess boxes, Orderly Room boxes, H.Q. cooking utensils, Canteen stores and other stores will be dumped at the Q.M.Stores ready for loading by 9.0 a.m. Company storemen will report to R.Q.M.S. HOLT at the Q.M.Stores for loading party by 8.45 a.m. Field kitchens will be ready for collection by the Transport Officer at 9.0 a.m.

4. Billets will be cleaned ready for inspection by Capt. BREEDEN at 8.30 a.m. Each company will detail 3 O.R's as rear party to report to Capt. BREEDEN at their company H.Q. at 8.30 a.m. A.Coy's party to include one N.C.O. Certificates that company billets have been left thoroughly clean will be handed to the Adjutant at the Starting Point.

5. Watches will be synchronised by Despatch Rider sent to companies about 7.0 a.m.

6. Condition of billets when taken over, Falling-out states and other returns will be sent to the Orderly Room as soon as possible after arrival in the new area.

7. ACKNOWLEDGE.

                                        J.W. Blanchard
                                        Capt. & Actg. Adjt.

Issued at 11.0 p.m.

Copy No. 1 to C.O.   Copy No. 7 to H.Q.
         2 to Adjutant,   8 to Transport Officer
         3 to A.Coy.   9 to Quartermaster,
         4 to B.Coy.   10   War Diary
         5 to C.Coy.   11   File
         6 to D.Coy.

SECRET.

RED SQUARE OPERATION ORDER, NO. 90   Copy No. 11
Reference — Sheet 51.B. 1/40000   September 23rd 1917.

1. The Battalion will relieve the 8th Battalion South Staffs. Regiment in Left support today, companies taking over trenches from corresponding companies. Gudies for all companies will be at CAM VALLEY on the ARRAS-FAMPOUX road as follows:—

    A. & C. Coys. & Battn. H.Qrs. ... ... 3.30 p.m.
    B. & D. Coys. ... ... 9.0 p.m.

    Three guides per company and one for Battalion H.Qrs. will be provided. Company Sergeant Majors and one N.C.O. per platoon will move forward to take over stores reporting to company H.Qrs. in the line at 3.0 p.m. today.

2. Companies will march by platoons at 100 yards interval.

3. The Transport Officer will arrange transport for Lewis Guns and drums, company stores and Officers' trench kits to be collected and taken up with the companies. The Medical cart and stores will go up with rations under orders of the Transport Officer.

4. Relief complete will be notified to Battalion H.Qrs. by the usual code word.

5. ACKNOWLEDGE.

                Major.
       Comdg. 2/5th R. Warwick. Regt.

Issued at 9.30 a.m.

Copy No. 1 to C.O.
       2 to Adjutant,
       3 to H.Qrs.
       4 to A. Coy.
       5 to B. Coy.
       6 to C. Coy.
       7 to D. Coy.
       8 to Transport Officer,
       9 to Quartermaster,
     10 to 8th South Staffs. Regt.
     11   War Diary
     12   File.

SECRET.
RED SQUARE OPERATION ORDER, NO. 91.   Copy No. 12
Reference — Trench Map 75.a. etc.   Sept. 29th 1917.

Appendix 9

1. The Battalion will relieve the 2/6th R.War.R. in the Right Sub-section today. Companies will take over from opposite numbers and will be disposed as follows:-
    - D.Coy.   On the Left front.
    - C.Coy.   Centre.
    - B.Coy.   On the Right front.
    - A.Coy.   In Strong Points and Support.

   Routes will be as follows:-
    - B. & D. Coys.   Via COLT RESERVE to TUNNEL.
    - A. & C. Coys.   Via LINCOLN LANE — NORTHUMBERLAND LANE — SINGLE ARCH — TUNNEL.
    - Batt. H.Q.   Via NORTHUMBERLAND LANE to SINGLE ARCH

   Relief will commence at dusk, and all movement will be by platoons at 200 yards distance.

2. Guides will be provided as follows:-
    - For D.Coy.   At TUNNEL at 7.0 p.m.
    - B.Coy.   At TUNNEL at 7.30 p.m.
    - C.Coy.   At SINGLE ARCH at 7.15 p.m.
    - A.Coy.   At SINGLE ARCH at 7.45 p.m.
    - Batt. H.Q.   At SINGLE ARCH at 8.0 p.m.

3. All inward traffic after passing TUNNEL will be via CORDITE Trench and CORFU Trench.

4. Signallers and O.P. will be relieved by day.

5. Scouts under Sec.Lieut. A.E.PALMER will hold NO MAN'S LAND during relief, being relieved by a patrol from C.Coy. not later than midnight. C.Coy's patrol will come in at dawn. Snipers arranged by Sec.Lieut. DONALDSON will occupy NO MAN'S LAND during the day throughout the tour.

6. The Transport Officer will arrange for one limber to be at the disposal of Battalion H.Q. at TANK DUMP at 8.0 p.m.

7. One officer and one N.C.O. per company will take over work in hand, trench stores, photographs, maps and defence schemes during daylight.

8. Disposition sketches, Trench Store Lists and lists of R.E. material taken over are to be sent to Batt. H.Q. by 10.0 a.m. on the 30th inst. Similar lists of material handed over to the 2/8th R.War.R. to be sent in at the same time.

9. Watches will be synchronised by runner sent to companies between 4.0 p.m. and 6.0 p.m.

10. Relief complete will be reported to Battalion H.Q. by the usual code word.

11. ACKNOWLEDGE.

                                           Major.
                                  Comdg. 2/5th R. Warwick. Regt

SECRET.

2/6 WARWICK OPERATION ORDER NO. 91.
Reference :- Trench Map 7B.n.etc.

Copy No.
Sept. 25th 1917.

Issued at 12.30 p.m.

Copy No. 1 to C.O.
       2 to Adjutant.
       3 to H.Q.
       4 to A.Coy.
       5 to B.Coy.
       6 to C.Coy.
       7 to D.Coy.
       8 to Quartermaster,
       9 to Transport Officer,
      10. to 2/6th Warwicks.
      11 to 2/8th Warwicks
      12   War Diary
      13   File

1. The Battalion will relieve the 2/8th N.War.R. In the Night Sub-section today. Companies will take over from opposite numbers and will be guided into position.
   D.Coy.   C's the left front.
   C.Coy.   Centre.
   B.Coy.   On the right.
   A.Coy.   In Reserve and in Support.

   Routes will be as follows:-
   B. & D. Coys. Via GOLD STREET.
   A. & C. Coys. Via LINCOLN REACH and LONGSHOREMAND LANE
                  TUNNEL.
   Batt. H.Q.   Via TUNNEL and CORDITE TRENCH to SINGLE ARCH.

   Relief will commence at 6.0 p.m. and movement will be by platoons at 200 yards distance.

2. Guides will be provided as follows:-
   For D.Coy.   At TUNNEL at 7.0 p.m.
       B.Coy.   At TUNNEL at 7.10 p.m.
       C.Coy.   At SINGLE ARCH at 7.15 p.m.
       A.Coy.   At SINGLE ARCH at 7.45 p.m.
       Batt. H.Q. At SINGLE ARCH at 8.0 p.m.

3. All inward traffic after passing TUNNEL will be via CORDITE Trench and DOWNC Trench.

4. Signallers and O.I. will be relieved by day.

5. Scouts under Sec.Lieut. A.E.PALMER will hold NO MAN'S LAND during relief, being relieved by a patrol from C.Coy. not later than midnight. C.Coy. patrol will come in at dawn. Snipers arranged by Sec.Lieut. DONALDSON will occupy NO MAN'S LAND during the day throughout the tour.

6. The Transport Officer will arrange for one limber to be at the disposal of Battalion H.Q. at TANK DUMP at 8.0 p.m.

7. One officer and one N.C.O. per company will take over work in hand, trench stores, photographs, maps and defence scheme during day light.

8. Disposition Sketches, Trench Store lists and lists of R.E. material taken over are to be sent to Batt. H.Q. by 10.0 a.m. on the 26th inst. Similar lists of material handed over to the 2/6th N.War.R. to be sent in at the same time.

9. Watches will be synchronised by runner sent to companies between 4.0 p.m. and 6.0 p.m.

10. Relief complete will be reported to Battalion H.Q. by the usual code word.

11. ACKNOWLEDGE.

Major.
Comdg. 2/6th R. Warwick. Regt.

Confidential.

War Diary

of

2/1st Bn. The Royal Warwickshire Regt.

From Oct 1st to Oct 31st 1917.

Army Form C. 2118.

WAR DIARY
or
INTELLIGENCE SUMMARY.

(Erase heading not required.)

Place	Date	Hour	Summary of Events and Information	Remarks and references to Appendices
CHEMICAL WORKS	1/10/17	-	Strength of Battn. 27 offrs 685 OR. In front line. Right Sub Sector	L.W.B.
"	2/10/17	-	"	L.W.B.
"	3/10/17	-	"	L.W.B.
"	4/10/17	-	"	L.W.B.
"	5/10/17	-	Relieved by the 2nd R.War. Reg. Relief completed 10.40pm	L.W.B. appendix 1
PUDDING TRENCH	6/10/17	-	In support. CHEMICAL WORKS SECTOR.	L.W.B.
"	7/10/17	-	In support	L.W.B.
"	8/10/17	-	"	L.W.B.
"	9/10/17	-	"	L.W.B.
"	10/10/17	-	"	L.W.B.
CHEMICAL WORKS	11/10/17	-	Relieved the 16th R.War. Reg. on CHEMICAL WORKS. Relief complete 9.45 pm	L.W.B. appendix 2
"	12/10/17	-	In front line.	L.W.B.
"	13/10/17	-	Battn. holding front line of right subsection CHEMICAL WORKS sector.	L.W.B.
"	14/10/17	-	B Coy successfully raided enemy trenches at 9.30pm	L.W.B. appendix 3
"	15/10/17	"		
"	16/10/17	-	Battn. relieved in front line by 1/8th WORCESTERS & moved to LANCASTER CAMP, ARRAS. Relief complete at 10.10 pm Appendix 4	L.W.B.

Army Form C. 2118.

WAR DIARY
or
INTELLIGENCE SUMMARY.

(Erase heading not required.)

Instructions regarding War Diaries and Intelligence Summaries are contained in F. S. Regs., Part II. and the Staff Manual respectively. Title pages will be prepared in manuscript.

Place	Date	Hour	Summary of Events and Information	Remarks and references to Appendices
LANCASTER CAMP	17/10/17	—	Bathing & general cleaning up	
ST NICHOLAS	18/10/17	—	Company Training. Range practice for Lewis Gunners	
"	19/10/17	—	Range practice	
"	20/10/17	—	Battn moved to the PRISON BARRACKS, ARRAS.	
ARRAS	21/10/17	9am	Battn Muster Parade. 10am Church Parade.	
"	22/10/17	9am	Battn Muster Parade. Company Specialist Training	
"	23/10/17	—	" " " Range practice.	
"	24/10/17	—	" " " "	
"	25/10/17	—	" " " "	
"	26/10/17	—	" " " "	
"	27/10/17	—	" " " "	
"	28/10/17	—	Battn relieved 2/1st BUCKS R. in LEFT SUPPORT, GREENLAND HILL SECTOR. Relief complete at 6.40 pm.	W/Appendix 5
GREENLAND HILL SECTOR	29/10/17	—	Battn in LEFT SUPPORT. Working parties.	
"	30/10/17	—	" " "	
"	31/10/17	—	" " "	

Strength of Battn 38 Offs. 709 O.R.
Casualties for month = 3 Offs. 52 O.R.
Reinforcements — 14 Offs. 76 O.R.

M80 Lt. Maj Cmdg 2/1st R. Ber. R.

SECRET.
RED SQUARE OPERATION ORDER, NO. 92.   Copy No.
Reference – FAMPOUX Map 1/10000   October 4th 1917.
            GREENLAND HILL Map 1/10000

1. The Battalion will be relieved by the 2/6th R.War.R. on the
   night of 5th/6th inst. the 2/5th R.War.R. withdrawing to right
   support. No movement except in the case of signallers and
   Lewis gunners, in connection with the relief, will take place
   before 7.15 p.m. Subsequently all movement will be by
   platoons at 200 yards distance.

   D.Coy. 2/6th R.War.R. will relieve D.Coy. 2/5th R.War.R.
         on the Left, who will move to PUDDING TRENCH.
   C.Coy. 2/6th R.War.R. will relieve C.Coy. 2/5th R.War.R.
         in the Centre, who will move to CRETE TRENCH.
   A.Coy. 2/6th R.War.R. will relieve B.Coy. 2/5th R.War.R.
         on the Right, who will move to PUDDING TRENCH.
   B.Coy. 2/6th R.War.R. will relieve A.Coy. 2/5th R.War.R.
         in support, who will move to FAMPOUX.
   Batt. H.Q. 2/6th R.War.R. will relieve Battn. H.Q. 2/5th
         R.War.R. who will move to PEPPER TRENCH.

2. One guide per platoon and one per company H.Q. will be at
   SINGLE ARCH at 7.45 p.m. Each guide will be provided with a
   note shewing which platoon he is to guide, and where to.
   They will arrive in the following order and move by the routes
   shewn:-
   D.Coy. & "B" Post, 2/6th R.War.R. via CHEMICAL TRENCH.
   A. & C. Companies, 2/6th R.War.R. via CORFU TRENCH.
   B.Coy. remainder 2/6th R.War.R. via CORFU TRENCH, "A" Post
         leading.
   Battalion H.Q. personnel will require no guide.

   2/5th R.War.R. troops moving out will use the following
   routes:-
   C. & D. Coys. via CHEMICAL TRENCH.
   A. & B. Coys. via CORFU TRENCH.

   The O.P. Signals, and two men per Lewis Gun team will move
   in by day, but no troops will move out except with their
   companies.

3. Sec.Lieut. PALMER and Battalion scouts will hold NO MAN'S LAND
   from dusk until 9.0 p.m. when they will return via CORFU TRENCH.

4. One N.C.O. and one man from each company will be sent out to
   take over billets and stores by daylight.

5. The Transport Officer will arrange for limbers to bring up
   Officers' kits for C.Coy. to SINGLE ARCH. These limbers will
   remain to take back Officers' kits and mess boxes, for A. Coy.
   to FAMPOUX; Battn. H.Q. (including Medical Stores and Orderly
   Room boxes), B. & D. Coys. to junction of PUDDING TRENCH and
   ARRAS-FAMPOUX road. Also to bring up Officers' valises, those
   for Battn. H.Q. B. & D. Coys. being dumped at PUDDING TRENCH
   and those for A.Coy. at FAMPOUX. For the information of the
   Transport Officer, four new officers arrived today and are
   posted as follows:-
           Sec.Lieut. A.W.BARNES,   A.Coy.
              "   A.E.WINTER,   B.Coy.
              "   E.T.HARRIS,   C.Coy.
              "   R.J.CROWE,   D.Coy.
   These Officers' kits will be distributed accordingly.

\- 2 -

O.C. Bttn. H.Q. Coy. will arrange for police sentry at SINGLE ARCH and PUDDING TRENCH for dumps of officers' kits, mess boxes, etc. until moved away by the Transport.

6. All maps, aeroplane photographs, defence schemes and trench stores will be handed over and receipts sent in to Battalion H.Q. on completion of relief.

7. All petrol tins in the line not originally taken over as Trench stores will be dumped at SINGLE ARCH, handed over to the police and equally divided between A. & C. Companies, who will give receipts to the Provost Corporal.

8. All work in hand will be fully explained to relieving companies in order to ensure continuity.

9. Watches will be synchronised by Despatch Rider sent to companies during the day.

10. Completion of relief will be reported to Battalion H.Q. by the usual code word.

11. ACKNOWLEDGE.

[signature] Major.
Comdg. 2/5th R. Warwick. Regt.

Issued at 9.0 p.m.

Copy No. 1 to C.O.
       2 to Adjutant,
       3 to H.Q.
       4 to A.Coy.
       5 to B.Coy.
       6 to C.Coy.
       7 to D.Coy.
       8 to Quartermaster,
       9 to Transport Officer,
     10 to 2/6th Warwicks
     11   War Diary
     12   File.

C O P Y.

Headquarters,
    182nd Infantry Brigade.

With reference to your Operation Order No. 135 of 9/10/17.

I beg to report that the raid was successfully carried out on the night of 14th/15th inst. the arrangements in my Operation Order No. 94 being exactly adhered to.

Zero was fixed at 9.30 p.m. but two hours previously a patrol under Lieut. R.K.SPURRELL was sent out to reconnoitre the gap. The night was clear and it was easily found, but the patrol was challenged and bombed. The parties were lying out before the gaps specially cut in our wire before Zero, and at Zero plus 3 rushed forward. A good gap was cut in the wire at exactly the position desired and the leading party entered the German gap which was considerably blown about, the head being almost obliterated. The left party on turning to the left found two dug-outs in the front line under the parapet with about eight steps leading down to each. The first one was unoccupied, but a sentry standing alone was taken prisoner. A second dug-out was encountered and three Germans killed after hard fighting. A bomb was then thrown down and two wounded and three unwounded prisoners taken. The area allotted to this party was almost completely searched when the whistle went, and on the way back two more unwounded prisoners were taken, who had evidently just left the last dug-out. This dug-out was blown up by the R.E. before retirement.

The right party found six small dug-outs in the front line to the right of the point of entry, each with about seven or eight steps. They bombed all of them, but only two prisoners were taken, the remaining occupants being probably killed. Owing to the number of dug-outs encountered, this party was unable to complete searching the area before the signal to retire. The remaining two parties searched the support trenches as far as possible, two more prisoners being taken.

The O.C. Raid wisely decided to withdraw his party at Zero plus 15, owing to the number of prisoners already through his hands and to the degree of enemy resistance.

All the German trenches are reported to be without duck-boards, except the communication trench leading back from the point of entry. They were about six feet deep and only about four feet wide. No concrete dug-outs or emplacements were encountered. The trenches generally were in good condition (unrevetted) although very badly knocked about by artillery and trench mortar fire.

The absence of enemy light signals was noticeable except for a few put up on the southern side of the SCARPE and one or two red lights near the railway cutting. There was little, if any retaliation, which shows that the enemy Trench Mortars were effectively dealt with.

The Artillery and Trench Mortar barrage opened to time and was exceedingly good. All targets were reported to have been effectively dealt with, and I do not think their shooting could have been improved upon.

Twelve prisoners were taken and at least five Germans were killed by hand to hand fighting in the trench. Other dug-outs were bombed and it is estimated that at least another thirty casualties were caused. Probably many other casualties were caused by the Artillery, Trench Mortar and Machine Gun fire.

Our casualties were four O.R's very slightly wounded (all at duty).

The strength of our raiding party was two officers and thirty O.R's actually entering the German trenches. One officer and twenty-three O.Rs. were on duty on the parapet and in NO MAN'S LAND.

The raid was excellently planned and carried out by Capt. F.J.BREEDEN, who shewed untiring energy training his party and whose cool courage gave the greatest confidence to his subordinates.

           (Signed)   P.L.COATES.

                      Lieut. Col.
         Comdg. 2/5th R. Warwick. Regt.

14/10/17.

SECRET.

RED SQUARE OPERATION ORDER, NO. 93   Copy No. 10
Reference – FAMPOUX MAP 1/10000   October 10th 1917.
          GREENLAND HILL Map 1/10000

Appendix 8

1. The Battalion will relieve the 2/6th R.War.R. on the night of 11th/12th inst. in the Right Front Sub-sector in accordance with the attached table.

2. No movement, except in the case of Signallers and Lewis gunners in connection with the relief will take place before 7.0 p.m. All movement will be by platoons at 200 yards distance.

3. Sec.Lieut. PALMER and Battalion Scouts will hold NO MAN'S LAND from dusk until 10.0 p.m. when they will be relieved by patrols from companies in the front line.

4. One N.C.O. and one man per company will be sent out to take over trench stores by daylight.

5. The Transport Officer will arrange for limbers to pick up Officers' kits and mess boxes for Battalion H.Q. from PUDDING TRENCH – A.Coy. from FAMPOUX – C.Coy. from SINGLE ARCH, and to carry Medical Stores and Orderly Room boxes from PUDDING TRENCH to SINGLE ARCH.

6. All maps, aeroplane photographs, defence schemes and trench stores will be taken over and receipts sent in to Battalion H.Q. on completion of relief.

7. All petrol tins belonging to the Battalion will remain with the companies now using them.

8. Relieving companies will obtain details of work in hand in order to ensure continuity.

9. Watches will be synchronised by Despatch Rider sent to companies during the day.

10. Completion of relief will be reported by the usual code word.

11. ACKNOWLEDGE.

                         J.W. Blanchard,
                         Capt. & A/Adjt.
                         2/5th R. Warwick. Regt.

Issued at 9.0 p.m.

Copy No. 1 to C.O.
        2 to Adjutant
        3 to H.Q.
        4 to A.Coy.
        5 to B.Coy.
        6 to C.Coy.
        7 to D.Coy.
        8 to Quartermaster,
        9 to Transport Officer,
     10   War Diary
     11   File

Relief Table issued with RED SQUARE OPERATION ORDER
No. 93. October 10th 1917.

Company	Position	Guide	Route in	Time Pass S.P.
C.Coy. 2/5th Warwicks relieve C.Coy. 2/6th Warwicks	Centre	One at junc. of CRETE and CORFU at 7.45 p.m.	SINGLE ARCH and CORFU	CRETE TRENCH at 7.45 p.m.
A.Coy. 2/5th Warwicks relieve D.Coy. 2/6th Warwicks	Left Front.	3 at CHEMICAL TRENCH at 7.45 p.m.	CHEMICAL, CROW and COCOA	Entrance to CHEMICAL AT 7.45 p.m.
"B" Post of B.Coy. 2/6th Warwicks. relieve "B" Post of A.Coy. 2/6th Warwicks	"B" Post	Nil	-do-	Entrance to CHEMICAL at 7.50 p.m.
B.Coy. 2/6th Warwicks with "A" Post leading relieve Remainder of A.Coy. 2/6th Warwicks.	"A" Post & Support	Nil	SINGLE ARCH & CORFU	SINGLE ARCH at 8.0 p.m.
H.Q. 2/5th Warwicks relieve H.Q. 2/6th Warwicks	CRETE	Nil	SINGLE ARCH	SINGLE ARCH at 8.15 p.m.

REMARKS.

Two men per Lewis Gun, Signaller for O.P. two Signallers per company and four for H.Q. Company will relieve by day.

Appendix 3

SECRET.

RED SQUARE OPERATION ORDER, NO. 94. Copy No. 16
Reference - Map 6I.M90 and attached sketch. Oct. 11th 1917.

1. "D" Company will raid the enemy front and support trenches between I.14.c.75.17 and I.14.c.88.46 on a date to be notified later. Objects of raid:-
    (a) To secure prisoners, wounded or unwounded and to inflict casualties.
    (b) To collect papers, maps and identifications.
    (c) To destroy any enemy M.Gs, T.Ms. or dug-outs.

2. Composition of parties:-
    O.C. Raid - Capt. F.J.BREEDEN.
    2 signallers with telephone and duplicate wire of D.5 cable.
    Two Wire cutters to improve passage in wire for exit.
    6 Parapet men.
    2 Tape men.
    2 Lewis gunners, with gun.
    4 S.B. with two stretchers.

    Four Storming Parties as follows:-
        4 Bayonet men for A. & D. parties.
        2 Bayonet Men for C. Party.
        8 Bayonet men for B. Party.
        Each party also having.
        1 Officer or N.C.O.
        2 Intelligence men.
        1 R.E. man with explosives.

    Rear party in our front line:-
    C.O.
    F.O.O. and signaller with telephone.
    2 signallers with telephone
    Lieut. DONALDSON and 8 O.R. for collection of stores and prisoners.

3. DRESS:- Box respirators in "Alert" position.
    Rifle with bayonet fixed and magazine charged.
    30 rounds in right jacket pocket.
    2 Mills' bombs (Storming & Parapet parties only)
    Faces blacked.
    White patches (size about 6 inches) sewn on back as follows:-

No. A. Storming Party	- Square.
B. -do-	- Triangular.
C. -do-	- Triangular, upside (down
D. -do-	- Oblong.
All others	- Circular.

    Leaders will also carry one "P" Bomb each.
    Intelligence men will also carry a sandbag, slung over one shoulder by a sling and an electric torch.
    2 Parapet men will carry shovels.
    Wire cutters will carry large wire cutters and red torch.
    R.E. men will also carry a mobile charge.
    Parapet men will also carry whistles.
    No papers, pay books, maps or badges will be worn or taken.
    All bombs will be carefully cleaned and oiled.

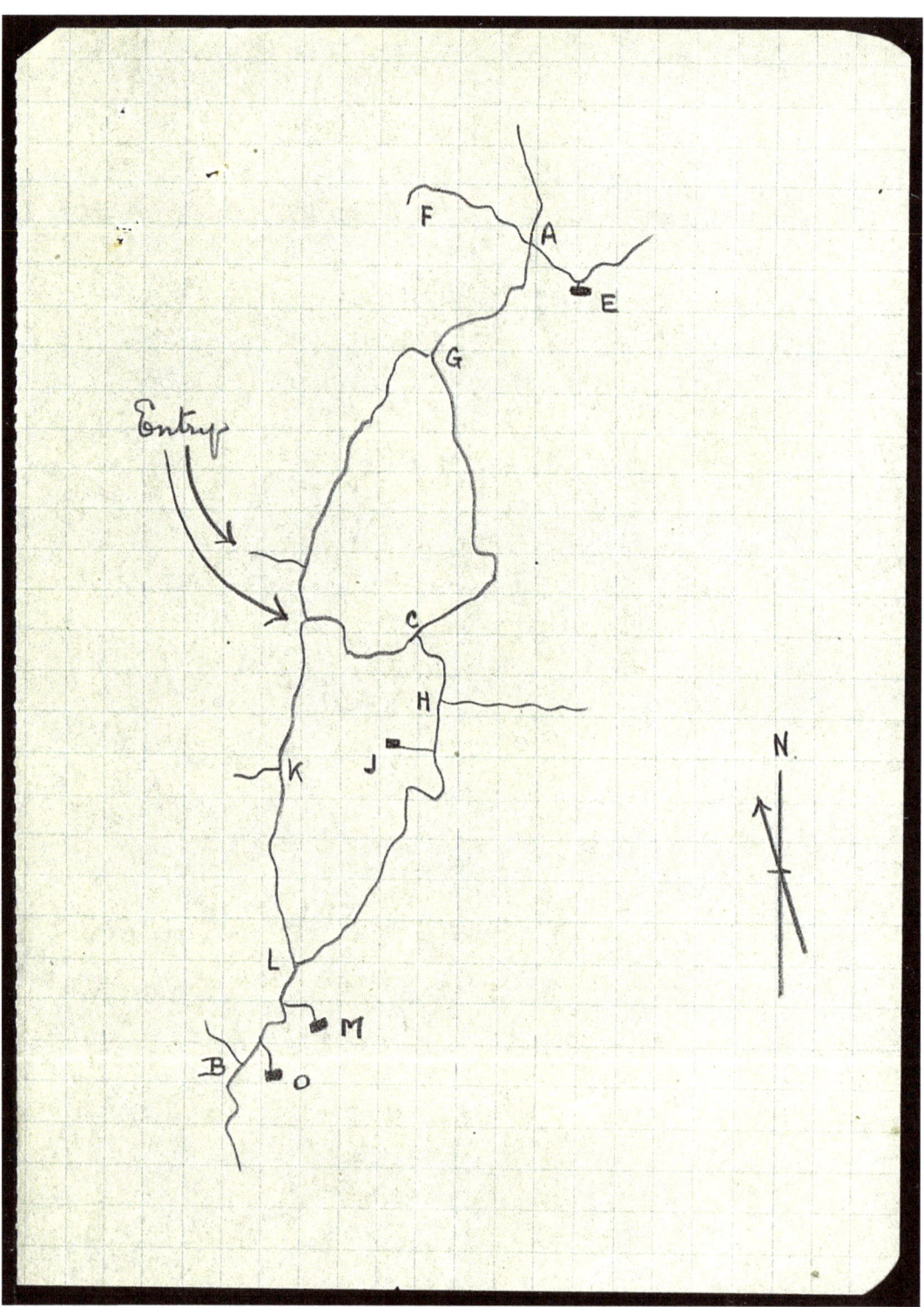

- 2 -

4. Artillery Programme – As per Appendix "A".

5. Trench Mortar Programme – As per Appendix "B"

6. Machine Gun Programme – As per Appendix "C".

7. The signal for the T.Ms. and M.Gs. to open fire will be the firing of a salvo at ZERO by the Artillery. In the event of the Officers' patrol finding the wire uncut, a message will be sent them and the raid postponed.

8. At ZERO, minus 90, the parties will arrive in our front line via CORFU AVENUE.
    At ZERO minus 60, an Officers' patrol will be sent out by "D" Coy. to examine the gap in the enemy wire. Two men will be left there to observe until ZERO minus 10.
    At ZERO minus 30, the parties will move over the parapet in position in front of the gaps specially cut in our wire. This assembly must be completed and all ranks lying flat before ZERO minus 5.
    At ZERO minus 5, saps 1, 3 & 4 will be cleared. They will be re-occupied immediately the blue rockets are fired.
    At ZERO plus 3, the parties will dash forward through the gap and enter the German trench in the following order:-
    No. A. Storming Party.
          B.   -do-
          C.   -do-
          D.   -do-
    O.C. Raid.
    Signallers.
    Parapet party.
    Tape men.
    Stretcher Bearers
    Wire Cutters
No. A. party via sap at I.14.c.76.35, remainder at I.14.c.79.30

9. No. A. Storming party will go to the left on reaching the main trench and block at point A, dropping two men at point G, sending two men to clear dug-out E, They will send two men to clear sap F when the supports arrive.
    No. B. Storming party will go to the right from point of entry and block at point B, dropping two men to clear sap K, two sentries at point L, and two men at each M. and O. to clear dug-outs there.
    No. C. Storming Party will go straight on from point of entry, turning to the right at point C, searching point J, and going on to support No. B. party at point L.
    No. D. Storming party will go straight on from point of entry, turning to the left at point C, leaving two sentries there and going on to support No. A. party at point G.
    All trenches will be cleared on the way and dug-outs bombed, prisoners and heavy booty being handed up to the parapet party.
    The Intelligence men will follow their own parties and carefully search all dug-outs and enemy dead for papers, maps and shoulder straps. They will report to O.C. Raid when their area is clear.
    R.E. men with parties will carry explosives to destroy any dug-outs or any T.Ms. or M.Gs. it may not be possible to remove.

Parapet men will line the enemy parapet and take over prisoners and salvage, working with A. & B. Storming parties. They will (in conjunction with the Lewis gunners) also see that the enemy do not come over the open in rear of their front line. Those near point of entry will shovel earth and push sandbags into the German trench to facilitate exit.

Wire cutters will immediately improve the gap in the enemy wire as soon as all parties are through. They will devote their attention to the track of the tape to facilitate the withdrawal. When the first golden rain rocket is fired, they will shine their red torches at intervals to guide the parties back.

Stretcher Bearers will remain near O.C. Raid.

Tape men and signallers will act as per para. 10. Both tape men will also act as parapet men after they have laid their tapes and will, in addition, cut the tapes on their return just our side of the German wire.

B.Coy's Lewis gunners will cover the flanks of the raiders.

The O.C. Raid will leave a cap of another regiment in the German trench.

10. COMMUNICATION.

Two lines of D.5 cable will be connected with advanced Battalion H.Q. at I.14.c.55.43. and to the right company H.Q. and carried out by the two signallers (one also having a telephone) who will be at least at 15 yards interval and at least 20 yards wide of all tape. They will both join up to O.C. Raid on the enemy parapet.

The two tape men will carry out two broad white tapes (one from front line near Sap 1 and one from front line near Sap 2) through the gaps in our wire to the enemy parapet where they will run outwards and lay them along the parapet as far as the Storming parties have gone.

A pass-word will be communicated to all ranks immediately beforehand.

11. RETURN.

When all the Intelligence men have reported and the O.C. Raid is satisfied that the area has been cleared, he will signal the withdrawal by blowing a whistle and ordering "C.I", both being repeated by all parapet men. The signaller with O.C. Raid will signal "C.I" to our line. For 20 minutes after this signal a golden rain rocket will be sent up every minute from CORFU AVENUE near the CHALKPIT to assist in guiding back the parties. When all the raiders are in, blue rockets will be sent up from our line.

    Order of return as follows:-
        Nos. C. & D. Storming parties.
        A. & B.   -do-
        Parapet men (on order of O.C. Raid, "Parapet party "C.I").
        Signallers.
        Stretcher bearers.
        Lewis Gunners.
        O.C. Raid.

Every effort will be made to bring in casualties, but this duty will not be performed by anybody except the stretcher bearers until after the signal to withdraw.

The parties will assemble in CORDITE RESERVE, where all leaders will check their parties and report to Sec.Lieut. PALMER. A traffic control sentry will be posted by Sec.Lieut. PALMER at the junction of CORFU AVENUE and CORDITE RESERVE.

The command "RETIRE" is not to be used or obeyed.

12. The advanced Regimental Aid Post will be established by the M.O. by the re-assembly point in CORDITE RESERVE.

13. Luminous watches will be carried by all leaders and will be synchronised by the Signalling Officer about 6.0 p.m.

14. Men with coughs and colds will not be taken.

15. Date and ZERO hour will be notified later.

16. ACKNOWLEDGE.

Lieut. Col.
Comdg. 2/5th R. Warwick. Regt.

Issued at 10.0 p.m.

Copies to:-

No. 1 to 61 Division (through 182 Inf. Brigade)
2. 182 Infantry Brigade.
3. C.O.
4. Major FOSTER.
5. Signalling Officer,
6. Lieut. DONALDSON.
7. A.Coy.
8. B.Coy.
9. C.Coy.
10)
11) D.Coy.
12. 182 T.M.B.
13. Medium T.M.B.
14. 182 M.G. Coy.
15. 307 Brigade, R.F.A.
16. War Diary
17. File

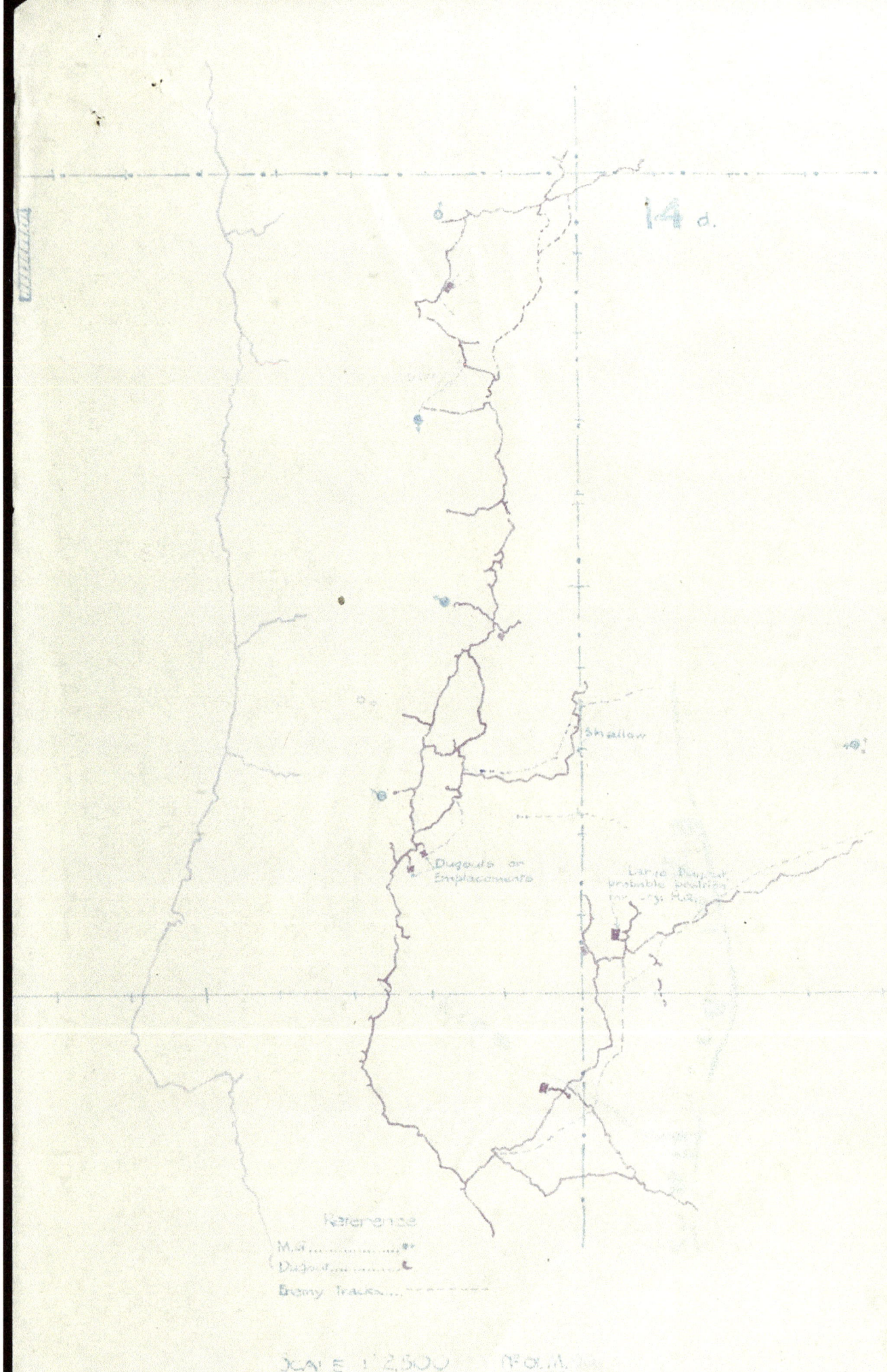

SECRET.   APPENDIX "A"

ARTILLERY PROGRAMME.

IN SUPPORT OF RAID BY 2/5 WARWICKS NIGHT 14/15 OCTOBER 1917.

Time. From	To.	Unit.	No. of Guns.	Objective.	Rate of Fire.	Remarks.
18-PDRS.						
0.0	0.3	70 Bde.	6	CORN TRENCH I.20.a.97.80. to I.14.d.20.15.	4 rds. p.g.p.m.	75% AX 25% A.
0.3	0.7	70 Bde.	6	do.	3 rds. p.g.p.m.	do.
0.7 onwards.		70 Bde.	6	do.	2 rds. p.g.p.m.	do.
18-PDRS.						
0.0	0.3	307 Bde.	4	I.20.b.10.90.-I.14.d.05.30.	4 rds. p.g.p.m.	do.
			4	I.14.c.90.75.-I.14.b.00.10.		
			8	I.20.a.90.65.-I.14.c.74.00.		
0.3	0.7	307 Bde.	4	I.14.b.6.3.-I.14.b.70.15.-I.14.d.52.25.	3 rds. p.g.p.m.	do.
			4	I.14.c.90.75.-I.14.b.00.10.		
			8	I.20.a.90.65.-I.14.c.74.00.		
0.7 onwards.		307 Bde.	4	I.14.b.6.3.-I.14.b.70.15.-I.14.d.52.25.	2 rds. p.g.p.m.	do.
			4	I.14.c.90.75.-I.14.b.00.10.		
			8	I.20.a.90.65.-I.14.c.74.00.		
18-PDRS.						
0.0	0.3	306 Bde.	12	I.14.b.00.10.-I.14.a.95.60.	4 rds. p.g.p.m.	do.
0.3	0.7	306 Bde.	6	CLOD I.14.b.00.10.-I.14.b.6.3.	3 rds. p.g.p.m.	do.
			6	CANDY I.14.b.6.3.-I.14.b.30.75.		
0.7 onwards.		306 Bde.	6	CLOD I.14.b.00.10.-I.14.b.6.3.	2 rds. p.g.p.m.	do.
			6	CANDY I.14.b.6.3.-I.14.b.30.75.		

P.T.O.

Time. From To.	Unit.	No. of Guns.	Objective.	Rate of Fire.	Remarks.

4.5" HOWITZERS.

Time. From To.	Unit.	No. of Guns.	Objective.	Rate of Fire.	Remarks.
0.0 onwards.	306 Bde.	2	I.15.d.1.4. - M.G.	1 rd per How per min.	
		1	Junction CLOD and CANDY I.14.b.65.35.	do.	
		1	Junction CLOD and CANDY I.14.b.67.25.	do.	
0.0 onwards	307 Bde.	1	I.14.d.3.3. - M.G. and dug-outs.	do.	
		1	Trench junction in CYRIL at I.15.c.15.65.	do.	
		1	HAUSA WOOD.	do.	
		1	WINDMILL COPSE.		

1. The signal for Trench Mortars and Machine Guns to open fire will be the firing of a Salvo at Zero by the Artillery.

2. GOLDEN RAIN Rockets will be fired from the vicinity of the CHALK PIT, I.13.d.45.40. as a signal for the raiders to return. This signal will continue at 1 minute intervals during the withdrawal as a guide for direction.

3. When Raid H.Q. have returned to our lines, BLUE Rockets will be fired by order of O.C. 2/5 Warwicks. from I.14.c.55.40., on which signal all Trench Mortars, Machine Guns and 18-pounders will cease fire, and 4.5" Hows. will switch on to the following T.M.E's for 10 minutes as follows :-

    307 Bde. (i) I.14.b.70.50.
              (ii) I.15.c.05.47.
             (iii) I.14.b.90.50.
             (iv) I.20.b.60.95.

    306 Bde. (i) I.8.d.45.10.
              (ii) I.14.b.20.15.
             (iii) I.8.d.50.60.
             (iv) I.8.d.35.25.

    Rate of fire :- 1 round per How. per minute.

4. No notice will be taken of any BLUE Rockets previous to the first GOLDEN RAIN Rocket.

SECRET.   APPENDIX "B".

TRENCH MORTAR PROGRAMME.
IN SUPPORT OF RAID BY 2/5 WARWICKS NIGHT 14/15 OCTOBER 1917.

Time. From. To.	Formation.	Unit.	Position.	Target.	Rate of fire.
0.0 0.3	Rt.H.T.M.Group. (61 Div)	6" Stokes No. A.1.	I.13.d.45.45.	I.14.c.84.23.	4 rounds per gun per minute.
		do. A.2.	do.	I.14.c.86.28.	do.
		do. A.3.	I.14.a.15.65.	I.14.c.88.46.	do.
do.	15th Div.T.M's.	2" M.T.M. No. 1	I.14.c.40.67.	I.14.c.85.27.	1 round per gun per minute.
do.		6" Stokes.(1 gun)		I.14.c.77.17.	4 rounds per gun per minute.
do.	182nd L.T.M.B.	3" Stokes.(5 guns)	Sunker road at I.14.c.43.10.	Front line from I.14.c.76.26. to I.14.c.85.42.	20 rounds per gun per minute.
		do. (1 gun)	I.8.c.05.30.	I.14.a.95.50.	do.
0.3 on-wards.	Rt.H.T.M.Group. (61 Div)	6" Stokes No. A.1.	I.13.d.45.45.	I.14.d.05.05.	1 round per gun per minute.
		do. A.2.	do.	I.14.d.38.30.	do.
		do. A.3.	I.14.a.15.85.	I.14.c.80.71.	do.
	15th Div.T.M's.	2" M.T.M. (1 gun)		I.20.a.97.86.	do.
0.0 on-wards.	Rt.H.T.M.Group.	2" M.T.M. No. 2.	I.14.c.40.76.	I.14.c.30.71.(L.G.E.)	1 round per gun per minute.
		do. 3.	I.14.a.10.03.	I.14.b.05.70.(M.G.E.)	do.
		do. 4.	I.14.a.15.05.	I.14.a.97.50.	do.
		do. 5.	I.14.a.30.95.	I.14.b.40.05.	do.
		do. (1 gun)		I.20.a.85.73.	do.
		do. (do.)		I.20.b.07.77.	do.
	15th Div.T.M's.	3" Stokes.(1 gun)	I.14.c.09.49.	I.14.c.85.X.	
	182nd L.T.M.B.	do. (do.)	I.14.a.35.23.	I.14.c.80.71. (H.G.E.)	(i) 10 rounds per gun per minute from Zero to Zero plus 15.
		do. (do.)	I.14.a.40.25.	I.14.c.79.84.	(ii) 5 rounds per gun per minute from Zero plus 15 onwards.

NOTE:- The following guns cease fire at 0.3 :-
   (i) The 5 3" Stokes at I.14.c.46.10.
   (ii) The 1 3" Stokes at I.8.c.05.30.
   (iii) 2" M.T.M. No. 1 at I.14.c.40.67.

1. The signal for Trench Mortars and Machine Guns to open fire will be the firing of a salvo at Zero by the Artillery.

2. GOLDEN RAIN Rockets will be fired from the vicinity of the CHALK PIT, I.13.d.45.40. as a signal for the raiders to return. This signal will be continued at 1 minute intervals during the withdrawal as a guide for direction.

3. When Raid H.Q. have returned to our lines, BLUE Rockets will be fired by order of O.C. 2/5 Warwicks, from I.14.c.55.40., on which signal all Trench Mortars, Machine Guns and 18-pounders will cease fire, and 4.5" Hows. will switch on to the following T.M.E's for 10 minutes as follows :-

```
307 Bde.    (i)   I.14.b.70.50.
            (ii)  I.15.c.05.47.
            (iii) I.14.b.90.50.
            (iv)  I.20.b.60.85.

306 Bde.    (i)   I.8.d.45.10.
            (ii)  I.14.b.20.15.
            (iii) I.8.d.50.60.
            (iv)  I.8.d.35.25.
```

Rate of fire :- 1 round per How. per minute.

4. No notice will be taken of any BLUE Rockets previous to the first GOLDEN RAIN Rocket.

S E C R E T.   APPENDIX "C".

MACHINE GUN PROGRAMME.

IN SUPPORT OF RAID BY 2/5 WARWICKS - NIGHT OF 14/15th OCTOBER 1917.

Time From — To.	Unit.	Gun No.	Position.	Target.	Rate of Fire.
Zero - Onwards.	182 M.G.Coy.	17 18	I.19.a.35.95. I.13.c.15.35.	Search railway embankment from I.14.b.35.80. to I.9.c.20.15.	(i) 250 rounds per gun per minute from Zero to Zero plus 5. (ii) 150 rounds per gun per minute from Zero plus 5 onwards.
do.	do.	19 20	I.13.c.10.70. H.18.b.95.20.	Traverse bank I.15.c.9.9. to I.15.d.C5.25.	do.
do.	do.	31 32	H.18.a.85.45. H.18.a.75.75.	Traverse and search road from CHALK PIT (I.20.b.8.9.) to I.15.c.00.25.	do.
do.	do.	21 22	H.12.d.70.35. H.12.d.70.50.	Search track from CHALK PIT (I.20.b.6.9.) to S.W. corner of DELBAR WOOD.	do.
do.	15th Div.M.G's.	4 guns		Search tracks leading from PLOUVAIN S.W. and N. to CRUST and CORN.	do.

1. The signal for Trench Morters and Machine Guns to open fire will be the firing of a salvo at Zero by the Artillery.
2. GOLDEN RAIN Rockets will be fired from the vicinity of the CHALK PIT, I.13.d.45.40. as a signal for the raiders to return. This signal will continue at 1 minute intervals during the withdrawal as a guide for direction to return.
3. "*her Raid H.Q. have returned to* our lines, BLUE Rockets will be fired from I.14.c.55.40., on which signal all Trench Morters, Machine Guns and 18-pounders will cease fire and 4.5" Hows. will switch on to the following T. E's for 10 minutes as follows:- → by order of O.C. 2/5 Warwicks
   307 Bde. (i) I.14.b.70.50. (ii) I.15.c.05.47. (iii) I.14.b.90.50. (iv) I.20.b.30.85.
   306 Bde. (i) I.8.d.45.10.   (ii) I.14.b.20.15. (iii) I.8.d.50.80.   (iv) I.8.d.35.25.
   Rate of Fire :- 1 round per Ho. per minute.
4. No notice will be taken of any BLUE Rockets previous to the first GOLDEN RAIN Rocket.

SECRET   Appendix 4
RED SQUARE OPERATION ORDER, NO. 95.   Copy No. 11
Reference – Sheet 51.B. N.W. 1/20000   October 15th 1917.
         FAMPOUX Map 1/20000

1. The Battalion will be relieved by the 2/8th Worcesters on the night of 16th/17th inst. the Battalion withdrawing to LANCASTER CAMP, via SINGLE ARCH and the main road.

2. No movement, except in the case of incoming signallers and Lewis gunners, will take place in connection with the relief before 7.15 p.m. Subsequently all movement will be by platoons at 200 yards distance.

3. Companies will be relieved as per attached table.

4. Companies will be responsible for holding NO MAN'S LAND in front of their sector until relief. Patrols will not be withdrawn until the last moment.

5. One Officer and one N.C.O. from relieving companies will come in by daylight to take over trench stores etc.

6. One officer and one N.C.O. per company will proceed to LANCASTER CAMP in time to take over the camp in daylight. Company cooks will be sent out immediately tea has been served to prepare a meal for the incoming troops.

7. The Transport Officer will arrange for limbers to pick up Officers' kits, mess boxes, Lewis guns and Lewis gun ammunition, Medical Stores, Orderly Room boxes and H.Q. cooking utensils. These will be dumped by companies at SINGLE ARCH after relief. He will also arrange to deliver cookers with dixies filled at LANCASTER CAMP not later than 5.0 p.m. leaving one man as guard to hand over to each company's cooks on their appearance.

8. All maps, aeroplane photographs, defence schemes and trench stores will be handed over and receipts obtained, as also certificates that the trenches were left in a clean condition. These will be handed in to Battalion Orderly Room by 6.0 p.m. *tomorrow* at latest.

9. All petrol tins belonging to the Battalion will be dumped at SINGLE ARCH and receipts obtained from the Regt.Sergt Major. All other petrol tins will be handed over and included in the Trench Store lists.

10. All work in hand will be explained to relieving companies.

11. Watches will be synchronised by Despatch Rider sent to companies during the day.

12. Completion of relief will be reported by the usual code word.

13. ACKNOWLEDGE.

                                                Capt. & Adjt.

Issued at 2.0 p.m.
Copy No. 1 to C.O.   Copy No. 7 to D.Coy.
        2 to Adjutant,   8 to Transport Officer
        3 to H.Q.   9 to Quartermaster,
        4 to A.Coy.   10 to 2/8th Worcesters.
        5 to B.Coy.   11   War Diary
        6 to C.Coy.   12   File

Relief Table issued with RED SQUARE OPERATION ORDER,
No. 95 — October 15th 1917.

Guides will lead in relieving troops in the following order:—

Relieving Coy.	Relieved Coy.	Route in	Route out	
D.Coy. 2/8th Worcs.	A.Coy. 2/5th R.War.R.	CHEMICAL	CHEMICAL	
B. Post of "B" Coy. 2/8th Worcs.	"B" Post of D.Coy 2/5th R.War.R.	—do—	—do—	
C.Coy. 2/8th Worcs.	C.Coy. 2/5th R.War.R.	SINGLE ARCH & CORFU	—do—	Thence by main road to
A.Coy. 2/8th Worcs	B.Coy. 2/5th R.War.R.	—do—	CORFU.	LANCASTER CAMP.
"A" Post of B.Coy. 2/8th Worcs.	"A" Post of D.Coy 2/5th R.War.R.	—do—	—do—	
Remainder of B.Coy. 2/8th Worcs	Remainder of D.Coy 2/5th R.War.R.	—do—	SINGLE ARCH	
H.Q. 2/8th Worcs.	H.Q. 2/5th R.War.R.	SINGLE ARCH	—do—	

Three guides per company and one for H.Q. will be at the junction of YORK ROAD and FAMPOUX ROAD in FAMPOUX (H.17.c.3.5) at 6.45 p.m. Each guide will have with him a note shewing the troops he is to lead and their destination.

SECRET.

RED SQUARE OPERATION ORDER, NO. 96.   Copy No. 11
Reference – Sheet 51B. N.W. 1/20000   October 27th 1917.
GREENLAND HILL Trench Map, 1/20000

1. The Battalion will relieve the 2/1st Bucks. Regiment in the GREENLAND HILL Sector, Left Support, tomorrow the 28th inst. in accordance with the attached table. East of the ARRAS – LENS railway, movement will be by platoons at 200 paces distance.

2. Field Kitchens will be taken with companies and tea served in CAM VALLEY before the troops enter the trenches.

3. One Officer and one N.C.O. per company will proceed into the line to take over by 12.0 noon tomorrow. All maps, aeroplane photographs, defence schemes and trench stores will be taken over and receipts sent in to Battalion H.Q. by 9.0 p.m. tomorrow.

4. Blankets, tied in bundles of ten, and all other stores not being taken into the line will be dumped in the main passage of the Prison ready for collection by the Transport by 9.0 a.m. Cpl. NOONAN will take charge of this dump and will give receipts.

5. The Transport Officer will detail one limber per company and two for Battalion H.Q. to carry Officers' kits, mess boxes, Lewis Guns, cooking utensils, and other stores being taken into the line, to report at the Prison at 12.30 p.m. These limbers will proceed to COOKHOUSE DUMP under the Transport Officer, arriving there not later than 5.45 p.m. Companies will detail parties to collect these stores from COOKHOUSE DUMP after relief is completed. In addition, one half limber will be detailed to report to D.Coy. at 12.30 p.m. to collect two Lewis guns and accompany "D" Coy's teams to POINT DU JOUR. This limber will bring back Lewis guns and kits of the 2/1st Bucks. relieved in the Post. The transport will deliver rations daily at COOKHOUSE DUMP by 5.45 p.m. Each company will supply its own ration carrying party

6. Billets will be cleaned ready for inspection before companies move off, and certificates that they have been left clean will be handed into the Orderly Room. Lists of billet stores are to be sent to the Orderly Room by 9.0 a.m. tomorrow.

7. Relief complete will be reported by the usual code word.

8. ACKNOWLEDGE.

Capt. & Adjt.
2/5th R. Warwick. Regt.

Issued at 6.0 p.m.
Copy No. 1 to C.O.
2 to Adjutant
3 to H.Q.
4 to A.Coy.
5 to B.Coy.
6 to C.Coy.
7. to D.Coy.
8 to Transport Officer
9 to Quartermaster
10 to 2/1st Bucks.
11 War Diary
12 File

Relief Table issued with RED SQUARE OPERATION ORDER, NO. 96.
October 27th 1917:

Order of Relief	Coy. 2/5th R.WAR.R.	Coy. 2/1st Bucks to be relieved	Position	Guides	Route in	Remarks.
1.	Batt. H.Q.	Batt. H.Q.	HUMID TRENCH	1 guide CAM VALLEY 2.0 p.m.	ST.NICHOLAS CAM VALLEY – CASTLE LANE – CABLE TRENCH	To follow 2/7 R.WAR.R. into CASTLE LANE
2.	D.Coy.	D.Coy.	COOKHOUSE DUMP	3 at CAM VALLEY at 4.0 p.m.	–do–	Not to enter CASTLE LANE till 2/4th Oxfords are clear.
3.	A.Coy.	A.Coy.	–do–	–do–	–do–	
4.	C.Coy.	C.Coy.	–do–	–do–	–do–	
5.	B.Coy.	B.Coy.	HARRY TRENCH	–do–	–do–	
6.	2 Lewis Gun teams (each 1 N.C.O. & 3 men) D.Coy.	2 Lewis Gun Teams. "B" Coy.	POINT DU JOUR	1 at ROAD JUNCTION at H.13.b.5.5 at 4.30 p.m.	ST.NICHOLAS FAMPOUX Road.	

Headquarter and "B" Coy. signallers, 4 Headquarter's and 2 company runners, Medical and water duty personnel will take over before 3.0 p.m.

Confidential.

War Diary

of

1st Battn The Royal Warwickshire Regt.

from Nov 1st to Nov 30th 1917

Army Form C. 2118.

WAR DIARY
or
INTELLIGENCE SUMMARY. M.C
(Erase heading not required.)

Instructions regarding War Diaries and Intelligence Summaries are contained in F. S. Regs. Part II. and the Staff Manual respectively. Title pages will be prepared in manuscript.

Place	Date	Hour	Summary of Events and Information	Remarks and references to Appendices
GREENLAND HILL SECTOR.	1/11/17	—	Battn. in LEFT SUPPORT GREENLAND HILL SECTOR.	M.C
"	2/11/17	—	"	M.C
"	3/11/17	—	Battn. relieved 2/6th Warwicks in FRONT LINE, LEFT SUBSECTOR. Relief complete at 8.45 p.m.	M.C appendix 1
"	4/11/17	—	Battn. holding front line, LEFT SUBSECTOR.	M.C
"	5/11/17	—	"	M.C
"	6/11/17	—	"	M.C
"	7/11/17	—	"	M.C
"	8/11/17	—	"	M.C
"	9/11/17	—	Battn. relieved by 2/6th Warwicks in FRONT LINE and withdrew to LEFT SUPPORT. Relief complete at 7.15 p.m.	M.C appendix 2
"	10/11/17	—	Battn. in LEFT SUPPORT, GREENLAND HILL SECTOR. Working parties.	M.C
"	11/11/17	—	"	M.C
"	12/11/17	—	"	M.C
"	13/11/17	—	"	M.C
"	14/11/17	—	"	M.C
"	15/11/17	—	Battn. relieved 2/6th Warwicks in FRONT LINE, LEFT SUBSECTOR. Relief completed 6.40 p.m.	M.C appendix 3
"	16/11/17	—	Battn. holding front line, LEFT SUBSECTOR.	M.C

WAR DIARY
or
INTELLIGENCE SUMMARY.

(Erase heading not required.)

Army Form C. 2118.

Place	Date	Hour	Summary of Events and Information	Remarks and references to Appendices
GREENLAND HILL SECTOR	17/11/17	—	Battn holding front line, LEFT SUBSECTOR.	M°C
"	18/11/17	—	"	M°C
"	19/11/17	—	"	M°C
"	20/11/17	—	"	M°C
"	21/11/17	—	Battn relieved by 1/4th GLOUCESTERS, Relief complete at 8.45pm, and withdrew to the PRISON, ARRAS, arriving 10.15am.	M°C
ARRAS	22/11/17	—	Resting, general cleaning up and refitting.	M°C
"	23/11/17	—	Company Training.	M°C
"	26/11/17	—	"	M°C
"	25/11/17	11.30am	Church Parade.	M°C
"	26/11/17	—	Company Training. Inspection of Transport by G.O.C. 183. Inf. Bde.	M°C
"	27/11/17	—	Company Training	M°C
"	28/11/17	—	Battn marched to billets at WARLUS BAPAUME, arriving at 1pm.	M°C Appendix 5
WARLUS	29/11/17	—	Refitting.	M°C
WARLUS	30/11/17	6.30am	Battn entrained at BEAUMETZ-LES-LOGES at 9am, proceeded to BAPAUME detraining at 10.30am, thence marched to METZ-EN-COUTURE, billets for night. at BAPAUME proceeded to RUYAULCOURT, marching from there to METZ-EN-COUTURE, billets for night.	M°C Appendix 6 10th

W. Cowler Lt Col
Commdg 2/7th R. Warwick R 1/12/17

SECRET.

Appendix 1

RED SQUARE OPERATION ORDER No. 97.   Copy No. 11
Reference — GREENLAND HILL Trench Map. 1/10000
            FAMPOUX Trench Map.   1/10000. November 2nd. 1917.

---

1. The Battalion will relieve the 2/6th. Royal Warwick Regt. in the Front line, left sub sector tomorrow November 3rd.

2. Dispositions.

   "A" Coy. 2/5th. Warwicks, relieves "A" Coy. 2/6th. in right front.
   "D" Coy. 2/5th. Warwicks. relieves "B" Coy. 2/6th. R. War. R. in centre front.
   "C" Coy. 2/5th. Warwicks. relieves "D" Coy. 2/6th. R. War. R. in left front.
   "B" Coy. 2/5th. Warwicks. relieves "C" Coy. 2/6th. R. War. R. in support.

   Any guides that may be necessary to be arranged by Company Commanders.

   "A" Coy. will proceed via CALEDONIAN AVENUE and CURSE SUPPORT, leaving the junction of HUMID TRENCH and CALEDONIAN AVENUE at 5 p.m.

   "B", "D" and "C" Coys. and Battalion H.Qrs., in that order, will proceed via CIVIL AVENUE, "B" Coy. leaving junction of CIVIL AVENUE and HUMID TRENCH at 5 p.m.

   Regimental Aid Post will remain in its present position.

3. All Lewis Gunners (with the exception of the teams in TRENT TRENCH and POINT du JOUR REDOUBT), Signallers, Runners, Water duty personnel, Snipers for O.P., and one Officer per Company and one N.C.O. per platoon to take over Trench Stores, will go into the line at 12 noon.

4. The Right and Centre front Coy. of the 2/6th. Warwicks will each leave two Lewis Guns in the Front line until the guns in TRENT TRENCH and POINT du JOUR REDOUBT are relieved.

   "A" and "D" Coys. will each detail 2 guides to report at the present Battalion Headquarters at 8-30 p.m. to guide the teams of the 2/6th. Warwicks. to TRENT TRENCH and POINT du JOUR REDOUBT respectively.

   The Transport Officer will detail one half limber to collect the Lewis Guns and mens' kits from POINT du JOUR REDOUBT at 9-30 p.m. and to accompany the teams to COOKHOUSE DUMP.

5. Officers' kits and all other stores not being taken forward will be dumped at COOKHOUSE DUMP ready for collection by the transport before companies move off. Corporal NOONAN will take charge of this Dump and give receipts.

6. The Transport Officer will deliver rations for "A", "B", "C" and "D" Coys. at TANK DUMP, from where they will be pushed up to CUBA DUMP, companies supplying their own carrying parties from this point. Headquarter rations will be

dumped at COOKHOUSE DUMP.

Petrol Tins will be taken over from the 2/6th. R. War. R. and Coys. will draw their own water.

Water tanks are in position at the junction of CHICKEN RESERVE and CALEDONIAN AVENUE and in CORK SUPPORT.

7. Aeroplane photographs, trench maps and trench stores will be handed over and receipts obtained.

Trench store Lists for the Reserve line will be sent into the Battalion Orderly Room by 12 noon, and those for the front line by 9 p.m. tomorrow.

"Relief complete" will be notified by the usual Code word.

8. Separate instructions are being issued with regard to Working parties tomorrow night.

9. Acknowledge.

Capt. & Adjt.
2/5th. R. Warwick. Regt.

Issued at 9 p.m.

Copy No. 1. C.O.
2. Adjutant.
3. Batt. H. Qrs.
4. A. Coy.
5. B. Coy.
6. C. Coy.
7. D. Coy.
8. Transport Officer.
9. Quartermaster.
10. 2/6th. R. Warwick. Regt.
11. War Diary.
12. File.

RED SQUARE OPERATION ORDER, No. 98.   Copy No. 11
Reference — GREENLAND HILL TRENCH MAP 1/10000.
             FAMPOUX TRENCH MAP,   1/10000.   November 8th, 1917.

---

1. The Battalion will be relieved by the 2/6th. Warwicks. on
   the night of 9th./10th. November, 1917., and on relief will
   withdraw to Left Support where companies will take over the
   same dispositions as before.

2. "C" Company will be relieved by "D" Coy. 2/6th. Warwicks.
   "D" Company   "   "   "   "B" Coy.   do.
   "A" Company   "   "   "   "C" Coy.   do.
   "B" Company   "   "   "   "A" Coy.   do.

   Any guides that may be necessary to be arranged by Coy.
   Commanders.

   Companies of the 2/6th. Warwicks. will leave the Support
   Line at about 5 p.m., "C" and "A" Coys. moving via CALEDONIAN
   AVENUE, "B", "D", and "H.Q." by CIVIL AVENUE.

3. The 2/6th. Warwicks. are sending into the line at 2.30 p.m.
   Lewis Gunners, Signallers, Runners, Water duty personnel,
   Snipers for Observation Post, and one Officer per Coy. and one
   N.C.O. per platoon to take over Trench Stores.
   One Officer and one N.C.O. per Coy. will be sent out
   during the afternoon to take over the Trench Stores in the
   Support Line.

4. "A" and "C" Coys. will each leave 2 Lewis Guns in the line
   until relieved by the guns of the 2/6th. Warwicks. at present
   in TRENT TRENCH and POINT DU JOUR REDOUBT.
   "A" Coy. will detail :—
   (a). 2 Lewis Gun Teams, each of one N.C.O. and 3 men to relieve
        the 2 guns of the 2/6th. Warwicks in TRENT TRENCH.
   C Coy will detail (b). 2 Lewis Gun Teams, each of one N.C.O. and 3 men to relieve
        2 guns of 2/6th. Warwicks. in POINT DU JOUR REDOUBT.
   The guides for (a) and (b) will be at the Left Support Battn.
   H.Q. in HUMID TRENCH at 7 p.m..

   The Transport Officer will detail one half limbers be at
   the junction of NORTHUMBERLAND AVENUE and the track to
   COOKHOUSE DUMP at 7.15 p.m. to carry the guns and kits of the
   teams going to POINT DU JOUR REDOUBT.

5. "D" Coy. will send out a patrol to cover the Battalion Front
   until 8.30 p.m., when they will report back to the O.C. "B" *Coy.*
   2/6th. Warwicks.

6. Any Officers' kits, mess boxes, or other stores required by Coys
   and rations, will be taken by the Transport to TANK DUMP and
   will be pushed up on the railway to the point where it crosses
   HARRY TRENCH.
   A party from H.Q. under L/Sgt. NOONAN will be responsible
   for unloading stores at this point and guarding them until
   carrying parties arrive from Companies.

7. All aeroplane photographs, trench maps and trench stores will
   be handed over and receipts obtained.
   "A" Coy. will hand over to "A" Coy 2/6th. Warwicks at the
   Support Company H.Q. in CORK SUPPORT, 30 filled Lewis Gun drums
   sent them today.

Trench Store lists for the Front line will be sent to the
Battalion Orderly Room by 5 p.m. and those for the Reserve
Line by 9 p.m. tomorrow.

g. "Relief complete" will be notified by usual Code word.

g. Separate instructions will be issued with regard to Working
Parties tomorrow night.

10. ACKNOWLEDGE.

                                                        Capt. & Adjt.

Copy No. 1. C.O.
        2. Adjutant.
        3. Batt. H.Q.
        4. "A" Coy.
        5. "B" Coy.
        6. "C" Coy.
        7. "D" Coy.
        8. Transport Officer.
        9. Quartermaster.
      10. 2/6th Warwicks.
      11. War Diary.
      12. File.

RED SQUARE BATTALION ORDERS, No. 99.   Appendix 3   Copy No. 11
Reference — GREENLAND HILL TRENCH MAP 1/10000.
             FAMPOUX TRENCH MAP.   1/10000.   November 14th 1917

1.   The Battalion will relieve the 2/6th. Warwicks. in the front line, left sub-sector tomorrow November 15th.

2.   Dispositions.

            "B" Coy. will relieve "A" Coy. 2/6th. Warwicks. in Left Front.
            "D" Coy. will relieve "B" Coy. 2/6th. Warwicks. in Centre Front.
            "C" Coy. will relieve "C" Coy. 2/6th. Warwicks. in Right Front.
            "A" Coy. will relieve "D" Coy. 2/6th. Warwicks. in Support.

        Any guides that may be necessary to be arranged between Company Commanders.

        "C" Coy will proceed via CALEDONIAN AVENUE leaving the junction of HUMID TRENCH and CALEDONIAN AVENUE at 5 p.m.
        "D", "B", and "A" Coys. and Battn. H.Qrs., in that order, will proceed via CIVIL AVENUE, "D" Coy. leaving junction of CIVIL AVENUE and HUMID TRENCH at 5 p.m.
        Regtl. Aid Post will remain in its present position.

3.   All Lewis Guns (with the exception of the teams in TRENT TRENCH and POINT DU JOUR REDOUBT), Signallers, Runners, Water Duty Personnel, Snipers for O.P., and one Officer per Company and one N.C.O. per Platoon to take over Trench Stores, will go into the line at 12 noon.
        One Officer per Company of the 2/6th. Warwicks. is being sent out to take over Trench Stores during the morning.

4.   The Right Front and Support Companies of the 2/6th. Warwicks. will each leave 2 Lewis Guns in the line until the guns in TRENT TRENCH and POINT DU JOUR REDOUBT are relieved.
        "A" and "C" Coys. will each detail two guides to report at the present Battalion H.Q. at 7.30 p.m. tomorrow to guide the teams of the 2/6th. Warwicks. to TRENT TRENCH and POINT DU JOUR REDOUBT respectively.
        The Transport Officer will detail one half limber to collect the Lewis Guns and mens' kits from POINT DU JOUR REDOUBT at 8.30 p.m. and to accompany the teams as far as TANK DUMP.

5.   The 1 N.C.O. and 2 men of "C" Coy. at the Gum Boot Store CIVIL AVENUE, and 1 N.C.O. and 2 men of "D" Coy at TANK DUMP will be relieved by the 2/6th. Warwicks. by 2 p.m. tomorrow and will return to their companies.

6.   The Centre Company of the 2/6th. Warwicks. will send out a patrol to cover the front until 7.30 p.m. when they will report back to the O.C. "D" Coy.

7.   Officers' kits and all other stores not being taken forward will be dumped at the point where LIGHT RAILWAY crosses HARRY TRENCH before companies move off.
        Battn. H.Q. will supply a party under L/Sgt. NOONAN to

take charge of this dump and take the stores by returning trucks to TANK DUMP where TRANSPORT will collect.

L/Sgt. NOONAN will give receipts for all Stores delivered at the Dump and obtain receipts on handing them over to the transport.

8. Rations for all companies will be delivered by the Transport at TANK DUMP nightly. Those of "A", "B", "C" and "D" Coys. being pushed up to CUBA DUMP, and H.Qrs. to the junction of the LIGHT RAILWAY and STAFFORD LANE.

Companies will supply their own ration and water carrying parties.

9. Aeroplane photographs, trench maps, and trench stores, including stoves, braziers and petrol tins will be handed over and receipts obtained.

Trench Store Lists for the Reserve Line will be sent into the Battalion Orderly Room by 12 noon, and those for the front line by 9 p.m. tomorrow.

10. "Relief complete" will be notified by the usual Code word.

11. Separate instructions will be issued with regard to Working Parties tomorrow night.

12. ACKNOWLEDGE.

Capt. & Adjt.

Issued at 2.30 p.m.

Copy No. 1. C.O.
2. Adjutant.
3. H.Qrs.
4. A. Coy.
5. B. Coy.
6. C. Coy.
7. D. Coy.
8. Transport Officer.
9. Quartermaster.
10. 2/6th. Warwicks.
11. War Diary.
12. File.

SECRET.
Appendix 4

RED SQUARE OPERATION ORDER No. 100.   Copy No. 11
Reference Maps:-
   GREENLAND HILL TRENCH MAP, 1/10000
   FAMPOUX TRENCH MAP, 1/10000.
   51 B. N.W. 1/20000.   November 20th. 1917.

---

1. The Battalion will be relieved by 2/4th. GLOSTERS tomorrow 21st. inst. and on relief will withdraw to PRISON BARRACKS, ARRAS, via NORTHUMBERLAND AVENUE — Road junction H.4.b.8.5. GAVRELLE — ARRAS Road.

    Officers' billets will be as before with the exception that "A" and "B" Companies will exchange, "A" Coy. taking over the Prison Quarters with Battn. H.Q.

    All movement East of the ARRAS — LENS Railway will be by platoons at 200 yards distance.

2. Dispositions.

    | "B" Coy. | will be relieved by | "D" Coy. 2/4th. GLOSTERS. |
    | "D" Coy. | do. | "A" Coy. do. |
    | "A" Coy. | do. | "B" Coy. do. |
    | "C" Coy. | do. | "C" Coy. do. |

    Three guides each from "A", "C" and "D" Coys. two from "B" Coy., one from "Bn.H.Q" will be at the junction of CAM VALLEY and the FAMPOUX ROAD at 4 p.m. tomorrow. They will be given written instructions as to whom they are to report to.

    "B" Coy. 2/4th. GLOSTERS. will come in via CALEDONIAN AVENUE, the remainder via CIVIL AVENUE.

3. The 2/4th. GLOSTERS are sending into the line during daylight hours, Lewis Gunners, Signallers, Runners, Observers for O.P., Water Duty Personnel, and 1 Officer and 1 N.C.O. per Company to take over Trench Stores.
    One Officer and one N.C.O. per company will be sent out of the line during the morning to take over billets in ARRAS.

4. Companies will arrange for their front to be patrolled until relief is completed.

5. Transport arrangements will be as per instructions already issued separately.
    Blankets, Officers' kits, mess boxes and other stores will be delivered at the ARRAS billets by the Transport tomorrow morning. C.Q.M.S's taking charge thereof.

6. All Trench Maps, aeroplane photographs, defence schemes and other documents relating to the Sector, S.O.S. grenades and other Trench Stores will be handed over and signed lists sent to the Orderly Room by 4 p.m. at the latest tomorrow.

7. "Relief complete" will be notified by the usual Code Word.

8. ACKNOWLEDGE.

                                              Capt. & Adjt.

Issued at 5-30 p.m.

Copy No. 1 - C.O.
2 - Bn. H.Q.
3 - A. Coy.
4 - B. Coy.
5 - C. Coy.
6 - D. Coy.
7 - Transport Officer.
8 - Quartermaster.
9 - Medical Officer.
10 - 2/4th. GLOSTERS.
11 - War Diary.
12 - File.

Appendix 5

SECRET.
RED SQUARE OPERATION ORDER, NO. 101.   Copy No. 10
Reference – Sheet 51. B. 1/40000   Nov. 28th 1917.
           LENS Sheet 11, 1/100000

1. The 182nd Infantry Brigade will move to the DAINVILLE area today, the Battalion proceeding to billets at WARLUS. Route:- road junction immediately north of the A. in FBG. D' AMIENS (Reference LENS Sheet 11) – DAINVILLE.

2. Companies will march in the following order, H.Qrs. A. B. C. & D. Coys. and Transport, the head of the column passing the Starting Point (road junction at G.27.a.2.9) at 11.0 a.m. Dress, Marching Order, service dress caps to be worn. Distances of 200 yards between companies and between the rear company and Transport will be observed. Field Kitchens will march with the Transport.

3. Orders for the Billeting Party have been issued separately.

4. Blankets, tightly rolled in bundles of ten and labelled, will be dumped in the passages leading to the Officers' quarters ready for collection by motor lorry at 9.0 a.m. One man per company will be detailed to look after blankets and to ride on the lorry. Canteen Stores will be collected by the motor lorry on its second journey. Officers' kits, Orderly Room boxes, H.Q. cooking utensils and other stores will be dumped at the entrance to the Prison ready for collection by the Transport at 10.0 a.m. except Officers' kits of B. & D. Coys. which will be dumped at D.Coy's mess at 9.45 a.m. Officers' mess boxes will be ready at 10.30 a.m. Each company will detail one man to march with its Lewis Gun Limber as brakesman.

5. Billets will be cleaned ready for inspection by Capt. R.E.COMBE at 10.30 a.m. Sec.Lieut. R.LOVE and 12 O.Rs. of "A" Coy. will remain behind to hand over to the Area Commandant all billets occupied by the Battalion and to ensure that they are left scrupulously clean. They will also take charge of all stores belonging to the Battalion until collected. Certificates that billets have been left clean will be handed to the Adjutant at the Starting Point.

6. Watches will be synchronised by D.R. sent to companies about 9.30 a.m.

7. Falling out states, Condition of billets when taken over and other returns will be rendered to the Orderly Room as soon as possible after arrival in the new area.

8. ACKNOWLEDGE.

                                        Capt. & Adjt.
                                        2/5th R. Warwick. Regt.

Issued at 2.0 a.m.

Copy No. 1 to C.O.   Copy No. 7 to D.Coy.
         2 to Adjutant.   8 to Quartermaster
         3 to H.Qrs.   9 to T'port Officer
         4 to A.Coy.   10   War Diary
         5 to B.Coy.   11   File
         6 to C.Coy.

SECRET.
D SQUARE OPERATION ORDER NO. 102.　　　　Copy No. 11
Reference - LENS Sheet 11. 1/100000.　　　November 29th. 1917.

1. The Battalion will move to the BARASTRE area tomorrow, November 30th. Dismounted personnel will move by rail entraining at BEAUMETZ-les-LOGES at 9 a.m. and detraining at BAPAUME at about 10 a.m. Transport will move by road under orders which have been issued separately to the Transport Officer.

2. Companies will march to the entraining station via BERNEVILLE in the following order, H.Qrs. B. A. C. & D. Coys. the head of the column passing the Starting Point (cross roads in WARLUS) at XX 6.50 a.m. Distances of 200 yards between Companies will be observed. Each man will carry Marching Order and one blanket strapped on top of the pack. Steel helmets will be worn and haversack rations carried.

3. Capt. F.W.BLANCHARD is detailed as Battalion Entraining Officer, and will report to the R.T.O. BEAUMETZ-les-LOGES at 7 a.m. with a statement shewing the entraining strength of the Battalion.

4. Orderly Room boxes, Mess boxes (with the exception of one per Company) and other stores not detailed below, Field Kitchens and Lewis Gun Limbers will be collected by the Transport before the Battalion moves off. Blankets (the extra one per man), rolled in bundles of ten and labelled, Officers' Kits, one mess box per Company, camp kettles containing remainder of days rations, will be taken by Companies before moving off to the Q.M.Stores ready for loading on the motor lorry.

5. Billets will be cleaned ready for inspection by Capt. S. GRANT at 6.30 a.m. Each Company will detail a rear party of 3 O.Rs. to report to Capt. GRANT at the Company billet and to carry out any necessary cleaning. They will march to the entraining station under Capt. GRANT. Certificates that billets have been left scrupulously clean will be handed to the Adjutant at the Starting Point.

6. Watches will be synchronised by Despatch Rider sent to Companies about 6 a.m.

7. Falling-out states, Condition of billets when taken over and other returns will be sent to the Orderly Room as soon as possible after arrival in the new area.

8. ACKNOWLEDGE.

　　　　　　　　　　　　　　　　　　　　　　　Capt. & Adjt.
　　　　　　　　　　　　　　　　　　　　　　　2/5th. R.Warwick.Regt.

Issued at 6.0 p.m.

Copy No. 1 to C.O.　　　　　　Copy No. 7 to D.Coy.
　　　　2 to Adjutant.　　　　　　　　8 to Transport Officer.
　　　　3 to H.Qrs.　　　　　　　　　　9 to Quartermaster.
　　　　4 to A.Coy.　　　　　　　　　10 to War Diary.
　　　　5 to B.Coy.　　　　　　　　　11 to File.
　　　　6 to C.Coy.

W 20

CONFIDENTIAL

WAR DIARY

2/5 ROYAL WARWICKSHIRE REGT

December 1st to 31st 1917.

VOLUME 20

Army Form C. 2118.

WAR DIARY
or
INTELLIGENCE SUMMARY.

(Erase heading not required.)

Instructions regarding War Diaries and Intelligence Summaries are contained in F. S. Regs., Part II. and the Staff Manual respectively. Title pages will be prepared in manuscript.

Place	Date	Hour	Summary of Events and Information	Remarks and references to Appendices
METZ-EN-COUTRE	1/12/17	5am	Battalion marched to HEUDECOURT and bivouaced in valley just EAST of village	
HEUDECOURT	2/12/17	9am	Battalion moved via FINS-METZ-EN-COUTRE - to GOUZEAUCOURT WOOD halting there till 4.45 p.m. & then moving to relieve the 2/8 WORCESTERS in the line NE of LA VACQUERIE	Appendices I & IA
LA VACQUERIE	3/12/17		see reports attached	Appendices I & IA
"	4/12/17			
EQUANCOURT	5/12/17		Remnants of the Battalion attached to other units of the 182 INF RDE, 1 Coy attached to 2/7 R.WAR.R and 1 Coy to 2/6 R.WAR.R	
"	6/12/17		Bn. H.Qrs consisting of C.O and R.S.M only proceeding to EQUANCOURT to reorganise	
"	7/12/17			
HAVRINCOURT WOOD	8/12/17		Bn re-organized into 2 Coys at HAVRINCOURT WOOD	
"	9/12/17		Bn. camp moved 9-10am to another part of the wood on account of hostile shelling	
"	10/12/17		Bn addressed by G.O.C. 61st DIVN 10 a.m. Bn relieved 2/6 GLOUCESTERS in line NW of LA VACQUERIE. Relief complete at 1-10am 11/12/17	
LA VACQUERIE	11/12/17		Bn in the line Relieved by 2/7 R.WAR.R and moved back to BDE RESERVE NE of BEAUCAMP. Relief complete by 12-10 am	
	12/12/17			

WAR DIARY
or
INTELLIGENCE SUMMARY.

(Erase heading not required.)

Army Form C. 2118.

Place	Date	Hour	Summary of Events and Information	Remarks and references to Appendices
BEAUCAMP	13/12/17		Bn in BDE RESERVE	
LA VACQUERIE	14/12/17		"	Relief complete by 2/4 R.WAR.R. 11.30 p.m.
"	15/12/17		Moved into the line and relieved 2/4 R.WAR.R.	
"	16/12/17	N.C	Bn in the line. Relieved by 1 Coy 2/4 O.B.L.I. and 1 Coy 2/5 GLOUCESTERS and moved back into DIV reserve N.E. of BEAUCAMP. Relief complete at 9.30 p.m.	
BEAUCAMP	16/12/17		In reserve line	
"	17/12/17		"	
"	18/12/17		"	
"	19/12/17		Relieved by "O" Coy NELSON BN 63rd DIVN 10 p.m. & Bn moved back to camp at MANANCOURT by motor lorries	
MANANCOURT	20/12/17		Bn reorganised into 4 Coys. Draft of 8 NCO's & 98 OR arrived	
"	21/12/17	10 am	Draft inspected. GOC 183 BDE. Bn refitting.	
"	22/12/17		Refitting & reorganising	appendix I
"	23/12/17	12 mn	Bn moved to rest billets at VAUX-SUR-SOMME by train, arriving at CORBIE at 3.30 p.m. & marching to VAUX arriving at 6 p.m.	appendix II
VAUX-SUR-SOMME	24/12/17		Clearing roads	
"	25/12/17		HOLIDAY	
"	26/12/17		Company training commenced	

Army Form C. 2118.

WAR DIARY
or
INTELLIGENCE SUMMARY.
(Erase heading not required.)

Instructions regarding War Diaries and Intelligence Summaries are contained in F. S. Regs., Part II. and the Staff Manual respectively. Title pages will be prepared in manuscript.

Place	Date	Hour	Summary of Events and Information	Remarks and references to Appendices
VAUX-SUR-SOMME	27/12/17		Cleaning roads	
"	28/12/17	9 am	Bn Muster Parade. Company training	
"	29/12/17	"	" " "	
"	29/12/17	"	" " "	
"	30/12/17	8 am	Bn marched to billets at CAYEUX-EN-SANTERRE via SAILLY LAURETTE — WARFUSÉE L'EQUIPPÉE	Appendix III
"	"		ABANCOURT — MARCELCAVE — WIENCOURT, arriving at 1.30 pm	
CAYEUX-EN-SANTERRE	31/12/17	9.45 am	Bn marched to billets at LE QUESNEL via BEAUCOURT-EN-SANTERRE arriving at 12.30 pm.	Appendix IV
			Strength 1/12/1917 38 Officers 723 O.Ranks	
			" 31/12/1917 21 " 591 "	

W. Coates Lt Col.
Comdg. 1/5 Leinster R.
1/1/18

Reference :- GONNELIEU Map, Edn. 3a. 1/20000.

On the night of 2nd/3rd December 1917, I relieved the 2/8th Worcesters N.E. of LA VACQUERIE, my dispositions being:-

One company (B) in trenches between R.16.b.85.35 to about R.16.b.4.7. and in touch with the unit on their left.

Two companies (A. & C.) in shell holes in front of trench between R.16.c.35.55 and R.16.c.50.50 ready to attack the trenches in R.16.d. lost by the 2/4th Gloucesters.

One company (D) in support between R.15.c.55.55 and R.16.c.50.50.

Battalion H.Q. at R.15.d.50.65 with one company of 2/8th Worcesters close by.

Touch was established on my right flank, about R.16.c.5.5. between my support company (D) and the support company of the 2/4th Gloucesters and my part of this line re-organised with new Lewis Gun positions. Touch was also gained with the advanced company of the 2/4th Gloucesters in VACANT ALLEY.

My attack commenced at 7.30 a.m. on December 3rd. covering fire being arranged for by Lewis Guns and R.Gs. on the left forward flank and by Lewis Guns of the 2/4th Gloucesters in VACANT ALLEY. Very heavy opposition was encountered and the remnants of the two companies disappeared, one or two men only returning to the support company.

At about 8.30 a.m. the enemy placed an intense and accurate barrage on my support company (D) and another across the southern edge of LA VACQUERIE, then lifting on to a line drawn almost E. & W. through Battalion H.Q.

About 8.30 a.m. my left company (B) was attacked by bombing parties on their right flank, but they held their ground until ordered to withdraw to the vicinity of R.17.c., I believe by the O.C. 2/7th Warwicks. They did so about 6 a.m. on December 4th.

About 8.45 a.m. on December 3rd. my support company was also attacked on its right flank and they therefore took up their position facing the attack along the road running almost E. & W. through R.16.c.5.5. They succeeded in keeping the enemy off, but few survivors remain and they retired when ordered to do so with my left company.

About 9.0 a.m. the 2nd in Command of the 2/4th Gloucesters reported to me that the whole of his line had gone and his Battalion Headquarters moved. The enemy attack had come almost at a right angle to my front and my flank was therefore left in the air.

Almost immediately afterwards the barrage lifted further North and I stood to with all details and manned the posts previously reconnoitred for defence, then the enemy were seen working up through the village. A strong attack developed, but was repulsed, the enemy signalling by firing white Very Lights. The fire fight continued until just before noon when the supply of ammunition became almost exhausted. The enemy then made bombing attacks up the communication trenches supported by Machine Gun fire and Granatenwerfer on our front posts and heavy shell fire on our rear line.

These were held off for a time, but our bomb supply also became exhausted and casualties had become heavy. There was no hope of continuing this fight without bombs and I therefore decided to abandon the front posts (which included Battalion Headquarters) but to continue to hold the line about 50 yards in rear, where we could not easily be bombed.

I therefore placed the MEN along WELSH ROAD from R.15.c.6.8 to R.15.d.05.70 with a left flank defence along CORNER SUPPORT with orders to all not to retire as I considered it could be

- 2 -

Some ammunition was salved and two later attacks repulsed.

When I posted my new left flank I gained touch with a part of a company of the 2/8th Warwicks, who informed me that they had been ordered to occupy the Northern part of CORNER COPSE. I also collected a few other odd troops and placed them in support in the trenches running roughly N. & S. through R.15.c.9.0 and R.15.a.9.3.

As the situation then seemed satisfactory, and the enemy well held, I searched for support to organise a counter-attack but only found two companies manning PARK TRENCH and the trenches running N.E. from R.15.a.25.20 to form a defensive flank under orders of 183 Infantry Brigade, and I presumed I was not at liberty to use them.

I then got into touch with the 2/5th Gloucesters, and reported personally to the G.O.C. 184 Infantry Brigade, afterwards establishing my Headquarters with the 2/5th Gloucesters. During the night the troops holding the vicinity of CORNER COPSE were relieved by the 2/4th Berks, and I withdrew my men to PARK RAVINE establishing my Headquarters there with the 2/7th Worcesters.

A large amount of gas shell was used by the enemy.

When it appeared possible that Battalion H.Q. would be rushed, all papers, maps and S.A.A. codes there were burnt, although some may have fallen into the hands of the enemy through my missing officers of the two attacking companies.

I wish to mention that I saw no backward movement of my own men and did not know the 2/4th Gloucester's line had gone until just before I was myself strongly attacked at Battalion H.Qrs. and then a counter-attack to restore the line there with my small force was impossible.

The times given above may not be exact as my notes were burnt.

I wish, further, to notice the gallant conduct of Captains PRITCHARD (killed) and HOLCROFT, of the 2/8th Worcesters. Other officers and men of their battalion, whose names I do not know, also did extremely well.

P.L. Coates,
Lieut. Col.
Comdg. 2/8th R.Warwick.Regt.

6/12/17.

Appendix IA

Reference — GONNELIEU MAP, Edn. 5a. 1/10000

Headquarters,
    182nd Infantry Brigade.

            In accordance with your G.1010 of 27/12/17, I beg
to amplify my report of 8/12/17 as follows:-
            I arrived at the Headquarters of the 2/8th WORCESTERS
at R.15.d.50.65. in the early hours of the morning of December 3rd.
and the O.C. 2/8th WORCESTERS informed me that a counter-attack
by one company of his Battalion was then in progress, the objective
being the trenches in R.16.d. lost by the 2/8th GLOUCESTERS the
previous (?) day. Later on a report came in that the attack had
failed and in accordance with the instructions of the G.O.C. 183rd
Infantry Brigade, I decided to attack about dawn with two companies —
all the troops I could spare. No previous reconnaissance was
possible in the few hours remaining for arrangements, but the
O.C. 2/8th WORCESTERS informed me that the wire in R.16.d. had
been considerably damaged and was passable in most places.
            My dispositions were as previously stated in my report
of 8/12/17. My orders were issued verbally to Company Commanders
and included the following instructions:-
            Objective — Trench between R.16.d.54.30 and R.16.d.40.95
(350 yards). Upon reaching this, touch to be gained with "B"
Company on the left via the communication trench running from
R.16.d.40.95 to R.16.b.65.20. and with the 2/4th GLOUCESTERS on
the right in VACANT ALLEY about R.16.d.57.05. Fighting patrols
then to be pushed forward into the trench about 200 yards EAST
of the objective. Line eventually to be consolidated from the
right of the existing left company front at R.16.b.65.20 to
R.17.c.05.30 — R.22.b.75.92. and thence to 2/4th GLOUCESTERS at
R.16.d.50.05.
            Frontage — 166 yards per company — "A" Company
on the left and "C" Company on the right. The left flank to
direct — the sunken road being prominent and the only natural
feature to be clearly distinguished.
            Method of attack — Each company on a frontage of
one platoon with the remaining platoon in support, company
headquarters (including two Lewis Gun sections) following as
a third wave. Each wave in two lines as per normal attack
formation of 61st Division.
            Covering Fire by "B" Company with Lewis Guns and
Rifle Grenades from their right flank in R.16.b. The 2/4th
GLOUCESTERS were also asked to co-operate with Lewis Gun fire
from VACANT ALLEY, but I cannot say whether this was actually
done. If advance checked by enemy fire — companies to cover
each other with fire.
            Advanced Battalion Headquarters were established
at R.16.c.60.35 under Capt. G.GRANT (acting Second in Command).
            Communication between the two attacking company
headquarters and advanced Battalion Headquarters was arranged
by visual signalling and by runner. Between Battalion
Headquarters and advanced Battalion Headquarters by telephone and
by runner, no visual being possible. No telephones had been
previously established and continuous searching through the
night only resulted in the salvage of 300 yards of wire. So
that communication eventually was by runner only between Battalion
Headquarters and advanced Battalion Headquarters.

ZERO – 7.30 a.m. at which time the advance commenced. Watches of Company Commanders were synchronized by me.

Communication was maintained until 7.35 a.m. at which hour a message was despatched from advanced Battalion Headquarters saying that the troops had advanced to time and that there was considerable hostile shelling.

Shortly after this, Capt. GRANT and the personnel remaining at Advanced Battalion Headquarters were killed and a message was received to that effect from the support company just as the barrage came down on Battalion Headquarters previous to the German attack.

There is no doubt that the two attacking companies advanced most gallantly, but unfortunately against German troops assembled in strength for an attack themselves. This is evident from the fact that my left company (B) was attacked on its right flank about 8.30 a.m. from the objective of my attack (see para. 9 of my report of 2/12/17).

All the Officers and N.C.Os. of the attacking companies were killed or wounded and missing and it is difficult to gather reliable evidence of the progress of the attack. The few privates who survived have been cross-examined by me and they agree that the machine gun and rifle fire directed against them was exceedingly severe, but that the companies continued the assault until practically all were casualties. Direction seems to have been well maintained, except by one section who apparently worked south into the trench at R.16.d.55.05. although this may have been done by the order of the right company commander.

R/Coates,
Lieut. Col.
Comdg. 2/5th R.Warwick.Regt.

30/12/17.

SECRET.
RED SQUARE OPERATION ORDER, NO.
Reference - Sheet 57C. 1/40000
         LENS Sheet 1/200000
         AMIENS Sheet 1/100000.

Copy No 10
Dec. 22nd 1917

Appendix II

1. The 182nd Infantry Brigade, less marching portion of Transport will move by rail on the 23rd inst. to the VAUX sur SOMME area. The Battalion will entrain at ESBICOURT and detrain at CORBIE.

2. Order of march:- H.Qrs. A. B. C. & D. Companies, the head of the column passing the Starting Point (Battalion H.Qrs.) at 11.0 a.m. Dress, marching order; steel helmets to be worn. H.Coy. will carry 35 shovels on the men. Distances of 200 yards will be maintained between companies.

3. Haversack rations will be carried. One full days rations will be carried on the cookers.

4. Capt. R.H.V.BARNES, M.C. is detailed for duty as Entraining Officer, and will report to Capt. J.J.SHATER, 2/8th R.War.R. at the R.T.O's Office, ESBICOURT, at 10.0 a.m.

5. Transport, moving by road will proceed under the orders issued separately to the Transport Officer. Remainder of Transport moving by rail will arrive at the entraining station, YPRES, at 11.30 a.m. The Transport Officer will send guides with details of numbers to receive instructions from the entraining officer at 11.0 a.m.

6. Blankets rolled in labelled bundles of ten, Officers' kits, mess boxes, Orderly Room boxes and Medical Stores will be dumped by the sunken road immediately in rear of the Officers' quarters, ready for collection by 8.30 a.m.

7. The camp will be cleaned ready for inspection by Capt. F.E. BRIDDEN, M.C. at 11.30 a.m.

8. Watches will be synchronised by Despatch Rider sent to companies about 7.30 a.m.

9. The usual returns will be rendered to the Orderly Room as soon as possible after arrival in the new area.

10. ACKNOWLEDGE.

Lieut. & Adjt.
2/8th R.Warwick.Regt.

Issued at 11.30 p.m.
Copy No. 1 to C.O.
         2 to Adjutant.
         3 to H.Qrs.
         4 to A.Coy.
         5 to B.Coy.
         6 to C.Coy
         7 to D.Coy.
         8 to Transport Officer.
         9 to Quartermaster.
         10 War Diary
         11 File

Appendix III

SECRET.
RED SQUARE OPERATION ORDER, No. 104.   Copy No. 10
Reference — AMIENS Map, 1/100000   December 29th 1917.

1. The 182nd Infantry Brigade moves tomorrow to the CAYEUX-EN-SANTERRE area, the Battalion being billeted in CAYEUX-EN-SANTERRE. Route:- SAILLY LE SEC — SAILLY LAURETTE — WARFUSEE ABANCOURT — MARCELCAVE STATION — WIENCOURT L'EQUIPPE.

2. Companies will march in the following order, H.Qrs. A. C. B. & D. Coys. and Transport, the head of the column passing the Starting Point (road by Battalion Football Ground) at 8.2 a.m. Two hundred yards interval will be maintained between each group of ten transport vehicles. Dress, Marching Order, steel helmets to be worn.

3. Blankets rolled in labelled bundles of ten, Officers' valises, H.Q. cooking utensils, Orderly Room boxes and other stores will be dumped at the Q.M.Stores by 6.45 a.m. Mess boxes will be ready for collection by the Transport at 7.0 a.m. Cookers will be ready for collection at 7.30 a.m.

4. An advance party of Sec.Lieut. J.L.KELLY and 20 O.R's. of "C" Company and the tool limber will march 250 yards in front of Battalion H.Q. and will be prepared to sprinkle earth and stones on any part of the road that is particularly slippery, especially over hills. The packs of these men will be carried on the Transport, and will be dumped at the Q.M.Stores with other stores. "B" and "D" Companies will each detail a party of 1 N.C.O. and 10 men to march behind the Transport and assist on bad ground if necessary.

5. Billets will be cleaned ready for inspection by Capt. F.J. BREEDEN, M.C. at 7.45 a.m. Certificates that billets have been left thoroughly clean will be handed to the Adjutant at the Starting Point.

6. Watches will be synchronised by Despatch Rider sent to companies about 7.0 a.m.

7. The usual returns will be rendered to the Orderly Room as soon as possible after arrival in the new area.

                                            Lieut. & Adjt.
                                            2/5th R.Warwick.Regt.

Issued at 7.0 p.m.
Copy No. 1 to C.O.
         2 to Adjutant,
         3 to H.Qrs.
         4 to A.Coy.
         5 to B.Coy.
         6 to C.Coy.
         7 to D.Coy.
         8 to Transport Officer,
         9 to Quartermaster,
        10   War Diary
        11   File

SECRET.
RED SQUARE OPERATION ORDER. NO. 105.   Copy No.
Reference — AMIENS Map 1/100000   December 30th 1917.

Appendix IV

1. The 182nd Infantry Brigade moves tomorrow the 31st
   to the LE QUESNEL area, the Battalion being billeted in
   LE QUESNEL. Route:— BEAUCOURT-EN-SANTERRE — Cross
   roads south of the C. in CHAU — LE PLEMANGEST.

2. Companies will march in the following order, D. C. B. A.
   and H.Qrs. Coys. and Transport, the head of the column
   passing the Starting Point (road junction 250 yards S.
   of the M. in FM.) at 9.45 a.m. Dress, Marching Order,
   steel helmets to be worn. Distances of 200 yards will
   be maintained between each group of ten transport vehicles.

3. An advance party consisting of Sec.Lieut. H.G. CHELLINGWORTH
   and 20 O.Rs. of "D" Coy. will march 250 yards in front
   of the head of the column, together with the tool limber,
   and will be prepared to sprinkle earth and stones on the
   road where necessary. The packs of these men will be
   dumped with other stores. "A" and "C" companies will
   each detail a party of 1 N.C.O. and 6 men to report to
   the Transport Officer at the Starting Point at 8.45 a.m.

4. Blankets rolled in labelled bundles of ten, Officers'
   valises, H.Q. cooking utensils, Orderly Room boxes and
   other stores will be dumped by the Church, CAYEUX-en-
   SANTERRE, at 8.30 a.m. Officers' mess boxes will be
   ready for collection by the Transport at 9.0 a.m.
   Field Kitchens will also be ready for collection by
   the Transport at 9.0 a.m.

5. Billets will be cleaned and ready for inspection by
   Capt. F.J.BREEDEN, M.C. at 9.15 a.m. Each company
   will detail two men to remain behind in their company
   billets until passed as satisfactory by Capt. BREEDEN,
   after which they will march collectively under orders
   to be issued by that officer. Certificates that
   billets have been left thoroughly clean will be handed
   to the Adjutant at the Starting Point.

6. Watches will be synchronised by Despatch Rider sent
   to companies about 8.30 a.m.

7. Falling out states, "Condition of billets when taken
   over" and other returns will be sent to the Orderly
   Room as soon as possible after arrival in the new area.

8. ACKNOWLEDGE.

                                        Lieut. & Adjt.
                                        2/5th R.Warwick.Regt.

Issued at 11.0 p.m.

Copy No. 1 to C.O.   Copy No. 7 to "D" Coy.
        2 to Adjutant.   8 to Quartermaster.
        3 to H.Qrs.   9 to T'port Officer.
        4 to A.Coy.   10   War Diary.
        5 to B.Coy.   11   File
        6 to C.Coy.

Vol 21

CONFIDENTIAL

WAR DIARY.

2/5th ROYAL WARWICKSHIRE REGIMENT.

January 1918.

Vol. 20

Army Form C. 2118.

WAR DIARY
or
INTELLIGENCE SUMMARY.
(Erase heading not required.)

Instructions regarding War Diaries and Intelligence Summaries are contained in F. S. Regs., Part II. and the Staff Manual respectively. Title pages will be prepared in manuscript.

Place	Date	Hour	Summary of Events and Information	Remarks and references to Appendices
LE QUESNEL	1/1/18	9.30	Bⁿ Muster parade. Organisation of Coys completed. Billets repaired. Range repaired	
	2/1/18	9.30	Bⁿ Muster parade. Company training & Range practice. Draft of 2 officers and 5 O.R's	
	3/1/18	9.30	Bⁿ Muster parade. Company training & Range practice.	
	4/1/18	9.30	Bⁿ Muster parade. Company training. Latest scheme hour 9.40 3.15 pm. Draft of 2 N.C.O's & 73 O.R. arrived	
	5/1/18		Company training. Platoon attack on strong point practised.	
	6/1/18		Church Parade.	
	7/1/18	8.30	Bⁿ marched to billets in NESLÉ via BOUCHOIR - ROYE - CARREPUITS - BETHONVILLERS, arriving	Appendix I
			at 5.15 pm.	
NESLÉ	8/1/18		C.O.'s Coy Commander went forward to reconnoitre the line. Parties worked coy arrangements	
	9/1/18	10.15	Bⁿ marched to billets in VAUX via VOYENNES - MATIGNY - DOUILLY - FORESTE - GERMAINE	Appendix II
			arriving at 6.15 pm	
VAUX	10/1/18		Parties under Coy Commanders	
	11/1/18 4.30pm		Bⁿ moved into support line in HENNON WOOD relieving the 2nd Bⁿ 7th French	Appendix III
			Regiment of Infantry. Relief complete by 9 pm	
HENNON WOOD	12/1/18		Bⁿ in Support line	
	13/1/18			

WAR DIARY
or
INTELLIGENCE SUMMARY.

Army Form C. 2118.

(Erase heading not required.)

Place	Date	Hour	Summary of Events and Information	Remarks and references to Appendices
HOLNON WOOD	14/4/18		Bn in Support. Bn Order to Attack received	Appx II / VRSgt
	15/4/18		Bn moved to B Rn R in FAYET instructor Patrol complete by 4.45 a.m night of 15/16	VRSgt
	16/4/18		The enemy shelled the Bn HQ dug-out heavily. No further action taken.	
	17/4/18	7 pm	Reinforcement of 15 Officers and 110 OR arrived	mg Rept
			Coy used to strengthen front as Right and Centre	
			Coy supported by 2 Aust Regt and moved to Willik in ATTACK Relief completed by 11.20 pm	Appx III
	18/4/18		Bn in reserve. Rdrumming and refitting	
			Coy ... was ... caught	
			Bn ... ... moved ... moved on night 17/4/18	
	19/4/18		... Sunken and Armits by GOC Division	
	20/4/18		Bn commenced work on the new "Battle Line"	
	21/4/18		Bn working on new "Battle Line". Court of Enquiry re-opened ut circumstances of	
	25/4/18		Bn working on new "Battle Line" relieving 2/4 Ox & Bucks	
			Bn moved up to support in OTTER COPSE Relief completed by 7.10 A.M	
FRESNOY LE PETIT	27/4/18		Bn in Support	
	28/4/18		Bn in Support	

Army Form C. 2118.

WAR DIARY
or
INTELLIGENCE SUMMARY.
(Erase heading not required.)

Instructions regarding War Diaries and Intelligence Summaries are contained in F. S. Regs., Part II. and the Staff Manual respectively. Title pages will be prepared in manuscript.

Place	Date	Hour	Summary of Events and Information	Remarks and references to Appendices
FRESNOY LE PETIT	29/1/18		Bn in Support	WDA2. Appx IX
"	30/1/18		Bn relieved 2/8th R.War.R. in GRICOURT subsector. Relief complete by 8.20 p.m.	Appx X
"	31/1/18		Bn in Front-line: Lt Col Coates re-assumed command upon return from leave in Paris.	
			Strength of Bn on January 1st 21 Officers 591 o.r.	
			" " " " 31st " 42 " 703	

W Coates Lt Col.
Comdg 1/5 R.War.R.
31/1/18

SECRET.   Copy No.
RED SQUARE OPERATION ORDER, NO. 106.
Reference — AMIENS Map, 1/F20000   January 6th 1918.

1. The 182nd Infantry Brigade group moves to the NESLE area
   tomorrow, the Battalion being billeted in NESLE.   Route:—
   LE_PT_HANGEST Cross roads — BOUCHOIR — ROYE — CARREPUIS —
   RETHONVILLERS.

2. Companies will march in the following order, H.Qrs. D. C.
   A. & B. Coys. and Transport, the head of the column passing
   the Starting Point (junction of track, road and wood 680
   yards North of the S. in LE_PT_HANGEST) at 8.25 a.m.
   Dress, Marching Order, less packs and steel helmets; caps
   to be worn.   Transport will march in groups of six vehicles
   and will maintain an interval of 25 yards between each group.
   A. B. C. & D. Coys. will each detail one section (roughly
   1 N.C.O. and 6 men) to report to the Transport Officer at
   the Starting Point, to march with the Transport (one section
   behind each group).

3. In addition to the usual 10 minute halt before each clock
   hour, there will be a halt from 12.30 p.m. to 1.30 p.m.
   for dinners and to water and feed horses.   Water for horses
   will be carried in petrol tins.

4. Blankets rolled in labelled bundles of ten, Officers' kits
   H.Q. cooking utensils, Orderly Room boxes, mens' packs
   which must be clearly marked on the side carried next the
   body, with number, name and company, will be dumped by
   companies at Battalion H.Q. ready for collection at 8.0 a.m.
   Steel helmets will be strapped tightly on the back of packs
   with the pack straps crossing above AND below the crown of
   helmet.   Officers' mess boxes, Medical Stores and Field
   Kitchens will be ready for collection by the Transport at
   7.45 a.m.

5. Billets will be cleaned and ready for inspection by Major
   L.E.V. BARNES, M.C. at 8.10 a.m.   The usual certificates that
   they have been left thoroughly clean will be handed to the
   Adjutant at the Starting Point.

6. Watches will be synchronised by Despatch Rider sent to
   companies about 7.— a.m.

7. Falling_out states, "Condition of billets when taken over"
   and other returns will be sent to the Orderly Room as soon
   as possible after arrival in the new area.

8. ACKNOWLEDGE.

                                                        Lieut. & Adjt.

Issued at 7.0 p.m.
Copy No. 1 to C.O.   Copy No. 7 to D.Coy.
         2 to Adjutant,   8 to Quartermaster
         3 to H.Qrs.   9 to Transport Officer
         4 to A.Coy.   10   War Diary
         5 to B.Coy.   11   File
         6 to C.Coy.

Appendix II

SECRET.
RED SQUARE OPERATION ORDER, NO. 106.   Copy No. 11
Reference — AMIENS Map 1/100000.   January 8th 1918.
            ST.QUENTIN, 1/100000
            62.C. S.E. 1/20000

1. The 182nd Infantry Brigade moves tomorrow to the GERMAINE —
   HOLNON WOOD area, the Battalion being billeted in VAUX.
   Route:— Bend in road North of the H. in HEBLE — VOYENNES —
   MATIGNY — DOUILLY — FORESTE — GERMAINE.

2. Companies will march in the following order, H.Qrs. C. A.
   B. & D. Coys. and Transport, the head of the column passing
   the Starting Point (Battalion Headquarters) at 10.15 a.m.
   Dress, Marching Order, steel helmets to be worn. Transport
   will march in groups of six vehicles and will maintain an
   interval of 25 yards between each group. A. B. C. & D. Coys.
   will each detail one section (1 N.C.O. & 8 men) to report
   to the Transport Officer at the Starting Point, to march
   with the Transport (one section behind each group).

3. In addition to the usual ten minutes halt before each clock
   hour, there will be a halt from 1.50 p.m. to 2.50 p.m. for
   dinner and to water and feed horses. Water for horses will
   be carried in petrol tins.

4. Blankets rolled in labelled bundles of ten, Officers' kits,
   H.Q. cooking utensils, Orderly Room boxes and other stores
   will be dumped by companies at the Q.M.Stores ready for
   collection at 8.0 a.m. Officers' mess boxes, Medical Stores
   and Field Kitchens will be ready for collection by the
   Transport at 9.30 a.m.

5. Billets will be cleaned and ready for inspection by Major
   L.E.V.BARNES, M.C. at 10.0 a.m. Two men per company will
   remain in billets until passed. They will afterwards proceed
   under orders to be issued by Major BARNES. The usual
   certificates that billets have been left thoroughly clean
   will be handed to the Adjutant at the Starting Point.

6. Watches will be synchronised by Despatch Rider sent to
   companies about 9.0 a.m.

7. Hallingbout states, "Condition of billets when taken over"
   and other returns will be sent to the Orderly Room as soon
   as possible after arrival in the new area.

8. ACKNOWLEDGE.

                                    J.R.S.May Capt. & Adjt.
                                    c/6th R. Warwick. Regt.

Issued at 6.0 p.m.

Copy No. 1 to C.O.   Copy No. 7 to D.Coy.
        2 to Adjutant.   8 to Quartermaster
        3 to H.Qrs.   9 to Transport Officer
        4 to A.Coy.   10   War Diary
        5 to B.Coy.   11   File
        6 to C.Coy.

SECRET.   Appendix III
RED SQUARE OPERATION ORDER, NO. 107.   Copy No. 11
Reference – ST.QUENTIN, 62B. S.W. Edn. 3. 1/10000   Jan. 10th 1918.
              62B. S.E. 1/20000
              62C. S.E. 1/20000
              66D. 1/40000
              ─────────

1. The 182nd Infantry Brigade relieves the 74th French Regiment in the Right Sector on the night of 11th/12th inst. the 2/5th Warwicks relieving the 2nd Battalion in Support.

2. Dispositions will be as follows:–
    Batt. H.Qrs. B. & C. Coys. and 2 platoons of A.Coy.
    about S.7.b.3.5.
    H.Qrs. and 1 platoon of A.Coy. about M.32.b.5.0.
    D.Coy. – Savy Railway Cutting and the Quarry.
    Guides will be provided as follows:–
    (a) 4 guides – 1 per Coy.   Road junction   4.30 p.m.
                   (A.B. & C.)   X.10.a.5.3.   onwards
                   1 Batt. H.Qrs.
    (b) 1 guide – H.Qrs. & one   Battalion   On
                  platoon A.Coy.   H.Qrs.   arrival
    (c) 2 guides – D.Company   road junction   4.30 p.m.
                                     S.20.d.35.30   onwards

3. The Battalion will move in the following order:– A. B. C. H.Qrs. and D. Companies, the head of the leading company passing the Starting Point (road junction at F.1.d.6.6) at 4.30 p.m. Route for A. B. C. & H.Qrs. Companies will be ETREILLERS – ATTILLY – road junction at X.10.a.5.3. Route for D.Company, ETREILLERS – SAVY – Road junction S.20.d.35.30. Dress, full marching order. Distances of 200 yards will be maintained between companies. Limbers with stores will march with companies.

4. Blankets rolled in labelled bundles of ten and surplus stores will be handed in to the Q.M.Stores by 12.0 noon. The Transport Officer will detail sufficient limbers to report to each company and Battalion H.Qrs. at 3.45 p.m. for the conveyance of dixies, Lewis Guns, Officers' kits and mess boxes, and one blanket per man. He will also detail the Officers' mess cart and Maltese Cart to report at Battalion H.Q. for loading at 1.45 p.m.

5. Advanced party as under will parade at Battalion H.Q. in full marching order, with the remainder of their days rations, at 9.0 a.m. to proceed to the line under Major L.T.V.BARNES, M.C.
          Batt. H.Qrs.   Rev. D.F.ROCHE
                             & Regt. Sergt. Major.
       Each Company   1 senior N.C.O.
    This party will report at the H.Qrs. 2nd Battalion, 74th French Regiment at 10.45 a.m. where guides will be provided for those proceeding to companies.
    Sergt. JENSON, together with 3 signallers and 2 runners, will proceed with the above party, but will report to the Signalling Officer, 74th French Regiment, at Regimental Headquarters, F.2.a.9.3. at 11.0 a.m.

6. All telephones will be operated by the French until the whole Brigade relief is complete and will not be taken over till then. On no account will any English be spoken over the telephone until after the relief is complete.

7. The greatest care will be taken to conceal from the enemy that a relief is taking place; this applies particularly to parties which go into the line by day. They must now allow themselves

P.T.O.

to be observed, and if the weather is clear communication trenches will be used in moving forward. Every endeavour will also be made to delay as long as possible the discovery by the enemy that the relief has taken place. All ranks must not unnecessarily shew themselves and conversations on the telephone strictly limited.

8. All billets will be cleaned and ready for inspection by Major L.T.V.BARNES, M.C. at 3.30 p.m.

9. Watches will be synchronised by Despatch Rider sent to companies about 2.0 p.m.

10. Relief complete will be notified to Battalion H.Q. by runner only and by usual code word.

11. ACKNOWLEDGE.

Lieut. & A/Adjt.

Issued at 9.0 p.m.

Copy No. 1 to C.O.
2 to Adjutant,
3 to H.Qrs.
4 to A.Coy.
5 to B.Coy.
6 to C.Coy.
7 to D.Coy.
8 to Quartermaster,
9 to Transport Officer,
10 War Diary
11 File.

Appendix V

SECRET.
RED SQUARE OPERATION ORDER, NO. 107   Copy No. 12
Reference – Sheet 62B. S.W. 1/20000   Jan. 14th 1918.
            " 62C. S.E. 1/20000

1. The 2/5th R.War.R. relieves the 2/8th R.War.R. in the Left Sub-sector (FAYET) on the night of the 15th/16th inst.

2. Dispositions will be as follows:—
   B.Coy. 2/5 R.War.R. relieves A.Coy. 2/8 R.War.R. on the right
   C.Coy.   —do—   "   C.Coy.   —do—   in the centre
   D.Coy.   —do—   "   D.Coy.   —do—   on the left
   A.Coy.   —do—   "   B.Coy.   —do—   in reserve

3. Guides will be provided as under, and will be at S.R.central from 4.30 p.m. onwards:—
        1 guide per platoon
        2 guides for Battalion H.Qrs.

4. There will be no movement (except in the case of signallers and Lewis Gunners) in connection with the relief before 4.30 p.m. Dress, Marching Order, less haversacks, packs only to contain greatcoats and small kit.

5. One officer and one N.C.O. per company, observers, signallers, three police to take over traffic post, and the Regt. Sergt Major will go forward to take over before midday.

6. All trench maps, air photographs, defence schemes, trench stores etc. will be handed over and receipts sent in to Battalion H.Qrs. by 9.0 a.m. on the 16th inst.

7. Blankets rolled in labelled bundles of ten, mens' packed haversacks (which must be distinctly marked on the back with Regt. No., Rank, Name and Company), Officers' mess boxes and kits and any company stores will be dumped in company dumps by 4.0 p.m. and handed over to Coy. Qr.Master Sergeants. The Transport Officer will provide sufficient limbers to convey the above to the Q.M.Stores. He will also detail limbers to report by 4.15 p.m. to take forward Lewis Guns, dixies and any stores companies wish to take with them.

8. Relief complete will be notified by the usual code word.

9. ACKNOWLEDGE.

                                    R/Coates,
                                    Lieut. Col.
                            Comdg. 2/5th R.Warwick.Regt.

Issued at 8.30 p.m.

Copy No. 1 to C.O.   Copy No. 7 to D.Coy.
        2 to Adjutant,   8 to Quartermaster,
        3 to H.Qrs.   9 to Transport Officer
        4 to A.Coy.   10 to 2/8th Warwicks
        5 to B.Coy.   11   War Diary
        6 to C.Coy.   12   File

Appendix VI

2/6TH. BN. ROYAL WARWICKSHIRE REGIMENT.

Report on Enemy Raid, January 17th 1918.

At about 9.0 p.m. on the 17th inst. the enemy carried out a raid on No. 6 Post of the Battalion front. At the time L/C. A.S.CHAPMAN and six men composed the post.

According to the report of the two unwounded men, the enemy numbered between 16 and 20 men, who approached the post in two parties from front and rear.

The sentry called the attention of L/C. CHAPMAN, who challenged them and a salvo of bombs then fell near, but to the right of the post, followed almost immediately by a bomb which fell into the post, knocking over the greater part of the garrison and mortally wounding No. 1 of the gun. The unwounded men then opened fire with their rifles and No. 2 of the Gun seized the Lewis Gun and attempted to turn it on the enemy, but a second bomb fell into the post knocking over all the remainder with the exception of L/C. CHAPMAN. He was seen to mount the parapet apparently to charge the enemy with his bayonet.

By the time the unwounded men extracted themselves from the mud, the L/Cpl. and the enemy party had disappeared.

A patrol subsequently went out visiting the adjoining posts and also examined the wire. A gap was found to have been cut on the right of No. 6 post. This has now been repaired and will be further strengthened tonight.

18/1/18.

Major.
Comdg. 2/6th R. Warwick. Regt.

Appendix VIII

SECRET.
RED SQUARE OPERATION ORDER, NO. 109.   Copy No. 11
Reference - Sheet 62B. S.W. 1/20000   January 17th 1918.
            "   62C. S.E. 1/20000

1. The 183rd Infantry Brigade relieves the 182nd Infantry
   Brigade in the Right Sector on the night of the 18th/19th
   inst. the 2/6th Gloucesters relieving the 2/5th Warwicks
   in the Left Sub-sector (FAYET). On completion of relief
   the Battalion will withdraw to billets in ATTILLY.

2. Dispositions will be as follows:-
   C.Coy. 2/6 Glosters relieves B.Coy. 2/5th R.War.R. on the right
   B.Coy.   _do_   " C.Coy.   _do_   in the centre
   A.Coy.   _do_   " D.Coy.   _do_   on the left
   D.Coy.   _do_   " A.Coy.   _do_   in reserve

3. Guides will be provided as under, and will be at the cross
   roads at S.2.c. from 5.0 p.m. onwards:-
            1 guide per platoon.
            2 guides for Battalion H.Q.
   Guides will be provided with statements in writing as to
   the platoon they are to guide and to where.

4. Two limbers per company for B. C. & D. Coys. will be in
   position on the road entering FAYET (approx. M.35.c.) at
   8.0 p.m. onwards to carry Lewis Guns, Lewis Gun magazines,
   mens' packs etc. Guides to this transport will be provided
   at Battalion H.Qrs.
            Two limbers will report to O.C. A.Coy. after dusk to
   carry Lewis Guns, Lewis Gun magazines, blankets etc.
   A.Coy's packs will not be carried by the Transport.
            One limber, Officers' mess cart and Maltese cart will
   be at Battalion H.Qrs. after dusk for the conveyance of
   H.Q. Stores, Medical Stores, Officers' mess boxes, etc.
            One limber will be at the disposal of the Medical
   Officer to carry men unfit to march.

5. All trench maps, air photographs, defence schemes, S.O.S.
   signals, trench stores etc. will be handed over and receipts
   sent to Battalion H.Q. by 2.0 p.m. on the 18th inst.

6. Relief complete will be notified by the usual code word.

7. ACKNOWLEDGE.

                                         H R B May
                                            Capt. & Adjt.
                                         2/5th R. Warwick. Regt.

Issued at 9.0 p.m.

Copy No. 1 to C.O.   Copy No. 7 to D.Coy.
        2 to Adjutant.   8 to Quartermaster.
        3 to H.Qrs.   9 to Transport Officer
        4 to A.Coy.   10   War Diary
        5 to B.Coy.   11   File
        6 to C.Coy.

Appendix VIII

SECRET.
RED SQUARE OPERATION ORDER, NO. 110.   Copy No. 4
Reference – Sheet 28B. N.W. 1/20000.   January 25/1918.
            Sheet 28C. S.E. 1/20000.
            Sheet 28D. 1/40000.

1. The 182nd Infantry Brigade relieves the 184th Infantry
   Brigade in the Left Sector on the night of 28th/29th inst.
   the 2/5th Warwicks relieving the 2/4th Ox. & Bucks. L.I.
   in Right Support.

2. Dispositions will be as under:-
   A.Coy. 2/5 Warwicks relieves A.Coy. 2/4 Ox. & Bucks L.I.
   B.Coy.   _do_   "   D.Coy.   _do_
   C.Coy.   _do_   "   C.Coy.   _do_
   D.Coy.   _do_   "   B.Coy.   _do_

3. Companies will move off independently, but no movement will
   take place before 4.30 p.m. in dress, full marching order and
   one blanket. Distances of 200 yards will be maintained
   between companies. Limbers with stores will march with companies.

4. Blankets rolled in labelled bundles of ten, Officers' kits
   and surplus stores for return to the Q.M.Stores will be dumped
   by companies ready for collection by the Transport at 8.30 a.m.
   A. & D. Coys. will form their dumps at a point on road nearest
   to their billets. B. C. & H.Qrs. Coys. will form their dumps
   by the Railway cutting at X.10.c.
       The Transport Officer will detail sufficient limbers to
   report to each company and Battalion H.Qrs. at 3.45 p.m. for
   the conveyance of dixies, Lewis Guns etc. and mess boxes.
   He will also detail the Officers' mess cart and Maltese Cart
   to report to Battalion H.Qrs. at the same time.

5. Advanced party as under will parade at Battalion H.Qrs. in
   full marching order, with remainder of days rations, at 10.0 a.m
   to proceed to the line:-
           Batt. H.Qrs.   Regt. Sergt. Major.
                          Sergt. W.A.JENSON,
                           3 Signallers,
                           2 Runners,
                          Sergt. H.F.BIRD,
                           2 snipers.
           Each Coy.   1 Officer or 1 senior N.C.O.

6. All aeroplane photographs, defence schemes, S.O.S. grenades,
   trench stores, etc. will be taken over, carefully checked,
   and receipts sent to Battalion H.Q. before completion of relief.
   No Gum Boots will be taken over.

7. All huts will be cleaned ready for inspection by Capt. C.W.
   SICKEL at 4.0 p.m. after which time they will not again be
   entered by troops.

8. Watches will be synchronised by Despatch Rider sent to
   companies about 3.0 p.m.

9. Relief complete will be notified by the usual code word.

10. ACKNOWLEDGE.

                                         Capt. & Adjt.

Issued at 6.0 p.m.

Copy No. 1 to C.O.
2 to Adjutant.
3 to H.Qrs.
4 to A.Coy.
5 to B.Coy.
6 to C.Coy.
7 to D.Coy.
8 to Quartermaster.
9 to Transport Officer.
10 War Diary
11 File

SECRET.
RED SQUARE OPERATION ORDER, NO. 111.   Copy No. 11
Reference — Sheet 62B. S.W. 1/20000   January 29th 1918.
           Sheet 62C. S.E. 1/20000

Appendix IX

1. The 2/5th R.War.R. relieves the 2/8th R.War.R. in the Right Sub-sector on the night of 30th/31st inst.

2. Dispositions will be as follows:-
   C.Coy. 2/5 R.War.R. relieves B.Coy. 2/8 R.War.R. on right front
   A.Coy.   -do-   "   A.Coy.   -do-   on left front
   B.Coy.   -do-   "   C.Coy.   -do-   counter-attack
                                                       company.
   D.Coy.   -do-   "   D.Coy.   -do-   Passive defence
                                                       company.

3. Any guides that may be necessary will be arranged for by Company Commanders concerned.

4. There will be no movement, except as shown in para. 5. in connection with the relief before 5.30 p.m.

5. One Officer and 1 N.C.O per company, observers, signallers, and the Regt. Sergt. Major, will go forward before midday to take over.

6. All trench maps, air photographs, defence schemes, S.O.S. grenades, trench stores etc. will be carefully checked and handed over. Receipts for stores handed and taken over will be forwarded to Battalion H.Qrs. before completion of relief.

7. Blankets rolled in labelled bundles of ten, except in the case of "D" Coy., Officers' mess boxes and any stores will be dumped in company dumps by 5.0 p.m. and handed over to Coy. Qr.Master Sergts.
   The Transport Officer will provide sufficient transport to convey these stores back to the Q.M.Stores.
   He will also detail limbers to report to Companies by 5.15 p.m. to take forward Lewis Guns, dixies, etc.

8. Relief complete will be notified by the usual code word.

9. ACKNOWLEDGE.

                                          Capt. & Adjt.

Issued at 0.0 p.m.

Copy. No. 1 to C.O.
         2 to Adjutant,
         3 to H.Qrs.
         4 to A.Coy.
         5 to B.Coy.
         6 to C.Coy.
         7 to D.Coy.
         8 to Quartermaster,
         9 to Transport Officer,
        10 to 2/8th Warwicks.
        11   War Diary
        12   File.

---CONFIDENTIAL---
o-o-o-o-o-o-o-o-o

W A R   D I A R Y.

- OF -

2/5th Battalion Royal Warwickshire Regiment.

FEBRUARY. 1918.

(VOLUME XXII.)

Army Form C. 2118.

WAR DIARY
or
INTELLIGENCE SUMMARY.
(Erase heading not required.)

Place	Date	Hour	Summary of Events and Information	Remarks and references to Appendices
FRESNOY LE PETIT	1/2/18		Enemy raided our No 1 Post & were successfully repelled, leaving one prisoner	WRSR
"	2/2/18		Bn in front-line in GRICOURT Subsector	WRSR Appx I
"	3/2/18		Bn relieved in front line by 2/8 R War R & moved to Support. Relief completed by 8.10 p.m.	WRSR
"	4/2/18		Bn in Support	LOI 1/2/18 WRSR
"	5/2/18		Bn in Support. 201389 Cpl W. Westwell awarded Military Medal for gallantry in repelling the raid	WRSR
"	6/2/18		Bn in Support	WRSR Appx II
"	7/2/18		Bn moved into front-line relieving 2/8 R War R. Relief complete by 8.0 p.m.	WRSR
"	8/2/18		Bn in front-line	WRSR
"	9/2/18		Bn in front line	WRSR
"	10/2/18		Bn in front line	WRSR Appx III
GERMAINE	11/2/18		Bn relieved by 5th Gordon Highlanders & moved to GERMAINE. Relief complete by 8.53 p.m.	WRSR
"	12/2/18		Bn in Reserve	WRSR
"	13/2/18		Bn in Reserve	WRSR
"	14/2/18		Bn inspected by G.O.C. 182 Inf. Bde	WRSR
"	15/2/18		17 Officers and 350 O.R. transferred to 2/6th R War R	WRSR
"	16/2/18		Bn marched to BRAY - ST CRISTOPHE	WRSR Appendix IV

WAR DIARY
or
INTELLIGENCE SUMMARY.
(Erase heading not required.)

Army Form C. 2118.

Place	Date	Hour	Summary of Events and Information	Remarks and references to Appendices
BRAY-ST CRISTOME	17/2/18		Bn at work under 179 Army Bde RFA. Capt O Sichel assumed command of the Bn, on Lieut Col Coates DSO assuming temporary command of the 182 Inf Bde	HRAn
"	18/2/18		Bn at work under 179 Army Bde RFA	HRAn
"	19/2/18		"	HRAn
"	20/2/18		Two C.O.'s this in Command. Bn moved to TANGUEVOISIN to join No. 12 Entrenching Batt. Orderly Room & Sergts surplus W.O.'s to Base depot. Major L.T.V. Barnes proceeded to 61 Div H.Q. War Diary closed on disbandment of unit to 61 Div H.Q.	Appendix V

R.J. Coates Lt Col
Comdg. 2/5- Rwarwick R
20/2/18

SECRET.
RED SQUARE OPERATION ORDER, NO. 112.   Copy No. 11
Reference — Sheet 62B. S.W. 1/20000   February 2nd 1918.
            Sheet 62C. S.E. 1/20000

1. The 2/5th. R.War.R. will be relieved in the Right Sub-sector on night of 3rd/4th inst. by 2/8th R.War.R. After relief 2/5th R.War.R. will withdraw to Right Support. Dispositions as before.

2. Dispositions of relieving unit will be as follows:—
   C.Coy. 2/8th Warwicks relieves C.Coy. 2/5 Warwicks on right front
   D.Coy.   —do—   "   A.Coy.   —do—   on left front
   A.Coy.   —do—   "   B.Coy.   —do—   counter-attack
                                                    company
   B.Coy.   —do—   "   D.Coy.   —do—   Passive defence
                                                    company.

3. Guides will be found by companies under arrangements to be made between company commanders concerned.

4. No movement in connection with the relief (except as shewn in para. 5) will take place before 5.30 p.m.

5. One officer and one N.C.O. per company of the 2/8th R.War.R will come in before mid-day to take over. One officer and one N.C.O. per company, Sgt. BENNETT and 5 signallers of Battalion H.Q. will go out before mid-day to take over.

6. The Transport Officer will arrange for blankets at the rate of one per man to be delivered to Company H.Q. in Support for A. B. C & H.Q. companies. He will also detail limbers to be at forward company dumps by 7.30 p.m. for the conveyance of Lewis Guns etc. Officers' mess boxes, Dixies etc. He will also detail the Maltese Cart to be at Battalion H.Q. at 6.0 p.m. and one limber at 7.0 p.m.

7. All aeroplane photographs, defence schemes, S.O.S. grenades, trench maps, trench stores etc. will be carefully checked and handed over. Receipts for stores handed over will be sent to Battalion H.Q. by 4.0 p.m. Lists of stores taken over will be sent in before 9.0 a.m. on the 4th inst.

8. Relief complete will be notified by the usual code word.

9. ACKNOWLEDGE.

                                          Capt. & Adjt.

Issued at 9.0 p.m.

Copy No. 1 to C.O.   Copy No. 7 to D.Coy.
         2 to Adjutant,   8 to Quartermaster,
         3 to H.Qrs.   9 to Transport Officer,
         4 to A.Coy.   10 to 2/8th Warwicks.
         5 to B.Coy.   11   War Diary
         6 to C.Coy.   12   File

Appendix II

SECRET.
RED SQUARE OPERATION ORDER, NO. 113.   Copy No. 11
Reference – Sheet 62B. S.W. 1/20000.   February 6th 1918.
          "   62C. S.E. 1/20000.

1. The 2/5th R.Warwick.R. relieves the 2/8th R.Warwick.R. in the Right Sub-sector on the night of the 7th/8th inst.

2. Dispositions will be as under:-
   D.Coy. 2/5 R.War.R. relieves C.Coy. 2/8th R.War.R. on right front
   A.Coy.   –do–   "   D.Coy.   –do–   on left front
   B.Coy.   –do–   "   A.Coy.   –do–   Counter-attack company.
   C.Coy.   –do–   "   B.Coy.   –do–   Passive Defence company.

3. Any guides that may be necessary will be arranged between company commander concerned.

4. No movement in connection with the relief (except as under) will take place before 5.30 p.m.
         1 officer & 1 N.C.O. per Coy.) Will go in
         Regt. Sergt. Major.   ) before mid-day
         Sgt. JENSON & 3 signallers   ) to take over.
         Sgt. BIRD & 3 snipers   )

5. Blankets of A. B. & D. Companies will be rolled in labelled bundles of ten, Officers' kits & mess boxes and any surplus stores will be dumped by companies by 5.15 p.m. and handed over to Coy. Qr.Master Sergeants.
   Blankets can be taken forward by C. & H.Q. companies, but must be carried by the men.

6. The Transport Officer will detail sufficient limbers to convey the above mentioned stores back to the Q.M.Stores.
   He will also arrange for conveyance forward of Lewis Guns etc. Officers' mess boxes, dixies etc. and medical stores, which will be ready for collection at 5.15 p.m.

7. All raid schemes, aeroplane photographs, defence schemes, S.O.S. grenades, trench maps, trench stores, to be handed and taken over, will be carefully checked and receipts obtained. Lists of stores to be handed over will be sent to the Orderly Room by 12.0 noon, 7/2/18, and receipts for stores taken over will be sent to Battalion H.Q. before completion of relief.

8. Relief complete will be notified by the usual code word.

9. ACKNOWLEDGE.

                                            Capt. & Adjt.

Issued at 6.30 p.m.
   Copy No. 1 to C.O.   Copy No. 7 to D.Coy.
          2 to Adjutant,   8 to Quartermaster,
          3 to H.Q.   9 to Transport Officer,
          4 to A.Coy.   10 to 2/8th Warwicks
          5 to B.Coy.   11   War Diary
          6 to C.Coy.   12   File

SECRET.

Red Square Operation Order No.114. Copy No. 11
Ref. Map. 62.c.S.E. (1/20000) 12th. February 1918.
           62.b.S.W. (1/20000)

Appendix III

1.- The 182nd. Infantry Brigade will be relieved by the 183rd. Infantry Brigade in the Left Sector of Division front on the night of the 11/12th inst., the 2/5th. WARWICKS being relieved by the 5th. GORDON HIGHLANDERS. On completion of relief the 2/5th WARWICKS will withdraw to reserve billets in GERMAINE.

2.- Each Company will detail 4 guides, who will report to Battalion H.Qrs. at 4 p.m. 11th inst.

3.- No movement in connection with the relief will take place before 5.45 p.m. Proportion of signals, No. 1 of Lewis Gun teams, and one Officer per Company will come into the line tonight to take over.

4.- Transport arrangements for conveyance of Lewis Guns, etc., mess boxes, packs, and blankets of C and H.Q. Company as per instructions issued separately.

5.- All defence schemes, aeroplane photographs, S.O.S. grenades, gum boots and other Trench Stores will be carefully checked, handed over, and receipts sent to Battalion H.Qrs. by 12 noon, 11th inst. Lists of all stores taken over in reserve billets will be sent to Battalion H.Qrs. by 9 a.m. 12th inst.

6.- Relief complete will be notified by the usual code word

7.- ACKNOWLEDGE.

Lieut & adj
for Capt. & Adjt.

Issued at 8.30 p.m.

Copy No.1 to C.O.   Copy No.7 to D.Coy.
     2 to Adjutant.   8 to Quartermaster
     3 to H.Q.   9 to T.O.
     4 to A.Coy   10   War Diary
     5 to B.Coy   11   File
     6 to C.Coy   12 to 5th. GORDON
                                     HIGHLANDERS

Appendix IV

SECRET.
RED SQUARE OPERATION ORDER, NO. 114.   Copy No. 8
Reference — ST. QUENTIN Map, 1/100000.   February 15th 1918.

1. The Battalion marches tomorrow to billets in BRAY — ST. CHRISTOPHE. Route:— FORESTE — POINT 92 — AUBIGNY.

2. The Battalion will march in the following order, H.Qrs. A. & C. Companies and Transport, the head of the column passing the Starting Point (200 yards W. of the junction of BEAUVOIS — FORESTE roads) at 11.0 a.m. Dress, Marching Order, Service Dress caps to be worn.

3. Blankets rolled in labelled bundles of ten, Officers' kits, Medical Stores, Canteen and other stores will be dumped ready for collection by the Transport at 9.30 a.m. Officers' mess boxes will be ready for collection at 10.0 a.m. and company cookers at 10.30 a.m.

4. Billets will be cleaned and ready for inspection by Lieut. J.E.TARVIN at 10.45 a.m. A. & C. Companies will each detail six O.R's to report to the Inspecting Officer at their company billets at that time. They will march under orders to be issued by him. The usual certificates that billets have been left thoroughly clean will be handed to the Adjutant at the Starting Point.

5. Watches will be synchronised by Despatch Rider sent to companies about 9.0 a.m.

6. Falling-out States, Condition of billets when taken over and other returns will be rendered to the Orderly Room as soon as possible after arrival in the new area.

7. ACKNOWLEDGE.

                                    H R O'may
                                    Capt. & Adjt.

Issued at 10.0 p.m.

Copy No. 1 to C.O.
        2 to Adjutant,
        3 to H.Qrs.
        4 to A.Coy.
        5 to C.Coy.
        6 to Quartermaster,
        7 to Transport Officer,
        8   War Diary
        9   File

Appendix V

SECRET.

RED SQUARE OPERATION ORDER, NO. 115.   Copy No. 8
Reference – ST.QUENTIN MAP, 1/100000   February 19th 1919.
            AMIENS MAP, 1/100000

1. The Battalion (less personnel detailed to proceed to the Base) will march to the LANGUEVOISIN area tomorrow, the 20th inst. to join the 24th Entrenching Battalion.

2. The Battalion will march in the following order, H.Qrs. A. & C. Companies and Transport, the head of the column passing the Starting Point (Church on AUBIGNY road) at 10.0 a.m.   Route:– AUBIGNY – VILLERS_ST_CHRISTOPHE – SANCOURT – TOUILLE – BUGNY – VOYENNES. Dress, Marching Order, Service Dress Caps to be worn. Intervals of 200 yards will be maintained between companies and the Transport.

3. Blankets rolled in labelled bundles of ten, Officers' kits, mess boxes and other stores will be dumped by companies ready for collection by the Transport at 8.30 a.m.

4. In addition to the usual ten minutes halt before each clock hour, there will be a halt for one hour at 1.0 p.m. for dinner. Companies will arrange for dinners to be ready at that time.

5. Billets will be thoroughly cleaned and ready for inspection by Lieut. J.E.TARVIN at 9.0 a.m. after which time they will not be entered again by the troops. "C" Company will detail a party of one sergeant and eight O.R's. to report to the Inspecting Officer at Battalion H.Q. at 8.45 a.m. in full marching order. Certificates that billets have been left clean will be sent to the Adjutant by 9.15 a.m.

6. Watches will be synchronised by Despatch Rider sent to Companies about 8.0 a.m.

7. The usual returns will be rendered to the Orderly Room as soon as possible after arrival in the new area.

8. ACKNOWLEDGE.

                                            Capt. & Adjt.

Issued at 11.0 p.m.

Copy No. 1 to C.O.
         2 to Adjutant,
         3 to H.Qrs.
         4 to A.Coy.
         5 to C.Coy.
         6 to Quartermaster,
         7 to Transport Officer,
         8   War Diary
         9   File

www.ingramcontent.com/pod-product-compliance
Lightning Source LLC
Chambersburg PA
CBHW080911230426
43667CB00015B/2654